Auditing and Finance Management

Auditing and Finance Management

Edward Sunderland

RANDOM PUBLICATIONS
NEW DELHI - 110 002 (INDIA)

Auditing and Finance Management

ISBN 978-93-51113-01-0

Published in 2014 in India by

RANDOM PUBLICATIONS

4376-A/4B, Gali Murari Lal, Ansari Road
New Delhi-110 002
Phone: +9111-43580356, 23289044
E-mail: randomexports@gmail.com; sales@randompublications.com;
info@randompublications.com

Reprinted 2026

Type Setting by: Friends Media, Delhi-110089

Preface

A financial audit, or more accurately, an audit of financial statements, is the verification of the financial statements of a legal entity, with a view to express an audit opinion. The audit opinion is intended to provide reasonable assurance, but not absolute assurance, that the financial statements are presented fairly, in all material respects, and/or give a true and fair view in accordance with the financial reporting framework. The purpose of an audit is provide an objective independent examination of the financial statements, which increases the value and credibility of the financial statements produced by management, thus increase user confidence in the financial statement, reduce investor risk and consequently reduce the cost of capital of the preparer of the financial statements. In accordance with the US GAAP, auditors must release an opinion of the overall financial statements in the auditor's report. Auditors can release three types of statements other than an unqualified/unmodified opinion. The unqualified auditor's opinion is the opinion that the financial statements are presented fairly. A qualified opinion is that the financial statements are presented fairly in all material respects in accordance with US GAAP, except for a material misstatement that does not however pervasively affect the user's ability to rely on the financial statements. A qualified opinion can also be issued for a scope limitation that is of limited significance. Further the auditor can instead issue a disclaimer, because there is insufficient and appropriate evidence to form an opinion or because of lack of independence. In a disclaimer the auditor explains the reasons for withholding an opinion and explicitly indicates that no opinion is expressed. Finally, an adverse audit opinion is issued when the financial statements do not present fairly due to departure from US GAAP and the departure materially affects the financial statements overall. In an adverse auditor's report the auditor must explain the nature and size of the misstatement and must state the opinion that the financial statements do not present fairly in accordance with US GAAP.

Financial audits are typically performed by firms of practicing accountants who are experts in financial reporting. The financial audit is one of many assurance functions provided by accounting firms. Many organizations separately employ or hire internal auditors, who do not attest to financial reports but focus mainly on the internal controls of the organization. External auditors may choose to place limited reliance on the work of internal auditors. Auditing promotes transparency and accuracy in the financial disclosures made by an organization, therefore would likely to reduce of such corporations to conceal unscrupulous dealings. Internationally, the International Standards on Auditing (ISA) issued by the International Auditing and Assurance Standards Board (IAASB) is considered as the benchmark for audit process. Almost all jurisdictions require auditors to follow the ISA or a local variation of the ISA. Financial audits exist to add credibility to the implied assertion by an organization's management that its financial statements fairly represent the organization's position and performance to the firm's stakeholders. The principal stakeholders of a company are typically its shareholders, but other parties such as tax authorities, banks, regulators, suppliers, customers and employees may also have an interest in knowing that the financial statements are presented fairly, in all material aspects. An audit is not designed to provide absolute assurance, being based on sampling and not the testing of all transactions and balances; rather it is designed to reduce the risk of a material financial statement misstatement whether cased by fraud or error. A misstatement is defined in ISA 450 as an error, omitted disclosure or inappropriate accounting policy. "Material" is an error or omission that would affect the users decision. Audits exist because they add value through easing the cost of information asymmetry and reducing information risk, not because they are required by law.

This book presents the information on some of the basic concept of this subject.

I thank all members of my team who have helped in the preparation of the book. My special thanks go to "Random Publications" who have published the book.

—Edward Sunderland

Contents

1

Introduction

State Audit is an activity sui generis, distinct from other forms of government checks and controls, aims and techniques. It is independent; it deals with problems of high level of State administration and various public organs; it has full access to accounts, files and records of all public organizations for scrutiny. The aim of State audit is collection of data on the activities of the organization it inspects and their comparison to norms in order to induce the correction of shortcomings and improve public administration. The Lima Declaration of INTOSAI (International Organisation of Supreme Audit Institutions) defines the purpose of audit as follows:

> *The concept and establishment of audit is inherent in public financial administration as the management of public funds represents a trust. Audit is not an end in itself but an indispensable part of a control system whose aim is to reveal deviations from accepted standards and violations of the principles of legality, efficiency, effectiveness and economy of resource management early enough so as to make it possible to take corrective measures in individual cases, to make accountable parties accept responsibility, to obtain compensation, or to take steps to prevent violations from recurring or at least to make this more difficult.*

State Audit is an activity distinct from commercial audit. The main purpose of commercial audit is to determine whether the financial statements represent fairly the actual financial position and the working results of an enterprise. The Institute of Chartered Accountants of India defines auditing as, "a systematic and independent examination of data, statements, records, operations and performances (financial or otherwise) of an enterprise for a stated purpose. In any auditing situation, the auditor perceives and recognizes the prepositions before him for examination, collects evidence and evaluates the same and on this basis formulates his judgement which is communicated through his audit reports." State audit has a much broader scope and extends its dimension to examination of whether governmental functions have been carried with due regard to wisdom, faithfulness and economy.

State audit conducted by Supreme Audit Authority (SAI) can be broadly classified in three categories: (a) Regularity audit; (b) Financial audit; (c) Value for Money audit. These concepts are explained below:

Regularity Audit

To check upon the legality of an action taken by a public official or a person using public funds is a central element of regularity audit. The legality of a decision has two basic elements: is the decision or its implementation according to the law, rules or regulations governing that activity, and those responsible have the right or duty to take such decisions or to implement them. Much traditional audit work was concerned with the regularity of expenses and actions taken, in what is called "tick and turn" check of expenditures, item by item and whether they have complied with rules. For this reason this type of audit is also known as compliance audit.

A few examples will illustrate the concept of Regularity audit, (a) A senior government official while on official tour to New York claims daily allowance at $ 75 per day without making 10 percent deduction for breakfast charges, although the room rent of $200, which has been separately reimbursed, as per prescribed scale, was inclusive of breakfast charges. This may be due to ignorance or incorrect interpretation of the orders of the Ministry of External Affairs. The audit has therefore to point out the excess drawl of money and see that it is recovered. (b) An Executive Engineer who has powers to award work for road resurfacing upto Rs 25 lacs, splits a work of Rs 30 lacs into two works of Rs 20 lacs and Rs 10 lacs, floats two tenders and awards the work, thus avoiding sanction of the Superintending engineer. When audit points out, the superior authority will come to know that his financial powers have been usurped, and will help help in enforcing administrative discipline. (c) Sales tax was being levied at acrylic yarn, in one of the States, at the rate of 2 percent treating the commodity as yarn. The audit pointed out that acrylic yarn is nothing but wool for which applicable rate is 8.8 percent. The department accepted the position and was able to recover additional revenue.

Financial Audit

Financial audit basically means audit of financial statements and financial related results and satisfying that they are accurate and complete and are consistent with primary records, books and ledgers. Audit provide reasonable assurance that the financial statements of an audited entity, present fairly the financial position, results of operations, and cash flow according to generally accepted accounting principles.

In case of financial audit the auditors are required to form an opinion on the accounts that, "they reflect a true and fair" picture of the state of affairs of an audited entity and they are free from material mis-statements. If auditors identify material mis-statements a qualified opinion is issued. Where there are no material mis-statements or error in accounts, nonetheless a report on other significant matters will be issued.

In Financial audit, the State auditors practically do the same job which Chartered Accountant's (CA) perform, while auditing a public limited company. The CA's. conduct audit according to the Auditing Standards laid down by the Institute of Chartered Accountants of India (ICAI). In view of globalization of business, ICAI is making efforts to align its norms to International Accounting Standards. Every corporate management wants its profit to look as good as possible, as this helps pushing share prices in the stock exchange. Auditors often act as willing partners and collaborate with management in creative accounting practices.

The collapse of Enron and WorldCom, in USA and many other large corporations worldwide, where auditors acted in collusion with companies top management, has placed the accounting profession at the crossroad. There is call for setting high ethical standards and their regulation by an independent body. The whole debate underlines the fact that auditors, whether public or private, must function 'independently' of the audited entity, if they have to discharge their duty professionally and effectively.

Performance or Value for Money Audit

Performance audit also known as Value for Money (VFM) audit is an independent assessment of the performance of an organization, programme, project or an activity in terms of its goals and objectives-how far expected results have been achieved in terms of available resources of money, men and material. Put it differently an examination is made regarding economy, efficiency, and effectiveness of public spending, which has come to be known as 3E's audit.

- Economy: minimizing the cost of resources used or required-spending less
- Efficiency: the relationship between the output of goods and services and the resources to produce them- spending well
- Effectiveness: the relationship between the intended and actual results of public spending- spending wisely.

INTOSAI auditing standards states that: performance audit is concerned with the audit of economy, efficiency and effectiveness, and embraces:

(i) audit of the economy of administrative activities in accordance with sound administrative principles and practices and management policies;

(ii) audit of the efficiency of utilization of human, financial and other resources, including examination of information systems, performance measures and monitoring arrangements and procedures followed by audited entities for remedying identified deficiencies; and

(iii) audit of the effectiveness of performance in relation to the achievements of the objectives of the audited entity and audit of the actual impact of activities compared with the intended impact.

Audit as Quality Assurance

Today in advanced societies there is an audit explosion. There is management audit, data audit, science audit, technology audit, education audit, medical audit, environment audit and so on. Basically it implies that services provided by these professions maintain certain measurable standards so that the consumer is assured that he is getting quality services. Today all over the world there is talk of good governance and countries like Britain have transformed public sector culture by providing citizen friendly administration in what is known as New Public Management. Citizens demand that public agencies give high quality efficient services of certain measurable standard to them. Michel Power a professor in the London School of Economics observes that there is an explosion of audit in Britain in what he describes as an audit society.

This is largely because the society demands an account to be given by the persons responsible for an activity not only in terms of money spent but a check that an activity was carried out efficiently. This implies that concrete technical practices be introduced to secure assurance that they get the right services with a problem solving attitude. Thus as society progresses and democracy takes deeper roots, public audit will become an important tool in quality management and integrate basic philosophy of TQM in its discipline.

The President Dr APJ Abdul Kalam while addressing a conference of Accountant Generals has emphasized that audit should act as quality assurance and observed (2005), "Auditing in the modern sense is a quality assurance phenomenon. It has to move from conventional quality control mechanism to a quality assurance of institutions through establishment of internal control and self control. Audit has to be pro-active and alert the system before the occurrence of low performance."

The Challenge of Auditing

A complex and big agenda is set before the public auditors. Prof W J M Mackenzie of Manchester University sums up the difficult job which auditors are required to do, "the trade of the auditor, private or public, covers a continuous spectrum; at the one end, routine checks of 'regularity', in the presentation of the vouchers, at the other extreme a check upon the effectiveness of an instrument in relation to the job for which it has been designed.

The humble process of 'tick and turn-over' has little meaning except as the basis for wider assessment of the honest and efficiency of government agencies that continuing assessment is one of the thing we mean by public accountability, under any form of government. Yet great issues often come to light only because of scrupulous verification of details."

How to fulfill this responsibility and satisfy varying expectations of its customers and clients- the audited institutions, the Government, the Parliament and the people in general, is a challenge set before the public auditors.

Performance Evaluation and Value for Money Audit

CAG took up the work of performance audit from 1970's and reviews started appearing in the Audit Reports. A pioneering work in the field of performance audit was report on Irrigation projects presented to Parliament in December 1977. A review of 20 irrigation projects, including 12 large projects, in different parts of the country was conducted. The review covered aspects such as extent of area irrigated as compared to target, efficiency of water utilization, drainage, cropping pattern etc.

The Ministry of irrigation took a view that irrigation is a state subject and the proper forum for discussion would be the Public Accounts Committee of the States. The Central Public Accounts committee did not buy the argument and observed that implementation the plan schemes is the responsibility of the Planning Commission and there should be coordinated approach between the Central and the State governments. The PAC's recommendations were accepted by the government. This set the pace for centrally sponsored schemes which are now included on both the Central as well as State audit reports. Thereafter CAG has produced large number of performance reviews covering almost every facet of government's working.

The reviews have covered major socio- economic programmes such as Food for Work, Jawahar Rozgar Yojna, IRDP, Urban Employment Generation Programme & PM Rozgar Yojna, Swaranjaynti Gram Swarozgar Yojna, Empowerment of the Disabled, Accelerated Rural and Urban Water Supply Programme, National Literacy Mission, Operation Blackboard, Non Formal Education, National Programme for Control of Blindness and Tuberculosis, National Disease Control Programme, National Family Welfare Programme, National Aids Programme, etc. The review contain vast amount of information and analytical data about the working of various development programmes not available anywhere else and greatly facilitated their evaluation by the Planning Commission.

Audit of Commercial Enterprises

In the 1950's when government companies were being set up to promote country's industrialization, there were attempts to exclude CAG's audit on the ground that their expenditure and revenue transactions were not part of Consolidated Fund and being commercial enterprises their independent functioning will be inhibited. This was resisted by the then CAG V Narhari Rao who felt that this would be an unconstitutional act. His demand was met by making a suitable provision in the India Companies Act.

Thus while Chartered Accountants are required to certify Annual Accounts of government companies, CAG has a right to conduct supplementary audit. However, realizing that government companies have to function as business entity, a system of appraising them through Audit Boards was introduced in 1970. Every year CAG brings comprehensive reviews on the performance of selected group of Public Sector Undertakings.

Nevertheless audit of Public Sector Undertakings (PSU's) has remained a controversial issue and time and again there is demand to remove it. The articles in Part II B of the book focus attention on various dimension of the issues and emphasize the need of CAG's audit, if they have to function within the democratic framework of accountability to Parliament.

As an illustration a case relating to ONGC's contract with a private party for exploration of oil, is cited which highlights the valuable work being done by audit in making transparent dubious deals entered by government and PSU's. A production sharing agreement termed Joint Venture (JV) was entered with Enron- Reliance Consortium in respect of three medium sized field Panna/ Mukta, Mid & South Tapti and Ravva.

The agreement showed serious deficiencies: past cost reimbursement of Rs 676 crs was not made to ONGC; the JV was shown special favour as roalty and cess on oil were frozen, and ONGC was discriminated in matters of price on crude oil and natural gas and customs duty. A subsequent review by audit ten years after the operation of contract(which has validity for 25 years) showed government's complete inaction to correct the infirmities in the agreement and continued favours to JV. ONGC has suffered loss of Rs 4625 crs due to discriminatory gas pricing; JV has held up a sum of Rs 578 crs for transportation and processing of gas; and it refuses to pay production bonus of Rs 48 crs disputing the formula for profit sharing.

Issues of Public Importance

Defence Deals

Impropriety in award of high value contracts, particularly defence contracts, when pointed out by audit invariably get a great deal of media and public attention as generally Ministers and high officials are involved. One of the earliest cases in post independence history was Jeep scandal in the 1950's, in which the role of V K Krishna Menon then High Commissioner in London came under scrutiny and was subject of heated discussion in Parliament. Audit had pointed severe irregularities in the award of contract and was supported by the Public Accounts Committee. Audit reports on defence deals such as Bofors Gun and HDW submarine received wide publicity largely due to its political fallout, although both the cases were already highlighted in the media. Often the audit reports take political colour due to inter party rivalry. The coffin purchase during Kargil war (1999-2001) belonged to this category. The Opposition (Congress) targeted the UPA government minister George Fernandez for financial improprieties and when came to power (2004) ordered a CBI enquiry. This was unfortunate as selective picking up of audit reports to settle political scores does not serve the purpose of streamlining defence purchases and making critical weapons and equipment available to armed forces in time of emergent need.

A report on Railway audit pointed out that, in order to circumvent government rules that individual ministries cannot buy aircrafts, the Ministry of Railway asked IRCON (Indian Railway Construction Company) a PSU under it, to purchase an aircraft by diverting Rs 15 crs budget allocation from broad gauge line conversion and advancing it the money, through an arrangement under which IRCON will lease the aircraft to Railways. The logbook of the aircraft showed that the plane was used only for personal/ political journeys of the then minister Jaffar Sharif. The Public Accounts Committee passed serious strictures against the minister and the issue raised a furor in Parliament.

A CAG's report on Disinvestment of PSU's (1993) pointed out that method of sale by clubbing shares of different enterprises lowered their value , the reserve price was reduced arbitrarily causing loss to exchequer and total value of shares off-loaded exceeded the available investable resources of the financial institutions. The examination by Public Accounts Committee lead to serious indictment of government.

CAG's two reports (1998 and 2001) on Member of Parliament Local Development Scheme (MPLAD) has raised fundamental issues relating to conduct of elected representatives. The report points out wastage of money, irregular award of contracts, excess payments to contractors, fraud and misappropriation. A sum of Rs 12180 crs has been spent upto March 2004 on the scheme since its inception (in 1993-94).

CAG's report has formed the basis of debate on the subject and experts pointing out that the scheme is fundamentally flawed as members of legislature are encroaching in areas which fall within the domain of executive functioning. Era Sezhiyan former chairman of Public Accounts Committee, who has done a perceptive study says, "the scheme is against the parliamentary system, democratic decentralization and responsibility and accountability for moneys withdrawn from the public exchequer ", and made a forceful case for its discontinuance.

The audit report of UP points to serious lapses in the release of money from Chief Minister's Discretionary Fund (1998-99 to 2001-02) to which an annual allocation of Rs 20 crs is being made. UP Chief Minister's have been doling money on the basis of caste, religion and purposes such as marriage, foreign travel, purchase of vehicle, as if it is their 'private money' without following any norms. The report points to fraud being committed by some ministers in their TA bills resulting in expenditure of Rs 22.85 crs from public coffer. In a little over three years (1998 -99 to 2001-02), 33 ministers have drawn amount ranging from Rs 33 lakhs to 137 lakhs as out of pocket expenses, without production of any bill or supporting voucher, there being no ceiling limit on daily allowance.

Duties and Organization of Comptroller and Auditor General

The Comptroller and Auditor General of India (CAG), derives his constitutional standing as the auditor of Union and the States from Articles 148 to 151 of the Constitution. Article 148 guarantees independent functioning of the CAG. He is appointed by the President of India by warrant under his hand and seal and his conditions of service are on par with that of a Supreme Court Judge. The duties and powers of CAG are laid down in The Comptroller and Auditor's General's (Duties, Powers and Condition of Service) Act, 1971.

Duties Relating to Accounts

For more than a century when the office of Auditor General of India was set up in 1860's, CAG has been performing both the accounting and audit functions of government. This position has been reflected in the CAG's Act. Under Section 10 of the Act, CAG is responsible for compiling the accounts of the Union and each State from the initial and subsidiary accounts rendered to him by the treasuries, offices or departments responsible for keeping such accounts.

The act has a provision that the President may relieve him from this responsibility. In 1976, the CAG has been relieved of the responsibility of compiling the accounts of the Central Government and its various establishments. However, the accounts of State governments continue to be compiled by Accountant General's in each State. Article 150 of the Constitution prescribes the form in which accounts of Union and States are to be kept. A uniform pattern of accounts is followed by Union and State. The position is as follows:

Union Government Accounts: the accounts of expenditure and revenue of Civil departments and ministries is compiled by Controller General of Accounts and of Defence, Post and Telecommunication and Railways by the respective departments. They are audited by C&AG with reference to Budget passed by Parliament and placed in Parliament by way of Appropriation Account and Finance Account.

State Government Accounts: The State government accounts continue to be maintained by CAG. The Accountant General (Accounts) of various States which are subordinate offices of CAG, compile the accounts from the vouchers and initial accounts which are sent by district treasuries every month. The Finance and Appropriation Accounts are certified by Accountant General (Audit), and placed in the State legislatures. The Accountant Generals in States have been traditionally performing entitlement functions of government employees and maintaining accounts of Provident Fund and authorizing its payment as well as pension payment at the time of retirement. In some States, salary payment of gazetted officers is also made by AG, a function which AG used to do traditionally, before the separation of accounts from audit in 1976.

Audit Techniques and Methodology

The Indian Audit and Accounts Department (IAAD) follows two methodologies in carrying out audit functions: Central audit and Local audit or inspection. Central Audit: involving examination of accounts, vouchers, government and administrative orders and other records called for or available centrally in various audit offices. Incase of State Governments, where accounts and audit are not separated all payment vouchers are sent by treasuries to Accountant General's Office, where besides compilation of accounts, test audit as per prescribed yardstick is done.

Local Audit or Inspection: involving examination of accounts and other records in the office or department of the government or authorities or bodies where expenditure or revenue transactions take place. The lowest formation for local audit is an office which has been given powers to draw and disburse government money in what is known as DDO (Drawing and Disbursing Officer).

The initial audit is done by a three member Audit Party generally headed by an Audit Officer accompanied by one Assistant Audit

Officer/ Section Officer and one Assistant. In case of important audits, the audit parties are periodically supervised by Deputy Accountant General/ Deputy Director of Audit or Senior Deputy Accountant General/ Director of Audit (called Group Officer) who give broad directions regarding manner in which audit should be conducted. After examination of various records and documents in the office inspected, the audit party issues audit memos, in cases where it finds that some irregularity has taken place and there has been violation of rules and procedures.

After eliciting reply from the office visited, the Audit Party discusses the issues with the dealing officers and thereafter weighs the evidence and decides whether the point in issue should feature in the Draft Inspection Report, which it submits to the headquarters of the audit office. The report is examined in the audit office with a view to see that audit objections are factually correct, have materiality and substance and thereafter edited and approved at the level of Group Officer. Thereafter it is issued as Audit Inspection Report to the next superior officer whose office was inspected, as well as the head of the office inspected, for giving comments on the various issues raised. The departmental officers often take corrective action or come forward with a satisfactory explanation why a particular course of action was adopted. In such a case the audit objection is settled or dropped.

In cases where irregularity noticed is of serious nature, the report is drafted by way of audit para or audit review and sent for comments of Head of the Department and the administrative ministry. On receipt of reply of head of department / government, the facts are weighed and if the reply is not convincing it is proposed as a final draft para/review and submitted to headquarter office of CAG. The draft paras are examined at the head office and approved at the level of Additional Dy CAG / Dy CAG. On receipt of CAG's office approval the audit paras/ reviews are included in the Audit Reports and the final report is placed before the CAG for his formal approval. After CAG's approval, Audit reports are printed and thereafter sent to Government for placing before the Parliament/ State legislature.

Anachronism in Existing Structure

There has been very little change in the structure and style of functioning of the IAAD in the last six decades since Independence, as a result serious anomaly in its functioning has cropped up. Just before Independence, in 1945-46, the total receipts and disbursements of the Government of India and Provinces were Rs 4254 crores and Rs 3980 crores.

The IAAD had one directing and controlling office of Auditor General at Simla and four offices engaged in accounting and audit of the federal government, including Indian Railways, Military department, Posts and telegraph and 11 Accountant Generals responsible for audit and accounting of 11 provinces. The expenditure of the department was Rs 1.49crs. The activities of the government both at the Center and the States have multiplied hundred fold as result of State assuming the responsibility of socio-economic development.

The expenditure of Centre and States has ballooned to over Rs 9,00,000 crs (2004-05). This has necessitated huge growth in the Audit department, which has now 97 Accountant General/ Director General's offices with a staff of 58000 and budget of Rs 1100crs. This has resulted into a highly centralized behemoth, seriously effecting its work efficiency, as there has been hardly any formalized delegation of powers to its field outfits. Serious anomaly in the functioning of the institution would be evident from following:

(1) One centralized entity conducts audit of both Central and State governments. The State Accountant General's have no legal status nor any functional autonomy. There is no federal country in the world which does not have separate Auditor General's for the States under the statute, enjoying full autonomy in their sphere of work. The existing structure results in ineffective and poor quality audit.

(2) For CAG to perform accounting functions for State government is anachronistic and results in lack of accountability on the part of State government officials. Realizing the anomaly of accounts and audit functions being combined in one institution, the accounts of Central government were separated in 1976 and a new set up Controller General of Accounts was created, and each ministry made responsible for maintaining its accounts. A half hearted attempt at reform was done in 1984, when CAG within his own department, separated accounts and audit functions in the States and created two different wings, Accountant General-Audit and Accountant General-Accounts. But this has hardly helped matters. Accounting is not an end in itself, it is an important management tool. Accounting information is a powerful instrument of financial

management, fiscal discipline, planning and performance evaluation. The absence of authority to maintain accounts, places severe limitations in developing good management practices in various departments of State government. One reason for the reluctance of CAG/ Central government to transfer work relating to account keeping to State governments is, absence of trained accounting staff (the accounts of State PSU's are in pathetic state, majority of which are in huge arrears).The solution lies in a long term strategic plan and developing trained accounts and finance manpower, rather than holding back much needed reform.

(3) Bulk of audit staff is ill equipped to meet the challenges of modern day audit. While only 300 Group A officers are assigned audit task, there is an army of 11000 Audit Officers and 19000 auditor/clerical level staff engaged in audit. Almost all the field audit at the cutting edge level, where there is interface with audited offices, is conducted by Audit Officers/ auditors. They are ill trained, incapable of doing performance audit which needs great deal of skill and imagination and often raise frivolous objections resented by auditees. This is the single most important reason for adversarial relationship between audit and administration and poor image of IAAD.

The Audit department today needs a major restructuring and improve its efficiency, if it has to truly become guardian of national finances.

Regularity Audit—No Power of Enforcement

Audit is a device as old as organized State itself. No State can exist without a proper system of accounting and control of money. Audit's primary function is to see that provisions of law, rules and regulation are properly applied while incurring expenditure or collecting revenue. It reports on violation so that loss to exchequer is made good and the delinquent official is punished or reprimanded to act as a deterrence. In order to regulate usage of money elaborate rules and regulations have been drawn by government.

They cover such diverse areas as personal pay and allowances, custody of cash and its drawl from treasury; norms of expenditure for government's multifarious activities, contractors payment, and collection and accounting of tax and non-tax revenue. These rules have been codified in books such as FR's and SR's (Fundamental and

Supplementary Rules), GFR (General Financial Rules), Treasury Rules, Account Code, and various manuals of the departments. The Manual of Standing Orders issued by CAG contains elaborate instructions for audit staff regarding conduct of audit of expenditure, audit of revenue, audit against provision of funds, audit of sanction etc.

Public officials frequently violate rules. Some common irregularities are: an advance has been drawn but not adjusted; the sanctioned amount has been exceeded; the sanctioning authority has exceeded its power of sanction; pay and allowances have been overdrawn; excess payment has been made to a contractor, the terms of a contract or supply order have been varied to favour the contractor/ supplier. While audit notices systematic violation of law, rules and regulations by departmental officers, it is unable to take an effective action to prevent them for want of an effective deterrence in its hand. Should Audit simply be content to report such matters to the concerned departments, who attempt to obfuscate the issue, or should have power to recover the money?

Public Servants Violating Rules

With declining moral standard in public administration in recent past, large number of public servants violate rules relating to drawl of pay, traveling, medical and other allowances. During the British days and right upto 1976 (before the accounts of the Central government were departmentalized and a new set-up under Controller General of Accounts was created), the drawl of pay and allowances of gazetted government servants belonging to both Central and State government was controlled by Accountant General (AG).

Thus if a government servant made unauthorized drawl of allowances, the A.G would issue a retrenchment order to the Treasury Officer concerned, who was obliged to implement it. To cite an instance, the Lt Governor of Manipur drew sumptuary allowance for two months he was on leave (1969). This was objected to by the AG and a clarification secured from Home Ministry that the Lt governor has no obligation for entertainment during leave, and the amount drawn was recovered.

But this is no longer possible. CAG's helplessness is illustrated by the following case, which featured in the Audit Report: The Secretary of the Telecom Regulatory Authority of India (TRAI) had claimed per-diem-halting allowance of $500 for foreign tour although he availed of free hotel accommodation facility from ADB Manila, while the Chairperson of the Authority during his stay in hotels at Hong Kong and Manila claimed entertainment allowance on the basis of vouchers, which were in fact his personal hotel bills.

To cap the irregularity the TRAI had adopted the ceiling rate of $500 per diem stipulated by RBI, for foreign tour for all its senior officials irrespective of the place of visit and status of the officer without following Ministry of External Affairs guidelines and the mandatory government approval as required under the Act. When confronted with audit objection, the defaulting officers of TRAI, instead of refunding the unauthorized drawl of money, indulged in obfuscation by pointing out that TRAI being statutory authority enjoys special status. Such a situation results in correspondence between the Audit officer and the Department getting dragged for years helping the defaulting government servant to get away with irregular payments.

The Bihar fodder scandal was facilitated due to the fact that the Treasury Officers who made fraudulent payments, suppressed the vouchers and monthly accounts and did not transmit them to Accountant General Bihar for months together, which prevented the detection of the irregularity. Accountant General has no administrative power over Treasury officers , though most of the work they do, is on his behalf.

The accounts keeping of public sector companies owned by State governments is in chaotic state. The Annual Accounts of most of these companies remains in arrears, sometimes for periods ranging from five to ten years. The Companies Act stipulates that the Annual Accounts of these companies should be got audited by statutory auditors (Chartered Accountants) and AG within six months of the close of financial year viz. 30th September. The Audit Report of the CAG laments, " The necessity for action under the Companies Act to get the accounts completed and presented for audit was impressed upon the Department of Company Affairs who have the necessary powers for taking action under the companies Act." In case of the Central government companies, there were as many as 60 companies (including deemed government companies) whose Accounts for 2002-03 or earlier years were in arrears and not submitted for audit by the due date (September 2004). These companies violate with impunity the legal provision laid down in the Companies Act.

Similar is the situation with large number of autonomous bodies, which are wholly or substantially funded by government grant. The delay in submission of their Annual Accounts for audit could range from a few months to several years. For the year 2002-03, out of 232 autonomous bodies only 69 submitted their Accounts within the prescribed time schedule. For example the Annual Accounts of Indira Gandhi National Center for Arts was in arrears for 4 years and National Commission for Backward Classes for 10 years.

Utilization certificates in 37900 cases where Grant of Rs 9882 crs was given to various autonomous institutions, were not submitted by March 2004.

The position has only been worsening in subsequent years. Utilization certificate for Grants amounting to Rs14425 crs, were not submitted by March 2005. In many cases Grants were released more than five to ten years ago, and yet the Ministries have been releasing Grants in subsequent years without satisfying that they have been utilized for the intended purpose.

In numerous cases Annual Accounts when prepared do not follow the accounting standards, contain numerous mistakes, sometimes manipulated and when these are pointed out, the concerned organizations refuse to rectify the errors. The Office of CAG has no power to take punitive action against management of these defaulting organizations.

A sub-committee of the Conference of the Chairmen of Public Accounts Committee chaired by E Ayyapu Reddy with eight chairman of State Public Accounts Committee as members observed, " It is very depressing to find that inspite of Audit reports revealing loss of public funds or misuse or misapplication of public funds, there is no investigating agency charged with the duty to probe into these aspects and identify the culprits responsible for them".

The sub-committee recommended, "We do not see any difficulty or objection as to why such of these Audit paras which prima facie establish loss of public funds should not be registered as First information Reports and should not be made the subject matter of investigation by concerned Vigilance Officers or the ACB and the CBI." However, no action was taken on committee's recommendation.

Position in Advanced Countries

Most Supreme Audit Institutions (SAI) have been vested with wide powers of investigation and can fix responsibility on the officials who have caused loss to the exchequer. They have also been entrusted with legal power for recovery of the loss of money or property and can compel their departments to initiate disciplinary action against delinquent public servants.

Japan

In Japan, the Board of Audit has an adjudication system which acts as an effective means to secure recovery of loss caused to State by a public official. The Board of Audit is also entitled to demand that the head of auditee agency take disciplinary action against an official, when it finds that he has caused grave loss to the State either deliberately or by gross negligence.

Whenever, the auditee agencies find loss of cash, security or other State assets they are required to notify the same to Board of Audit. While adjudicating the cases, the Board examines whether the official in charge of cash or State property caused loss due to lack of due professional care and /or by deliberation and if finds him guilty, the Board orders that the official responsible indemnify the loss. Disciplinary action can also be demanded when an official does not submit statement of accounts and /or voucher in violation of legal regulations.

New Zealand

In New Zealand the Controller and Auditor General (CAG) is empowered to hold an enquiry under the Public Finance Act of 1977. He may require any person to attend and give evidence before him and to produce book of accounts. He has also powers to require such official to give evidence in writing and on oath with provisions of Crimes Act relating to perjury applying incase of false evidence.

The CAG has powers for surcharge if he finds that there is deficiency or loss of money or store caused through fraud, mistake, default, negligence, error or improper or unauthorized use. If there is any unsatisfied surcharge it is liable to be recovered as a debt in any Court of competent jurisdiction.

France

In France the Cour des Comptes (Court of Accounts) functions like a court and is assisted by a Public Prosecutor. The Cour is responsible for verifying whether income has been collected and expenses have been paid in accordance with all applicable accounting laws. Financial transactions of the State and its autonomous agencies are performed by accounting officers who are in charge of collecting revenue and approving and paying expenses. They are personally answerable for fulfillment of their duties.

These accounting officers must submit yearly accounts to the Cour. If the accounts are in order the Court grants the discharge for accounts in question. During an investigation, the officials may be ordered to show cause why they did not collect revenue or pay expenses which resulted in breach of financial regulations or rules. If they fail to provide a satisfactory justification, they may be ordered to settle uncollected revenue or irregular expenses out of their own resources - thus accounting officers have formal personal responsibility.

The magistrates and examiners of the Court have very broad investigative powers. All organizations within the mandatory jurisdiction of the Court must submit the basic legally stipulated documents. They cannot be denied any accounting or management documents. Hindering the Courts investigation may give rise to a fine of up to FRF 100,000. The judgements of Cour are legally binding and can be appealed only on points of law. If there are cases of fraud they are communicated to the State prosecutors with a view to take criminal action.

South Korea

In Korea, under the Board of Audit and Inspection (BAI) law, the Board has power to examine and adjudicate whether an accounting official or any other person is liable for reparation and if so the manner in which recovery is to be made. In case the BAI has adjudicated that there is a liability to make reparation, it will transmit the same to the supervisory agency, who shall serve it to the person concerned and order him to make reparation.

In case the person liable for reparation fails to fulfill his obligation, the supervisory agency has powers to execute collection by applying mutatis mutandis provisions concerning disposition of taxes in arrears under the National Tax Collection Act. The BAI may request the appointing authority to take disciplinary action, against persons who fall under the provisions of Civil Service Act. BAI has powers to impose penal servitude up to one year or fine up to 5 million won, if a person has refused audit or inspection or impeded the process of audit.

China

In China under the State Audit Act, an audited unit violating financial and economic laws and regulations, the audit organ may handle them according to the following stipulations: (1) Give warning and circulate a notice of criticism; (2) Order them to correct the revenues and expenditure in violation of the relevant regulations of the State; (3) Confiscate or instruct them to return the illegal gain;

(4)Take over the embezzled state assets; (5) In the case of an audited unit misusing financial misappropriations or bank loans and gravely jeopardizing State interests, take decisions to cut off such appropriations or loans; and (6) impose fines according to the relevant regulations. If the audited units refuse to hand over the illegal gains or pay fines as ordered, audit organs may inform the banks to withhold the money.

If the audit organs find that there are personnel directly liable as well as the leaders of the audited units, they will advise disciplinary sanction to the supervisory department or other competent departments. If their cases are serious enough to constitute criminal offences, they shall be referred to the judicial organs to affix the responsibility in accordance with law. Audit organs have powers to impose fines as well as advise disciplinary sanction to the supervisory authority in case the concerned officers: refuse to provide the relevant documents, vouchers, books of account, financial statements, data and evidential matters; obstruct the functions of the auditing personnel and resist or sabotage supervision and examination; practice fraud, or withhold the truth; refuse to implement the audit conclusions and decisions; and retaliate against the auditing personnel or those who expose the wrong doings.

Thailand

In Thailand the State Audit Act of 1979 gives extensive power to the Auditor General regarding conduct of audit and enforcement of its findings. The act authorizes the Auditor General to summon any official to deliver accounts and registers; attach money, properties, accounts registers, documents etc. of the audited agency; and summon a person to testify as witness. In case the result of examination indicates that there are errors or non- compliance with laws, rules, regulations, the office of the Auditor General shall notify the audited agency to furnish explanation or rectify the errors or correctly comply therewith within the prescribed period.

If the result of examination shows that there is a reasonable cause indicating dishonesty, the Auditor General is required to notify the inquiry official to institute legal proceedings. If a person who has the duty to keep in his custody money or property or documents etc., damages, destroys, or causes loss, he is liable for imprisonment up to five years or a fine up to fifty thousand baht. If a person fails to comply the order of the Auditor General or obstructs his work, he is liable for imprisonment for a term not exceeding three years or a fine not exceeding three thousand baths. The Auditor General and the competent officials while performing their duties under the State Audit Act, are treated as officials under the Penal Code.

Australia

Under the Auditor General Act of 1997, the Auditor General may direct a person to provide with any information that he may ask, attend and give evidence before him; and to produce any documents in the custody or under the control of the person.

A person must not make a statement to an audit official that the person knows is false or misleading in a material particular. A person has a criminal responsibility under the Criminal Code for giving information which is false and for which a penalty up to 12 months imprisonment can be imposed.

Power to Adjudicate

In no other country of the world State audit finds itself in such a helpless situation as in India. Audit is unable to take corrective action even after it has discovered that public officials have caused loss to State by their action or negligence.

The situation needs to be remedied by conferring powers of adjudication to senior Audit personnel. During the course of audit scrutiny, when cases of loss of public money or property come to the notice, audit authorities may be given powers as following:

(a) power to summon the concerned officers before it, to give evidence on oath;

(b) where default is established, after giving due opportunity, the concerned officer be required to make good the loss, if need be from his own resources. This is on the principle that officials handling public money and property are personally accountable for its proper upkeep;

(c) in case the official does not make good the loss, the audit authorities be authorized to refer the cases to revenue authorities to make recovery as arrears of land revenue;

(d) where grave default or neglect of public official is established, the audit authorities be required to make a report to the superior officer of the department where the official was working, for taking disciplinary action under the Civil Services rules;

(e) where action of public official involves criminal liability, the public prosecutor be informed for initiating criminal action under the Penal code.

For adjudicating cases, a three tier system may be adopted. The Senior Dy Accountant General/ Director of Audit could adjudicate cases come upto certain monetary limit (say Rs 10000). For cases of higher monetary value (and those involving senior officers of the government, say Jt Secretary and above) the adjudicating authority should be Accountant General/ Principal Director of Audit. To make the system transparent and fair, there should also be a provision of appeal at each stage with final appellate stage at the level of Deputy Comptroller and Auditor General at the headquarters of CAG's office.

Regularity Audit a Fundamental Task

While public audit has extended its dimension to new areas of audit, such as efficiency and performance audit, Regularity audit, which implies that public officials have followed provisions of laws and regulations while handling public money, will always remain its most fundamental task. A failure to realize this has lead to serious erosion in credibility and effectiveness of the IA&AD. In recent years CAG has produced voluminous performance audit reports, but they will have value, only if it is done, without neglecting the regularity audit. The public wants an assurance that no misuse, fraud or misappropriation of government money is being done by public officials who are given its custody as a public trust.

One of the task set for itself, by the US GAO is to investigate allegations of illegal and improper activities. It operates a website Fraudnet where any member of the public can report, 'allegations of fraud, waste, abuse and mismanagement of federal funds.' The UK NAO operates a whistle blowers hotline. Under the Public Interest Disclosure Act, C&AG is one of the prescribed authority to whom external disclosure can be made relating to, 'the proper conduct of public business, fraud, value for money and corruption in relation to the provision of Centrally funded public services.'

It is time the Office of CAG and the Government adopts a working methodology for audit, keeping in view the declining moral standards of public officials and a tendency to use public office for private gain. During British rule and two decades after independence, the audit observations were treated with great deal of respect and invariably complied with. Today it is no longer so.

There is an increasing tendency on the part of public officials to flout rules, procedures and norms and misuse public funds. Audit is the institutional machinery to safeguard public money. It is unable to effectively discharge its mandate as it has very limited power of investigation and no legal power to enforce its findings. It has simply become a 'barking dog' whose voice is so shrill that it cannot awake the master who is in deep slumber.

Public audit should be provided necessary sinews to effectively perform the task entrusted to it. Keiichi Tsuji President Board of Audit Japan says that regularity/ compliance audit, is sometimes criticized as inflexible for too much reliant on laws and regulations but, 'we cannot neglect this aspect of government audit'. The Office of CAG must realize that without effective regularity audit it will loose its very raison d'etre.

2

Overview of Audit

While both Central and State government transactions are subject to audit by the CAG under the Constitution, all the institutions which are recipient of government funds do not automatically fall within the audit jurisdiction of CAG. There are large number of bodies or authorities which though financed by government grants, escape CAG's audit jurisdiction due to complex arrangements through which funds are routed to them.

Partially Privatised Government Companies

Government in our country has launched a privatization programme and in several companies such as Maruti Udyog, Hindustan Zinc, BALCO, CMC, government equity has come below 51 percent. These companies have gone out of CAG's audit purview. However, government continues to hold substantial shareholding in these companies and has its nominees on their Board and a say in decision making process. They should therefore be subject to some kind of broad performance audit by CAG, with a view to see that their operations are consistent with government's larger objectives, and they remain accountable to Parliament as long as public funds are invested in them.

In several countries where government has substantial investment holding in private corporate sector, irrespective of majority holding, it is subject to State audit. In Germany the Bundesrechnunghof (Court of Audit), has powers to 'examine with due regard to commercial principles, the management of the federation's direct or indirect shareholding in private law enterprises'. In Japan the Board of Audit can audit a body in which less than half of the capital is invested by the State.' The principle of democratic accountability requires that companies where government has substantial investment by way of shareholding (even if it does not have majority stake) should be subject to CAG's audit.

Grant in Aid Bodies

While the CAG's Act (Section 14) stipulates that any body or authority substantially funded by government grants or loans will be subject to his audit, due to some infirmities in the Act, large number of bodies escape CAG's audit. The Act stipulates that: (a) such bodies or authorities should be substantially financed by grants or loans by government. Substantially financed is defined as the body or authority receiving more than Rs 25 lakhs and the grant is not less than seventy-five percent of its expenditure- if these two conditions are not fulfilled, it would not fall within the ambit of CAG's audit. (b) audit be subject to the 'provisions of any law' applicable to that body or authority.

Thus an authority can be set up under a statute, it may not provide for CAG's audit, though fully funded by Government. A case in point is Noida Authority, which is not subject to CAG's audit. Similarly bodies registered under the Societies Registration Act 1860, are also not subject to CAG's audit, as they are subject to jurisdiction of Registrar of Societies. A glaring example is District Rural Development Authority (DRDA).

District Rural Development Authority

DRDA are set up in every district of the country as an autonomous society under the Societies Registration Act to administer governments poverty alleviation and rural employment schemes. The Chairman of the Zila Parishad is its Chairman and a full time government officer on deputation as its chief executive designated, as Project Officer. Grants of the order of Rs 10000 crs annually for various poverty alleviation and rural employment programmes are given to DRDO by the Central and State governments.

The accounting and audit arrangements of DRDO leaves much to be desired. While the Ministry of Rural Development has drawn a detailed Accounts Manual, there is hardly any trained staff to keep accounts and exercise financial control. Under rules framed, Chartered Accountants (CA) have been entrusted the responsibility to audit the accounts. Most of them issue audit certificates after doing perfunctory audit, and do not have access to original records of the organizations which have spent the money. While under rules framed by the ministry, CAG is entitled to conduct supplementary audit, this is inadequate. CAG's audit, which is his constitutional responsibility can not be governed by administrative orders.

International Practice

The Lima Declaration of SAI says, 'All public financial management, irrespective of whether and in what manner it is reflected in the general budget, shall be subject to audit by Supreme Audit Institutions. Excluding parts of public financial management from the national budget shall not result in these parts being exempted from audit of the Supreme audit Institutions'. In France under the law, the Cour Des Comptes has discretion to cover organizations which receive support from the public, even if their accounts are audited by other organizations such as, private sector organizations including voluntary sector, charities and other non-profit sector. In Germany, the Bundesrechnungshof shall be entitled to audit bodies outside the federal administration if they:

(i) implement parts of the federal budget or have expenses reimbursed by the Federation;
(ii) administer federal funds or assets;
(iii) receive grants from the Federation

There is need for statutory provision that all bodies or authorities which receive government grants or funds, irrespective of conduit through which they flow, will fall within CAG's audit jurisdiction.

Panchayati Raj Institutions

Consistent with the philosophy of devolution of powers and strengthening of the local self government institutions, the constitution, composition and duties of Panchayats and Municipalities were enshrined in the Constitution by making 73rd amendment in 1993. Bulk of the finances of the Panchayats / Municipalities come from the Government but there is no satisfactory arrangement for their audit. Article 243 J and 243 Z state that, "the Legislature of a Sate may, by law, make provisions with respect to the maintenance of accounts by the Panchayats / Municipalities, and the auditing of such accounts." However no such law has been framed by any of the States. In most of the States, the Examiner Local Funds Accounts, which functions under the Finance department audits them. They have untrained staff and the audit remains in huge arrears. The existing audit arrangements are unsatisfactory.

Noting the unsatisfactory position of accounts keeping and audit, the 11th Finance Commission has recommended that, "The C&AG should be entrusted with the responsibility of exercising control and supervision over the proper maintenance of accounts and audit by all the tiers/ levels of panchayats and urban local bodies" and, "agency made responsible for the audit of accounts of local bodies, should work under the technical and administrative supervision of the C&AG." Following the recommendations of the Finance Commission, CAG has prescribed the budget and accounts formats of Panchayti Raj Institutions (PRI) and Urban Local Body (ULB). Most of the States have also accepted the proposal relating to CAG's technical guidance and supervision over accounts and audit of PRI and ULB. While this is welcome step in bringing some degree of discipline in accounting and audit of PRI/ ULB, this will not be able to solve the problem unless a proper institutional machinery is created for accounting and audit of these institutions.

There are 240000 Village Level Panchayats, 5900 Intermediate level panchayats and 500 district level Zila Parishads in the country. Bigger States like UP has 58600 panchayats, MP 31100 and Maharastra 27600. There is need to position trained staff for account keeping of PRI. The Accountant General jointly with the State government may develop training programme and conduct examination. One accountant may be made responsible for keeping accounts of one block consisting of 20 -25 panchayats.

Keeping the volume and importance of work, it is necessary to create a separate statutory authority for audit in each State, which may function under the technical control and guidance of Accountant General. The authority will be responsible for laying down standards for audit, appointment of auditors of PRI/ ULB, laying down qualification for them and overseeing the work done by them. The audit report containing observations of the designated auditor may be dealt with finally at the Zila Parishad level. Suggestions have been made that the Audit reports of the PRI be submitted to a committee of Legislature which may be constituted for the purpose. This would be a retrograde step and against the principle of devolution of authority.

In UK a separate Audit Commission has been constituted under an act, which audits areas of local government, health, housing, community safety, fire and rescue services. The Commission has a staff of 2500 and audits 11000 bodies. For carrying on audit, the Commission appoints auditors from its own staff and from professional audit firms, who have to audit as per Standard Code of Audit Practice laid down by the Commission.

The Audit Commission appointed auditors issue three types of reports: (a) an Inspection Report regarding a particular service within the council (which is available on website), (b) A Public Interest Report on matters such as fraud, corruption or failure of government, which is available to public, (c) An Annual Audit Letter to each audited body, which contains auditor's views on key workings of the audited body. In France the Regional Court of Accounts were created in 1982 as part of wider policy of decentralization for auditing local government and associated public bodies. The Regional Courts can fine Public Accountants who fail to submit accounts by due date and have power to make restitution, if a Public Accountant fails to correct any error identified in the Accounts.

In view of growing importance of PRI in development of rural India and Urban Local Bodies in city life, there is need to place their accounting and audit arrangements on sound footing. A separate statutory body to audit them should be created in each State, on the UK pattern, which may function under the technical guidance of Accountant General of the State/ CAG.

Quality of Audit—Outdated Methodology and Lack of Perspective

While there is need to strengthen public audit by giving it more powers, and bringing all the bodies which receive public funds within its purview, it will be able to fulfill its objective, only if its work is of excellent standard and brings out high quality products, which earns the respect of its clients.

Negative Image

The wide spread impression about public audit is that it is a negative fault finding activity, largely doing post mortem. The Administrative Reforms Commission had commented (1968), "It has been observed that vast multitude of audit objections relate to individual instances of lapses and arise from deviations from administrative rules and regulations. While it is inevitable that individual instances should be exposed to scrutiny of audit, it should be recognized that it is more important for audit to focus attention on deficiencies in the system of procedures as a whole with a view to making suggestions for remedial action. Audit instead of being content with playing a negative and neutral role, should aim at positive and constructive approach directed towards seeking improvements in organizational efficiency and in the effectiveness in financial rules and procedures." Commenting on audit concerning itself with past transactions, in what is known as post audit, the Commission said that the exercise of 'hindsight' does not take into account the surroundings circumstances in which the decisions were taken. The Committee recommended, "Audit should endeavour to consider and present its comments against the background of relevant circumstances existing at the time of decision and the overall objectives and achievements of the related programme and activities."

Experts have also been voicing concern about the methodology for conducting audit. K.S. Ramachandran veteran journalist and economist says that audit teams must know their priorities. "In evaluating performance, what should matter is the systems failure or inadequacy and not the shortcoming in the sense that the auditor has, over the years, been accustomed to seeing. A shortcoming or omission is only the tip of the iceberg while the iceberg is the systems failures itself. When the system is bad it breeds inefficiency. When an organization is run inefficiently, the losses will be in several crore of rupees." Commenting on the poor style of presentation of audit reports, Ramchandran says that an auditor should look himself as an editor of a good newspaper. In order to have maximum impact of his findings he should have a lead, conclusion should come first and the style of presentation should be less academic and more journalistic.

Y. Krishna former Dy CAG and doyen of Audit department says that audit is weak and ineffective, "The auditors have also been responsible for making it a faceless institution making little contribution to public life. Often, the audit reports are belated- dealing with ancient transactions- either flogging a dead horse or locking the stable after the horse has bolted. In fact, government auditors have come to be looked upon as impediments to development and progress, possessing narrow and negative attitude who, by their petty and hair splitting objections weaken or undermine the decision making ability and confidence of conscientious officers whereas the unscrupulous know how to get round. To many audit has become a constitutional evil to be suffered and ignored." A survey amongst top government officials conducted by R. Ramanathan gives interesting insights.

The widespread impression amongst them was that, audit tends to take a purely mechanical view on the application of rules and procedures without giving allowances for specific situation or circumstances and this makes people afraid to take positive decisions. Audit comments range from incisive and valuable to ridiculous. Most uninformed comments are due to lack of expertise on the part of audit staff. A general complaint was that audit comments come too late, the persons responsible generally leave the organization with successors having to reply. If reviews come during the currency of the project, it will enable mid-course correction.

Despite shortcomings in the style of functioning of Audit department being pointed out for the last four decades, things have not substantially changed. Prime Minster Atal Behari Vajpayee while addressing a conference of Accountant General's (2003), said that unimaginative audit damages administrative morale and observed,

Senior officers whose duty it is to take decisions and produce results, are often afraid of possible audit remarks and shy away from taking commercial decisions in a timely manner. Instead, they play it safe, preferring to take shelter under procedures and technicalities. Thus, the executive becomes a prisoner of procedures, rather than an achiever of purpose. An atmosphere in which the auditor is on the offensive and executive is on the defensive is detrimental to good governance.

Similar concerns, have been expressed by the President Dr AP J Kalam Azad, while inaugurating a conference of Accountant General's (2005). He suggested that audit teams should work alongside the project managers, design guidelines for efficient execution of various missions and provide constructive solutions and develop a systems approach to audit, so that they become partners in development. He observed,

Auditors audit after the event is over or the mission is completed, they will see with many deviations but they are too late to correct. I am sure you will realize the importance of providing online corrections to the deviations.

Outdated Methodology

Much of the problems faced by Audit department in producing quality work is due to its sticking to an outdated methodology and technique of audit. The basic approach is to audit a DDO (Drawing and Disbursing Officer) of every department, who handle receipt and payment transactions and are spread all over the country, in every State and district headquarters and run into thousands. Every year hundreds of audit parties visit the DDO's and issue an Audit Inspection

Report containing various irregularities mostly procedural, a good part of which is beyond the control of the office inspected.

The dimension of the problem can be realized by looking at the following data for one year 2003-04: For audit of Union government establishments, 24000 units were inspected and 22000 Audit Inspection reports were issued. For the States all taken together, 57000 units were inspected and 52000 reports issued.

In the States there is a system of central audit as all payments vouchers are sent to AG for accounts compilation. 11.75 million vouchers were audited and 48000 audit notes were issued involving a money value of Rs 1800 crores. Through Audit Inspection Reports huge amount of money spent by various departments is placed under objection, which leads to interminable correspondence and huge paper work, with no body knowing how to find a solution. Most of these audit objections die a natural death through efflux of time.

The current system has a great danger. Out of hundreds of audit objections, a few are of very serious nature such as overpayment of money, or cheating the government through misapplication of rules or a case of pure fraud. These serious irregularities also get lost in the volume of audit inspection reports, as there is no real follow up of the audit objections save those which appear in Audit Reports placed in legislature.

There is need to change current methodology for audit. Audit should be organized ministry and major department wise. Audit inspection reports of all the units under one departmental head (Chief Engineer, Director of Agriculture, Industries etc) should be consolidated and findings and broad conclusions about the working of the department drawn and issued to the Head of the department for response and compliance. In UK, USA, France audit is organized Ministry/ sector wise such as industry, energy, infrastructure etc. There is also need to change current methodology of audit. There is need to look into financial control and internal audit systems in various ministries/ departments and field outfits and ensure that an effective internal machinery is installed Modern sampling and statistical techniques would help in doing more effective audit.

The evolution and reform in audit methodology in other countries gives us valuable lessons. The American GAO founded in 1921, as a result of Budget and Accounting Act, primarily checked legality and adequacy of government expenditure until the end of World War II. The work was done centrally, which meant that government agencies had to send piles of accounting records to GAO's headquarters. Legions of audit clerks reviewed individual financial transactions and by 1945, GAO's staff had grown to 14000, but it still faced a huge backlog of 35 million unaudited vouchers. GAO changed its approach of work, and as a result of reform measures in early 50's, transferred a good part of its responsibilities such as voucher checking to the executive branch.

Instead of scrutinizing every fiscal transaction, GAO began to review financial control and management in federal agencies and urged them to improve their accounting systems and control over spending. In 70's GAO gradually shifted its work towards programme evaluation and started recruiting scientists, computer specialists and experts in public policy and built a team of professional investigators.

During last 20 years, GAO has worked with executive branch agencies to strengthen financial management and discard outmoded financial practices. Today with a strength of 3300 employees it is a lean professional outfit evaluating everything from computer security to challenges of an aging population and is the real force behind Congressional oversight of the Executive.

Evasion of Audit Responsibility—Audit of Privatisation

While the office of CAG is spending a great deal of its time and energy in auditing insignificant activities, it is neglecting to audit some critical areas of government's functioning. During last fifteen years Government has carried on large scale disinvestment and privatization but CAG has produced only two reports. CAG's first report was brought out in 1993, covering the first round of disinvestment during 1991-92. The second report relates to sale of Hotel Corporation of India's, Juhu Centur and Airport Centur hotel, submitted to Parliament in mid 2005.

Why have reports on sale of other transactions not brought out by CAG? Disinvestment has been of two kinds: (a) During NDA regime (2000-2004), majority equity of 14 PSU's such as BALCO, VSNL, CMC, IPCL was transferred into private hands, mainly through strategic sale route; (b) In other cases, while Government has retained majority control, equity has been disinvested through various methodologies such as transfer to public financial institutions, cross holding among PSU's, GDR (Global depository Receipt), auction of shares and offer to public through stock exchange. A sum of Rs 47600 crs has been realized between 1991-92- 2004-05.

Privatization of profitable PSU's such as BALCO became highly controversial and there were heated debates in Parliament and the matter came up before the Supreme Court. From the Supreme Court judgement and debates in Parliament it became clear, that while it is the prerogative of the Government to follow a policy of privatization, it has to be done in a fair and transparent manner, for which CAG has to give his satisfaction to the Parliament. The then Minister for Disinvestment Arun shourie had made a statement in the House that, after transactions are completed, all the papers and documents, will be turned over to CAG, to prepare an evaluation for sending to Parliament and releasing to the public. Why has CAG not discharged this responsibility?

It is not necessary that CAG should report to Parliament only when lapses are noticed. If CAG finds that transactions were done with due regard to financial prudence and propriety, he should say so in his report, which would give satisfaction to Parliament that the business of Government is being carried out properly and public interest has been safeguarded.

In UK, where large scale privatization was done during 1980's and 1990's, the National Audit Office (NAO) prepared an evaluation report in every case and submitted to Parliament. For example in case of Sale of Scottish Power and Hydro-Electric the NAO made the evaluation with reference to the objective set for sale, which were: completing the sale to time table; maximizing the net proceeds of sale; and promoting increased individual ownership.

NAO concluded that Department met the objectives of the sale and the sale was done on favourable terms and secured proceeds as high as expected. Audit reports on sale of Mining Operations of British Coal Corporation, London Transport, Residual Shareholdings in BP, BAA and other Privatised Companies, Sale of Freight Distribution, all concluded that sale process was effectively managed and secured best proceeds for the Treasury. C&AG's reports which received wide publicity, helped in securing public's favourable response to the policy of privatization and reassured the policy makers that they were on right track, emboldening them to pursue a more vigorous policy.

Realizing the importance of audit of privatization, INTOSAI (International Organisation of Supreme Audit Institution) has issued detailed guidelines on audit of privatization. India was one of the members of the sub group constituted to draft INTOSAI guidelines. One is therefore at a loss to understand why the office of CAG has not been bringing out audit reports on various privatization deals. One cannot but help getting the impression that CAG has abdicated this responsibility.

Collegiate Decision-Making—An Audit Commission

From the time India attained independence there has been multifold increase in the role and responsibilities of the government, largely due to government assuming responsibility for social and economic development of the people. This has resulted in tremendous growth in public expenditure. When India attained independence (1946-47) the receipt of the Government of India were of the order of Rs 3700 crs and expenditure Rs 3500 crs. The total receipt of 11 provinces was 548 crs and expenditure Rs 537 crs. Presently the expenditure of Central and State Government together has ballooned to Rs 9,00,000 crs, with Central government accounting for more than half of it at Rs 4,70,000 crs (2004-05). In 1947, there was one head office of the Auditor General in Simla and 4 federal offices, one each for federal government transactions, Railways, Military and Post & telegraph, and 11 offices engaged in provincial government accounts and audit. The total staff strength was 15000 with a budget of Rs 1.49 crs. Today the IAAD has a staff strength of 60000 with a annual budget of Rs 1100crs.

Despite tremendous growth in activities of government with consequent increase in the work of Audit department there has been no change in the organizational structure of the office of CAG. All powers have been centralized in the person holding the post of CAG - he being responsible for signing more than 100 audit reports presented to parliament and state legislature every year. This has telling impact on the efficiency of the working of the Audit department. There is no system of discussion of draft audit reports with Ministers and Secretaries to Government so that significant findings are brought to their notice for taking corrective action. This is possible only if responsibilities are shared and there are senior officers of appropriate status available in the Audit department to hold meaningful discussions with government This leaves yawning gap in the audit report, facts and conclusions are often challenged with the result that the main purpose of audit viz. improvement of the administrative machinery and the systems and procedure takes a back seat.

Most advanced countries have introduced a system of collegiate decision making. Audit Reports which are placed in Parliament are finalised through an Audit Board or Audit Commission of which all the senior officers of the State audit department are members enjoying legal authority.

In **France** the Cour des Comptes is presided by Premier President. The Cour has seven chambers each having jurisdictional authority over a defined range of central government activity. Each chamber is headed by a President. The Cour always acts as a collegiate body, whether in a judicial or non-judicial capacity. The Cour finalises its report after a collegial hearing, either before the entire Chamber which has 15 members or a single section which has at least three members. Audit findings are reported to a chamber of senior auditors chaired by one of the president of the Cour. Decisions, which may result in sanctions or fines, are made by majority vote in the chamber. The Cour is assisted by a Prosecutor General who gives legal advice and acts as intermediary between Government and the Court. The draft annual reports on the accounts of the state and the management of the state services, agencies and companies are brought before the complete bench presided over by the First President of the Cour. The report is adopted by Cour only after two conditions are met: the audited body has finally commented on the findings of the report and a collegial hearing of the Chamber has approved the report following organizational comments.

In **Germany** the Federal Court of Audit Act sets out the constitutional status of Bundesrechnungshof. All its members enjoy judicial independence and a constitutional status similar to that of judges. The final output from individual audit is in practice moderated by the collegiate (committees) decision making process. There is a three tier system- a college of two or three Directors, a Divisional Senate and a Large Senate which is the main decision making body. Large senate consists of 16 members- the President, the Vice President, the Directors of audit, the three Audit Managers and two rapporteurs. In addition to hearing and arbitration role the Large Senate decides the contents of Bundesrechnungshofs Annual Report.

In **Japan** there is an Audit Commission consisting of three Commissioners. All major decisions pertaining to audit are taken by the Audit Commission including finalisation of the Audit report. In **Korea** the Board of Audit is composed of seven Commissioners including the chairman. Decisions on policy issues, such as audit and inspection, are taken with the approval of the Council of Commissioners who are required to reach a decision by majority of constituent commissioners.

In **Sweden**, the State audit office known as Rikrevisionen has been completely reorganized from July 2003, enhancing its status as an independent organization guaranteed by the constitution. Parliament has created three posts of Auditor Generals, instead of one. Their appointment is approved by Parliament for a seven year term. The three Auditor jointly decide on matters of mutual interest and administrative issues of the organization but enjoy full autonomy for each of their areas of responsibility.

In **UK**, while the statutory authority for auditing Central government vests in the C&AG, a Management Board has been constituted to advise C&AG on discharge of his statutory duties. The Board is chaired by the C&AG, and comprises, the Dy CAG, six Assistant CAG's and the non-executive chairman of the Audit Committee.

Appointment of Comptroller and Auditor General

The Comptroller and Auditor General embodies an institution of great importance in maintaining discipline and probity in the management of national finances and helps establishing supremacy of the Parliament over the Executive. The Indian Constitution grants CAG an exalted status - he is appointed by President by a warrant under his hand and seal, has the same status as a Supreme Court judge; he cannot be removed from office save by an impeachment by Parliament; his conditions of service cannot be varied to his disadvantage; his salary is charged on the Consolidated fund of India. It is therefore important that persons of great professional competence and integrity are appointed to the post.

During last three decades the appointment of CAG has always been mired with controversy. From the time the Constitution came into being in 1950, the first three CAG's and the fifth were professionals from the Indian Audit & Accounts Service. However from 1978 onwards the last five incumbents, are from the Indian Administrative Service (IAS). The appointment of CAG who do not possess the requisite background of auditing and accounting has been subject of severe criticism by the members of the parliament, press, and the public.

The Indian Constitution does not lay down qualification for the post of CAG nor the manner of his selection. However the matter came up for discussion during the Constituent Assembly debates held in May 1949. An amendment was moved by Prof. K T Shah stating that, "The Auditor General shall be appointed from among persons qualified as registered Accountants or holding any other equivalent qualification". Replying to the debate T T Krishnamchari observed, "We had some very good Auditor Generals who were administrators and who had been in Finance Department and who have functioned as Accountant General in various places...All the knowledge of a registered accountant is certainly known to a person who holds the position of Auditor General in Government of India or Accountant General".

From the debates it is clear that framers of the Constitution's intention was that a person who had sufficient knowledge of finance and accounting systems and had practical experience of the work of Finance department and had worked as Accountant General would only be appointed. However, in practice this assurance has not been honored by successive governments.

In most of the countries of the world, the head of Supreme Audit Institution (SAI) is chosen after great deal of deliberation and care. In recent years most advanced democratic countries have made statutory enactments which requires appointment of head of SAI to be ratified by the Parliament. This is in recognition of the fact that national audit institutions work for the parliament and its main mandate is to secure effective parliamentary control over national finances.

In **U.K** an act to strengthen Parliamentary control and supervision of expenditure of public money by making new provision for appointment and status of C&AG and estab-lishing a Public Accounts Commission was enacted in 1983. The relevant provision regarding appointment of C&AG states that the, power of her Majesty to appoint C&AG shall be exercisable, "on an address presented by the House of Commons, and no motion shall be made for an address except by the Prime Minister acting with the agreement of the Chairman of the Committee of Public Accounts." Thus the person appointed as C&AG has to be jointly approved by the Prime Minister and Chairman of the Committee on Public Accounts and ratified by the House of Commons. The CAG is also made an officer of the House of Commons.

In **USA** under the Budget and Accounting Act of 1921, the Comptroller General of the United States and the Assistant Comptroller General of the United States shall be appointed by the President with the advise and consent of the Senate. The Congress participates in the selection of the Comptroller General by providing a list of candidates from which the President may choose and by confirming the appointment. The Act further amplifies the selection process of Controller General, and stipulates establishing a Commi-ssion to recommend the name for the post. The Commission shall consist of: (a) the Speaker of the House of Represen-tative, (b) the President of the Senate, (c) the majority and minority leaders of the House of representatives and Senate, (d) the Chairman and the ranking minority member of the Commission on Government Operations of the House of Representative and of the Committee on Government Affairs of the Senate. The Commission is required to recommend the name of at least three persons.

In **Australia** under the Auditor General Act of 1997, he is appointed by the Governor General on the recommendation of the Minister, after the Minister has referred his recommendation to the Joint Committee of Public Accounts and Audit and the Committee has approved the same.

In **Germany** the President and Vice President of the Federal Court of Audit (Bundesrechnuhof) is elected by Bundestag and Bundesrat (Parliament) without debate upon a proposal made by the Federal government. Before the proposal is made by the Federal President, he shall consult the standing committee of the large Senate of the Federal Court of audit.

In **Japan** the Board of Audit has three Commissioners. The Commissioners are appointed by the Cabinet, with the consent of both Houses of the Diet. In **South Korea** the Chairman of the Board of Audit is appointed by the President with the consent of the National Assembly. Similarly in **Thailand** the appointment of Auditor General must receive prior approval of National Assembly.

Most countries have not prescribed any qualification for the person to be appointed as the Head of Supreme Audit Institution in the Act governing SAI's. However, in Canada the Auditor General's Act prescribes that Governor in Council shall appoint a "qualified auditor" to be the officer called Auditor General of Canada. In practice it is seen that Auditor General's are appointed from amongst the officers who have considerable experience of work in their national audit offices and have been holding the post of Dy Auditor General / Members of Audit Court/ Board of Audit. Some countries have appointed professional Accountants holding qualification of Certified Public Accountant and possessing rich experience of public service to head the SAI.

Controversy Surrounding the Appointment of CAG

The appointment of IAS officers who do not possess adequate knowledge of accounts, audit and finance to the post of CAG had devastating effect on the morale of the Audit Department and lead to severe decline in its efficiency and effectiveness. The Members of Parliament, press and public men have time and again emphasizing the need for transparency in the appointment of CAG. The appointment of a non- professional as CAG has been continuously resisted by the members of the Indian Audit & Accounts Service and staff associations of audit department and representations made to President, Prime Minister and Finance Minister. K P Joseph former Accountant General and a perceptive commentator of financial management in government says that, " This is like appointing an IAS officer without a law degree as the Chief Justice of the Supreme Court".

In January 1996, just before the new CAG was to be appointed, the veteran social activist H D Shourie filed a PIL (Public Interest Litigation) in the Supreme Court, raising a public grievance with respect to the arbitrary and unfair manner and procedure being adopted by the Government in making the appointment of the CAG, pointing out that, 'the duties cast upon the CAG by the Constitution and Act 65 of 1971 are such as can be performed by a person possessing sound knowledge of auditing and accounting and also of wide experience in this kind of work which is of a highly technical nature.'

In March 1996 Ram Naik, the then Chairman of Public Accounts Committee took up the matter with the highest echelons of the government and met the President of India and the Prime Minister and submitted them a petition. However despite these efforts Government remained unmoved and appointed VK Shunglu as CAG in March 1996. Commenting on the appointment the veteran journalist Inder Malhotra wrote in the Hindu that it, 'is something of a shock and an extremely depressing one', and described his appointment as a politico-administrative coup. The Indian Express columnist Neerja Choudhry observed that appointment, 'gives an insight into the proximity that the country's top civil servants have with the center of power'. The appointment of VK Shunglu was widely believed to be due to his influence with the PMO (Prime Minister's Office).

The appointment of V N Kaul in March 2002 came as a surprise to the audit community and those concerned with public administration. He was holding the post of Secretary Ministry of Petroleum before the appointment. No body knows the criteria followed by Government in making the appointment. Ramaswamy R. Iyer a distinguished former member of Indian Audit & Accounts Service says that, without casting aspersion on the merit of an individual appointed to the post, "the great institution of the comptroller and auditor general of India stands eroded and diminished in credibility and moral authority by the manner in which the incumbent is appointed", and pleads for transparency in his appointment.

The Prime Minister apparently enjoys unfettered powers to appoint 'anyone' as CAG. The fact that the views of Chairman of Public Accounts Committee, Members of Parliament, eminent public men, press, the entire audit fraternity and public opinion were ignored by successive Prime Minster's when the issue of appointment of CAG came up before them , reflects an arbitrary style of functioning. This is reminiscent of dictatorial style of Nazi Germany, when the German Audit Office was completely emasculated and Adolf Hitler issued a decree that he can appoint and dismiss officers of German Audit Office at will.

Demoralising Impact on Audit Department

When the post of CAG is filled by non- professionals, even if they are otherwise, competent persons, it has serious repercussion on the efficient working of the Audit department. They are unable to give leadership and lack confidence in taking bold decisions, which comes from years of grind and expert knowledge of the subject. Being outsiders, CAG's often fall prey to inner power play of Audit Service Officers and start playing favorites. This has devastating effect on the morale of the officers, with adverse impact on the efficiency of the department.

The head of the Institution has to play a leadership role and become a change leader. During last three decades, for want of leadership, the institution of CAG has not been able to introduce new and innovative methods of doing audit and modernize the department, to keep pace with the changing times and the credibility of the institution has been seriously eroded. This is in contrast to first two decades, after independence when CAG's played key role in management of nations finances. V Narhari Rao the first CAG brought far reaching reforms and set up a well structured organization reeling under problems created as a result of partition of the country and integration of finances of the erstwhile princely states in the Union. The second CAG, Ashok Chanda helped setting up the system of Financial Adviser in Central government ministries to deal with the huge volume of work generated as a result of development planning. The third CAG, AK Roy took up the responsibility to audit revenue and improve the government tax collection machinery. The CAG's held meetings with the Prime Minister Pt Jawaharlal Nehru and

Finance Ministers, enjoyed great respect and credibility and worked in close rapport with the government.

Is Audit Independent?

Supreme Audit Institutions (SAI) can fulfill their tasks objectively and effectively only if they are independent of the audited entity and are protected against outside influence. However, executive wing of the government, which yields power may try to subvert its independence. Franz Fiedler Secretary General of INTOSAI and President Austrian Court of Audit says that, "This implies a constant risk of the executive branch influencing the activities of the government audit authorities and interfering with their independence. If such influence were indeed exercised over government audit, the SAI would soon find itself in a state of dependency upon the government it is auditing. Thus, the objective and effective control of the financial management of the state would be impaired and any government audit would deteriorate into an act of self-control or an 'alibi' of the government for its actions. The SAI would become nothing more than a puppet of the government."

The Indian Constitution guarantees independence of CAG. Under Article 148 he is appointed by President by warrant under his hand and seal and can be removed from office only in the like manner and grounds as a judge of the Supreme Court, his salary and conditions of service are laid down by law and cannot be varied to his disadvantage after his appointment. The Constitution, is however silent regarding the manner of selection and appointment of C&AG and if the Executive can make an appointment without following a transparent criteria, how does it guarantee independence of the SAI ?

Ramaswamy Iyer a doyen of audit department arguing for transparency in appointment of CAG says, "unfortunately, the constitutional provisions which are intended to protect a good and independent CAG will also protect an undistinguished or even a bad CAG." It is therefore necessary that CAG's are appointed by following transparent criteria and Executive should not have final say in his appointment as discussed in previous chapter.

To maintain independence of audit, most advanced democratic countries such as UK, USA, Germany, Japan, Australia, Austria, Belgium, Israel, and newly emerging countries such as South Korea and Thailand have all adopted a system under which the appointment of head of SAI requires approval of national legislative assembly.

The Determinants of Independence

There are three main components of the independence of Supreme Audit Institutions (SAI): (a) Organizational Independence, which includes the SAI's exclusive sovereignty in matters of human resources, including recruitment of personnel; (b) Functional Independence. The SAI should be free to set its own priorities and apply the audit method and techniques it considers appropriate and enjoy complete freedom regarding the substance of its reports. There should be exclusion of any possibility of government influencing its activity. (c) Financial Independence. The effectiveness of audit will be impaired if a chronic shortage of funds prevents the SAI from exercising the control function properly.

While the office of CAG enjoys functional independence and is free to decide its own priorities regarding conduct of audit and reporting, it suffers from severe organizational constraints. In personnel matters it has to follow the norms laid down by Government for recruitment, promotion and other staff perquisites which impairs its efficient functioning. In financial matters CAG follows the guidelines laid down by Ministry of Finance, but it has not been a major constraint, as it is generally granted whatever budget allocation it seeks for carrying on its activity.

No Independence for Senior Audit Personnel

It is claimed that in India, the office of CAG functions independent of the Executive. This statement needs closer examination. There is little doubt that the person holding the post of CAG has been given great deal of independence. But it must be realized that while discussing independence of state audit, the constitutional guarantee of independence of head of the SAI is only one of the issues. The larger issue is: does independence of one person who heads the department, guarantees independence of the Audit Department as a whole?

The Lima Declaration regarding the independence of members and officials of SAI states as follows:

1. The independence of Supreme Audit Institutions is inseparably linked to the independence of its members. Members are defined as those persons who have to make the decisions for the Supreme Audit Institutions and are answerable for these decisions to third parties, consequently the members of a decision-making collegiate body or the head of a monocratically organize Supreme Audit Institutions.

2. The independence of the members, too, shall be guaranteed by the Constitution. In particular the recall procedures, also to be embodied in the Constitution, may not impair the independence of the members. The method of appointment and recall of members depends on the constitutional structure of the country in question.
3. With regard to their professional career, the auditors of Supreme Audit Institutions may not be exposed to influences by the audited entities and may not be dependent on such entities.

The top functionaries of Audit Department, Dy CAG's, Director General/ Principal Directors of Audit responsible for Union Government audit and Principal Accountant Generals/ Accountant Generals in the States are responsible for all policy decisions, including preparation of Audit Reports.

They take decisions for the Audit department and fall in the category of those whose independence should be guaranteed as per the norms set by Lima declaration. But no independence or protection has been given to them under any of the statutes. There is not even a mention of any of them, in the CAG's Act of 1971. In the absence of any legally defined independent status to senior functionaries of Audit Department all the administrative and technical powers have been concentrated in the person of CAG. This impinges on their independent functioning.

The internal functioning of the Audit department can hardly be called democratic. CAG heads the Departmental Promotion Committees for promotion to the posts of Accountant General/ Principal Director of Audit and upto the level of Deputy CAG (the appointment of Dy CAG, though approved by Appointments Committee of the Cabinet is also made on the basis of CAG's recommendations). CAG is also the Reviewing Officer or himself writes the Confidential Reports of all the officers of the rank of AG / Principal Director and above.

Thus if CAG takes an adverse view about the work or character of a particular officer, he has no 'Court of Appeal' where to seek redressal and his career can be completely jeopardized.

CAG's wide powers to distribute patronage, such as posting to lucrative posts abroad and UN assignments, breeds a tendency on the part of large majority of IA&AS officers to seek favours from him and develop a tendency of sycophancy and servility. This has disastrous effect on their independent functioning which the job demands.

Situation of Double Squeeze

Vesting all the powers in one person often results in a dictatorial and arbitrary style of functioning. It is a fact of history that if power gets concentrated in one person, he tends to become unresponsive and autocratic. Absolute power has a very corrupting influence. Modern management practices emphasize importance of delegation, decentralization and sharing of power. The senior officers of the Audit department face a situation of double squeeze. Within the department they have to suffer an authoritarian rule where dissent is not tolerated. While dealing with outside world, they have no legal protection to discharge their responsibility without fear or favour. The situation needs to be corrected by making the functioning of the office of CAG more democratic. In previous chapters we have argued for restructuring the office of CAG, by constituting a multi-member Audit Commission at the apex level at the Centre and strengthening the position of Accountant General in the States by a suitable legal enactment.

There are numerous instances of intimidation of senior officers of audit department, when they have raised uncomfortable questions against persons in authority. The Chief Minister of Tamilnadu Jaylalitha took severe exception, to Accountant General Tamilnadu talking to the press about the State finances, threatened him and wanted him to be transferred out of the State. When the audit report on fodder scandal in Bihar was released, former Chief Minister Laloo Prasad Yadav launched a tirade against AG Bihar and demanded that he should be jailed for not being able to detect the irregularity! The Director General of Audit responsible for investigating the Bofors Gun case, was kept under surveillance, his phone taped and harassed by Intelligence agencies. Because of the sensitive nature of work which audit is required to do there is need for legal protection of officers who take decisions on behalf of the department.

European Countries- Independence Guaranteed by law

In West European countries such as France, Germany, Belgium and Austria state auditors are considered high officers of judicial standing and their independence is guaranteed by law. The French Cour des Comptes, has seven chambers each headed by a President and acts as a collegiate body. Its reports on the accounts of the state and the management of the state services are adopted only after a collegial hearing by a complete bench presided by First President of the Court. Each chamber has a jurisdictional authority over defined range of central government activity and is headed by a President and employs about thirty magistrates. The French law gives the magistrates irremovable status.

In Germany all the members of the Federal Court of Audit (FCA) - Bundesrechungshof enjoy judicial independence and a status similar to that of judges. The transfer, retirement, removal from office and the discipline of the members with judicial status are regulated in accordance with the rules for judges of the Federal High Court. The President, Vice President, the head of audit divisions and audit units, which number about 60, are members of Bundesrechungshof. The appointment of President and Vice President of Bundesrechungsh of needs approval of Parliament, and its members are appointed by Federal President on the proposal made by President of the Audit Office. In Germany there is great deal of emphasis on the personal independence of members of Bundesrechungshof, which includes professional independence even against the head of the audit body. Similar is the position in other European counties such as Austria and Belgium.

The independence of audit cannot be secured by limiting it to only one person who heads the department. The independence of all the senior functionaries, such as Accountant General, Director General and Deputy CAG should also be guaranteed and their powers should be laid down by legal enactment. This is a necessary caveat for Audit department to be able to function independently and discharge its duties as laid down in the Constitution.

Personnel Management

Public audit today faces a major challenge to establish its identity as an effective instrument of public accountability. This demands a highly professional approach to audit. As a result of changes in the role and functions of government and government entering into new areas such as electronic data processing (EDP), establishment of regulatory agencies, privatization, and public-private participation, new skills are required for auditing.

In addition to developing expertise in performance audit, there is also need to develop techniques of systems audit to examine areas such as, soundness of financial and accounting rules, control systems; working of internal audit and norms set for quality management. Audit will have to master knowledge of distinguishing wheat from the chaff, so that it does not get lost in vast jungle of data, figures and irrelevant details of an organization it audits. There is need for great deal of professionalism in the working of the India Audit and Accounts Department (IA&AD) which can come only if high priority is given to human resource management.

Personnel Management- A Weak Area

The personnel and human resource management in IA&AD is a weak area. The department is highly clerk oriented. An army 34000 persons work in the audit wing of the department out of which 11500 are in Group B (Audit Officers/Section Officers), 19000 in Group C (assistants and clerks) and 3000 in Group D- peons etc (the Audit department as a whole, including accounts wing has a staff strength of 58000 comprising 16000 in Group B, 36500 in Group C and 5000 in Group D). The strength of Group A (IA&AS) is a meager 500 out of which about 300 work in audit stream. Due to lop sided staff composition, heavily oriented towards low skilled junior level work force, the department is not able to produce high quality work.

The composition and character of audit parties which does initial investigation and visits various offices has not changed during the last fifty years. An audit party consists generally of a three member team, headed by an Audit Officer and accompanied by a Section Officer and an Assistant. Senior officers of the level of Deputy Accountant General / Director of Audit do not, as a normal practice supervise audit, visit field and hold discussions with their counterpart in administrative departments before findings are drawn by way of Audit Inspection Reports. The staff is recruited at the level of Upper Division Clerk or Assistant who after some years of service pass the departmental Subordinate Account Service (SAS) Examination and qualify to hold the post of Section Officer and by seniority get promoted as Audit Officers and are responsible for conducting most of the field inspections. The staff recruited at clerical level and the temperament they possess after remaining in subordinate position for many years does not equip them to conduct quality audit.

There is need to reorient the personnel policies. Bright young boys/girls from colleges and universities should be recruited directly into the SAS, given two years of training in modern techniques of audit, accounts and financial management and required to pass an examination before inducting in the cadre of Group B service. To make the job attractive there should be an opportunity for their career progression to Group A Service, after rendering 15-20 years of service,. This would help in building a cadre of professionally competent Audit Managers and provide valuable support to top management of IA&AD.

Modernizing Audit Department

For efficient functioning, the Audit department needs to be transformed from a babu oriented to an officer oriented department. The Audit department should shed its fat and do away completely with the role of Group C staff in audit work. The recruitment of staff for audit work should only be at the SAS level who may constitute second tier in audit investigation machinery. There is severe shortage of Group A officers to do quality work. The strength of IA&AS needs to be raised to 1000, and gradually to 2000, from present level of 500, through massive recruitment both direct and promotional route. In view of technical nature of work there is need to recruit Computer specialists, Economists, Chartered and Cost Accountants, Engineers and other specialists through lateral entry in Group A cadre. Expertise can also be drawn by enlisting services of professionals and technical groups by entering short term contracts with them.

The US GAO has a staff of 3200 which includes accountants, health experts, engineers, environment specialists, economists, social scientists, actuaries and statisticians. GAO's performance auditors are supported by experts in technical discipline such as data collection and survey methods, statistics, econometric modeling, information technology and law. In Canada audit staff includes a mix of academic discipline and experience in their work. Accountants, engineers, lawyers, management specialists, information technology professionals etc make up for the multidisciplinary staff. Where the necessary skills are not available in-house, expertise is arranged on contractual basis. UK recruits professionally qualified accountants for financial audit and for doing performance audit it has on its roll specialists from disciplines such statistics, environment issues, defence and business policy.

Human Resource Management -Key to Efficiency

The importance of people as the most important resource for efficient working of the Audit department has not found recognition from policy makers. The staff is generally de-motivated and suffers from frustration. Most of the audit staff works in very trying conditions. They have to do touring round the year and inspect various offices spread in different parts of the State. There are no proper facilities for their stay and travel. Due to nature of work they do, there is an atmosphere of indifference if not hostility in the offices which they audit. They have to use considerable ingenuity to access records and elicit response of the departmental officers. The poor response of administration to audit inspection reports and a general feeling that audit is at best to be suffered and ignored leads to frustration among audit personnel. Y Krishna a distinguished former Dy CAG says, "This attitude towards audit has seriously demoralized the auditors in the performance of their duties and they often suffer from a sense of futility in their work." There are numerous instances of audit personnel at different levels such as auditors, audit officers and IA&AS officers, doing brilliant work resulting in savings of lakhs of rupees for the government, but the office of CAG has no system of recognizing their merit. It has not instituted even a system of annual award to outstanding workers, a common practice in other departments of the government. All this results in low morale of the staff and poor productivity.

There is need to inspire the audit staff and give them a feeling that they are doing an important job and are the principal instrument in making administration accountable, for service of the people. Management guru Peter Drucker emphasizes that management is all about human beings. The task of management is to make people capable of joint performance, make their strength effective and inspire and motivate them to run their organization efficiently. Tom Peters and Waterman say that most management systems treat people as, "factors of production", as cogs in the industrial machine. They pay lip service to the fact that people are important, but having said that, they don't pay much attention to the people. People are the most neglected factors in the management scheme of the Audit department.

W Edward Denning the Quality guru has said, that 90 percent problems in an organization are general problems relating to bad systems and only 10 percent are specific problem relating to people. Most management misinterpret this data, and presume that if they correct the structure and systems, the problem with people will go away. Motivational expert Stephen Covey says, the reverse is actually true: if you correct the 10 percent first, the other problems will go away, " If you want to improve the programme, work first on the programmer; people produce the strategy, structure and styles of the organization. These are the arms and hands of the minds and hearts of the people". The same thought was echoed by Jack Welch the visionary Chairman of General Electric when he said, "People first, strategy and everything else second".

In this study we have emphasized the need for changing the existing systems and structure of the Audit department to make it an effective instrument of enforcing financial discipline and public accountability. However, systems and structures can be changed only by people, and therefore in any scheme of reform, the people who do audit will have to be given the highest priority.

Transforming the department into a lean and dynamic organization and developing technically competent, motivated and professional staff to undertake multifaceted and complex audit assignments should be the central agenda for the personnel policy planners in the Audit department.

Accountability of Comptroller and Auditor General—Who Audits the Auditor?

Independence of CAG should not be equated with immunity from a review and evaluation of its operations. As a matter of fact, the importance of audit mission, and what audit entails by way of resources deployed by agencies subject to audit, underlines the importance of subjecting the State audit to regular and perceptive scrutiny. It is necessary the state audit demonstrates that its own operations stand the test of professional soundness, efficiency and effectiveness.

In India while the CAG conducts audit of expenditure incurred by President of India, Governors of State , Lok Sabha / Rajya Sabha, the Supreme Court / High Court, UPSC and other constitutional functionaries there is no independent external audit, even of the expenditure of CAG's outfit, leave apart a review of his performance.

In practice CAG nominates one of the Accountant General under him as an auditor for his office. Under the existing arrangement the AG can at best conduct some regularity audit functions- though even for this task there would be a technical snag , as CAG has issued a regulation that no subordinate office can question the merits of a sanction issued by his office. This is obviously an unsatisfactory arrangement .

Peer Review

A fundamental goal in doing performance audit is to promote good governance practices in government department and agencies. Therefore audit practices should reflect recognized professional standards and it should be able to produce independent, objective and supportable information that parliament can rely on to examine government's performance and hold it to account. A peer review by Supreme Audit Institutions (SAI's) has several advantages: first the review team would be free of any conflict of interest or other impairment to its independence. Second those engaged in review be competent to perform the necessary work. Third the approach adopted for the review be widely understood and recognized as credible.

Peer Review of Canadian Auditor General

In 2004 a peer review of the office of the Auditor General (OAG) of Canada was done by a team led by UK National Audit Office with representatives of SAI's from Norway, Netherlands and France. US GAO participated as an observer. The peers adopted a principle- based approach focusing on independence, objectivity and reliability. It was felt that SAI's should be assessed against standards of professional practice applicable in their countries and that peer review should be carried on in accordance with commonly accepted auditing principles consistent with INTOSAI's (International Organization of Supreme Audit Institution) Code of Ethics and Auditing Standards. The peers adopted an open, transparent peer review process with three key elements: design assessment which included quality management framework; reliance assessment; and implementation assessment.

The peer team concluded that Australian Audit Office performance audit practices reflected, recognized professional standards and operated effectively to produce independent, objective, and supportable information that can be relied on to examine the governments performance. The report also provided several suggestions for improvement. In its report to the House of Commons, the Public Accounts Committee said the following, "Having independent and external confirmation of the soundness of the Office's value-for-money practices provides additional assurances about the integrity of the Office of the Auditor General of Canada and adds credibility to its efforts to provide objective, supportable and reliable information on the administration of government programme and activities". Canada had also appointed an external audit firm (1999) to review the quality management system for financial audit. The reviewers concluded that the system was suitably designed and operated effectively.

Peer Review, US GAO

A peer review of Government Accountability Office (GAO) of USA was done in April 2005, by an international team with representatives from Canada, Australia, Mexico, Netherlands, Norway and South Africa. GAO's Quality Assurance System as laid down in Government Auditing Standards is intended to provide confidence that: work is professional, independent, and objectively designed; evidence is complete and reliable; conclusions are supported; products are fair and balanced and recommendations are sound. The peer review concluded that the GAO's quality assurance system is suitably designed and in addition to providing reasonable assurance of conformance with Government Auditing Standards, reinforces the independence, objectivity, and reliability of the office and its work.

Comptroller and Auditor General and Parliament Relationship

Public audit institutions, all over the world, have developed over time to help legislatures implement power of the purse. This power had two essential elements: the granting of moneys by parliament and supervision of expenditure by the state audit institutions. In England the main component of Exchequer and Audit Act 1886 was to create an audit department with a view to audit all government departments and make a report to parliament. The results of C&AG investigations were considered by a special parliamentary committee called Committee of Public Accounts. This arrangement solved a dilemma which baffled parliament for years- how could non-expert parliamentarians control expenditure? The creation of an independent expert institution which reports its findings to parliament and a dedicated parliamentary committee scrutinizing the reports, resolved the problem.

The special relationship that CAG enjoys with parliament raises an issue of political theory- is CAG a legislative branch agency and belongs to one of the three classical power domain, the other two being executive and judiciary, or does CAG belong to fourth power not classifiable among the three.

CAG - A Legislative Branch Agency

In **UK** and other advanced countries such as Australia, Canada and New Zealand which follow British parliamentary tradition C&AG is now recognized as a legislative branch agency. In **UK** with the passing of National Audit Act in 1983, the position of C&AG was strengthened and he has been made 'an officer of the house of commons'. While C&AG has complete discretion in the discharge of his functions, in determining whether to carry out an examination ' he shall take into account any proposals made by the Committee on Public Accounts' In **Australia** under the Auditor General Act of 1997, the Auditor General will be an independent officer of Parliament. The act also stipulates that, Auditor General while discharging his functions will keep in view the priorities of Parliament and joint committee of Public Accounts and Audit. Similar is the position in **New Zealand** and **Canada**, where as a result of recent amplification of the Audit Act, the Auditor General has been made an officer of the parliament.

In **USA** the General Accounting Office(GAO) since its inception in 1921, has been recognized as an agency within the legislative branch of the government and enjoys special working relationship with the American Congress. Initially, GAO's location in the structure of government was ambiguous.

GAO was created at the instigation of the Congress, to satisfy the wishes for an independent auditor to whom it could look for information. At the same time the presidential appointment of the Comptroller General, together with GAO's inheritance from the Treasury of some executive functions, led some to conclude that GAO straddled the executive/ legislature boundary, having a foot in both the camps.

The matter was settled in 1985, when the US Supreme Court ruled, that GAO is a legislative branch agency. GAO's recent history shows a continuing evolution in response to the needs of the Congress. Until 1970's virtually all GAO's work responded to its own sense of need and priorities and hardly 10 percent of reports were in response to Congressional requests. However, by end of 1980's more than 80 percent of GAO's resources were involved in responding to specific Congressional requests.

In countries where there is a system of Audit Courts such as France, Germany and Italy, State audit, while it performs functions of expenditure control on behalf of Parliament, enjoys much wider powers and functions and acts like a judicial body. For example in France, the Cour des Comptes is assisted by a Prosecutor General responsible for providing legal advice and acts as an intermediary between Government and the Court.

The Cour is not only in a position to rectify faulty accounts but also to recover improperly expended public funds or cash deficits from accounting officers. However, while it comes close to resembling judicial branch, it cannot be regarded as part of the judiciary because it has the additional function of assisting parliament and the government in the process of political accountability and budget management.

Hans Schaffer, a former President of German Court of Audit observes, that German Supreme Audit Institution does not stand the test of autonomous "fourth power", more so because it has no power of enforcement. Schafer says that the aim of separation of powers must be realization of a system of check and balances with a view to serve the protection of the individual and state audit contributes to realization of a balance within the State power system.

Ambiguous Position In India

In India where we have adopted Westminster model of parliamentary democracy his position is analogous to that of UK and other Commonwealth countries such as Australia, Canada and New Zealand. He should therefore be legitimately considered as part of legislative wing of the government. Somehow there is considerable ambiguity in the mind of the office of CAG. The official web cite of the CAG says, "the Comptroller and Auditor General of India has a dual role to perform- firstly as an agency to function on behalf of the Legislature to ensure that the Executive complies with the various laws, passed by the legislature in letter and spirit, and secondly, on behalf of the Executive to ensure compliance by subordinate authorities with the rules and orders issued by it.

The Comptroller and Auditor General is thus, as head of the Indian Audit and Accounts Department, is neither a part of the Legislature nor the Executive but is an officer created by the Constitution to see that diverse authorities act in regard to all matters in accordance with the Constitution; and the laws and rules framed there under." Similar views have been held by some of the persons who have donned the mantle of C&AG in the past, and virtually claimed that they are an independent fourth branch of government.

There is a serious conceptual error, if the Office of CAG does not regard itself as part of parliamentary wing of government, if we consider three classical power domains- the Executive, Judiciary and Legislature which constitute government. CAG's main job is to see that budget passed by Parliament is faithfully executed by the Executive and report to it deviations from its intent. Unlike Executive and Judiciary, CAG enjoys no inherent or enforcement powers of its own. It is the backing and support it receives from the Parliament and its Financial Committees which is his main strength. Due to this conceptual error, the Indian CAG has not kept a close working relationship with the Parliament and Public Accounts Committee. Most CAG's in the past have not even been attending the meetings of the PAC on regular basis and have left the task to his deputies.

The position in the States is particularly pathetic and anomalous. Under the Constitution CAG is required to place Audit Report on State Accounts to respective Legislatures which in turn gets remitted to State Public Accounts Committees. This implies that CAG in person should be available to State PAC's to assist in the examination of Audit Reports. But how could one individual make himself available to 28 PAC's in 28 different States? The original draft of the Constitution proposed by Dr B R Ambedkar had proposed separate Auditor-in Chief for the States, but the provision got deleted at the stage of final passing of the Constitution.

The function of CAG is discharged by State Accountant General's (AG's). Unfortunately the State Accountant Generals function under a fragmented structure. There is no single functionary (AG) in the State responsible for all the auditing responsibilities nor any meaningful delegation given to him. One would have expected that for such an important functionary, statutory recognition would have at least been accorded. But there is not even a mention of AG and his duties and functions in the CAG's Act of 1971. Due to this basic flaw Accountant General's are in a weak position in the States and are unable to bear their authority on the working of government. AG's are also not able to influence the working of PAC's and in most States they are non-functional for all practical purposes.

Due to the conceptual error of not recognizing himself as part of parliamentary/legislative wing of the government, the institution of CAG has landed itself in a situation which can be described as an agency which is 'disowned by Parliament and despised by Government'.

3

Public Audit

Good Governance is the most important issue facing the country today. This implies gearing up the government machinery to provide a responsive, transparent, clean and people-friendly administration. Good governance is also linked with the role of the State: what it can do and cannot do matching its capability and resources to undertake the task assigned for itself. During the last *50* years, the view regarding the role of State in economic and social development of a country has shifted dramatically.

The collapse of the command economies of Soviet Union and Eastern Europe and the retreat from the concept of welfare State in the Western industrialised countries which has engulfed them in fiscal crisis has shown the limitation of State action. At the same time, economic, social and sustainable development cannot take place without State taking an active part. From the time the institution of the State was founded, its basic task has been cut out as follows: establishing a foundation of law; investing in basic services like education and health and infrastructure, and protecting the vulnerable sections.

However, after the World War II, the size and scope of government has expanded enormously. Japan and the newly industrialised countries of East Asia are discharging the role of an activist state in promoting development notwithstanding the recent economic crisis facing them. In these countries, the State has played a people and market-friendly role—building the infrastructure, educating and training the workers and providing a stable climate to enable release of creative urge of the people and help the economy to grow and flourish. The message from international experience is clear: *what is required is not minimal government but an effective government.*

For an effective government, it is necessary that in a democratic polity the executive wing of the government is accountable to Parliament and through it to the people to whom it is supposed to serve. Thus, public accountability is a key ingredient of good governance. Public accountability means the obligation of persons and authorities entrusted with public resources for proper management of such resources and be answerable for the fiscal, managerial and programme responsibilities that are conferred on them. Every democratic country provides a formalised set-up in the shape of public audit to ensure that public funds are properly used and make a report to the Parliament who has the final authority for passing the national budget and giving sanction for spending money and levying of taxes. The Indian Constitution provides for the institution of Comptroller and Auditor General (C&AG) as the custodian of national finance. The Comptroller and Auditor General, Act of 1971 lays down the duties and functions of C&AG.

Development of Public Audit In India

From Voucher Audit to Programme Evaluation

The system of accounting and audit that we inherited at the time of independence required that Accountant General (AG) in every state and in Centre (AGCR) as representative of C&AG to compile accounts and audit them. The audit was characterised by a highly formal, legalistic review of each payment and examining whether payment is conforming to an elaborate set of rules governing public expenditure. In 1976, a major reform in accounting and payment system was introduced and the accounts of Central Government departments were separated and transferred to ministries and individual departments. Thus, individual departments were required to make payments through the nationalised banks, compile their accounts and do their own voucher checking. The C&AG's role was limited to prescribing accounting principles and checking adequacy of financial procedure and control. This reform brought a major shift in the working of the audit department—giving more emphasis towards the wisdom of public expenditure rather than only to its legality. It may be noted that separation of accounting from audit has not yet taken place in the state governments where AGs continue to shoulder responsibility for accounting through a highly centralised system of compiling individual vouchers. Thus, huge volumes of vouchers are required to be carted from individual treasury in every district of the state to the headquarters of AG's office.

With the launching of Five Year Plans for economic and social development, there has been change in the role of State. This has necessitated shift in emphasis, concept and practice of audit. Earlier Government Audit was confined to check against provision of funds, and rules or orders or sanctions for expenditures. Their application to individual transactions were quite effective in detection of cases of improper, irregular, extravagant, wasteful and uneconomical expenditure.

However, when the pattern of governmental expenditure underwent rapid and radical transformation in the wake of increasing outlays on development activities, the scrutiny of individual transactions became inadequate as it tended to mistake wood for the tree. Parliament and the public were now interested to know whether various development and welfare programmes were being executed efficiently, whether their operations were conducted economically and whether these were producing the expected results. This lead the audit department to enter in the area of programme evaluation and value for money audit.

Financial Anarchy in Bihar

The fodder scandal in Bihar that was facilitated due to the withdrawal hundreads of crores of public funds without budgetary appropriation has made a mockery of the financial provisions of the Indian Constitution which has prescribed an elaborate machinery of control over public funds. The latest Audit Report of the Comptroller and Auditor General for the year ending March 1995 presented to the State Legislature on July 23, 1996 points out that "excess drawal" over voted provisions has been continuing since 1977-78—and during the 18-year period from 1977-78 to 1994-95 an excess drawal of over Rs 5383.68 crores has taken place without regularization by the State Legislature: while the amount of "excess drawal" was not very significant in earlier years (Rs 14.51 crores in 1977-78 and Rs 31.11 crores in 1978-79), the "excess drawal" over the voted budgetary provision jumped to Rs 1228.67, crores in 1991-92, Rs 1462.10 crores in 1992-93, Rs 702.17 crores in 1993-94 and was Rs 318.23 crores in 1994-95.

A large part of the excess expenditure has been taking place in grants relating to Animal Husbandry though there are several departments like Pensions and General Services, Public Works and Medical which have been exceeding budgetary limits with impunity. In eight years from 1987-88 the excess drawal in the Animal Husbandry

Department was of the order of Rs 505.12 crores against the budgetary allocation of Rs 442.13 crores (during 1994-95 against the budgetary sanction of Rs 74.40 crores a sum of Rs 345.01 crores was drawn).

What was the Finance Department of the State Government, which is responsible for presenting the Budget to the State Legislature, doing all these years? If money can be drawn from the government treasury in total disregard of the budgets approved by the State Legislature what use are the provisions of Articles 202, 203 and 204 of the Constitution (parallel Articles 112, 113 and 114 in the case of the Central Government) which enjoin that an annual financial statement will be laid before the Houses of the Legislature of the State and an Appropriation Bill will be introduced and no money shall be withdrawn from the Consolidated Fund of the State except the appropriation made by law?

The aforesaid situation under which money has been drawn from the treasury in total disregard of the budgetary ceilings approved by the State Legislature has perhaps been allowed to continue due to the misunderstanding of the true import of Article 205 (b) of the Constitution (parallel Article 115 (b) in the case of the Central Government) which enjoins that if "any money has been spent on any service during a financial year in excess of the amount granted for that service and for that year" a statement be presented to the House for a demand of such excess.

In the author's view, Articles 115(b) and 205(b) are basically enabling provisions which permit regularization of excess expenditure in grants where accurate forecast of expenditure is difficult to make (the Central Government's Budget for 1996-97 lists 101 demands for grants covering expenditure of each Ministry/Department, UT, transfers to State Governments, etc. and there are certain grants such as repayment of debt, drawal/discharge of Treasury Bills, or pension payment where it becomes difficult to make correct estimates of expenditure due to a variety of reasons). The financial rules framed by the Central as well as State Governments nowhere permit spending departments to exceed the budgetary allotment voted by the Legislature. The delegation of financial power rules issued by the Ministry of Finance of the Government of India permits only a limited reappropriation of savings within a grant and the maximum reappropriation which can be made in certain specific situations is Rs 15 crores beyond which prior approval of Parliament is required. The financial rules of Bihar stipulate that

> *the authority administering a grant is ultimately responsible for watching the progress of expenditure on public services under its control and for keeping the expenditure within the grant.*

After the Budget is passed each head of the department makes an allotment under various suit-heads to the individual drawing and disbursing officers spread all over the State indicating callings within which expenditure can be incurred. It is therefore, difficult to understand how in the Animal Husbandry Department in Bihar individual field officers could have spent money beyond their allotment and if they have done so they have violated the provisions of the Bihar financial rules and are guilty of misconduct under the Service Rules. This is also indicative of the fact that the entire financial control machinery of the State has collapsed.

LEGISLATIVE control over national finance will be meaningful only if there is an effective machinery to monitor that money has been spent against each expenditure-head voted by the Legislature, and there is a time period within which such reports are made available to the Legislature? This brings in the role of the Comptroller and Auditor General (C&AG) and the Public Accounts Committee (PAC).

Under Article 151 of the Constitution the annual accounts of the Union Government as well as the State Governments together with the Adudit Report of the C&AG are required to be laid before each House of Parliament/State Legislature. These include Appropriation Accounts and Finance Accounts. The Appropriation Accounts record grant-wise expenditures against votes as approved by the Legislature and offer explanations for variations between the actual and the funds voted. Under the rules of business framed by parliament/State Legislatures, the reports of the C&AG are demitted to the Public Accounts Committee. The Parliament (and State Legislatures) have prescribed the functions of the PAC which enjoins that the Committee shall examine the accounts showing the appropriation of sums granted by the House for the expenditure of the government and in scrutinizing the Appropriation Accounts and the report of the C&AG the Committee shall satisfy itself that moneys shown in the accounts as having been disbursed were legally available for, and applicable to, the service or purpose to which they have been applied or charged. In order that the system or parliamentary control as prescribed in the Constitution and in the Rules of Business of the Lok Sabha/State Legislature functions effectively, it is necessary that Appropriation Accounts certified by the C&AG and the report of the PAC are placed in Parliament/State Legislature within the next financial year and before next year's Budget is passed. Unfortunately this seldom happens. The Appropriation Audit Report of the C&AG for 1994-95 was placed in Parliament in July 1996 and would hopefully be examined by the PAC in the next few months as the new PAC has been constituted by the House only in early September (the latest Central PAC Report relating to 1993-94 was submitted on November 24, 1995 based on the C&AG's Appropriation Audit Report placed in Parliament on May 31, 1995). Fortunately the Central Government departments by and large observe the discipline of budgetary ceilings—during 1994-95 excess over grants reported in the C&AG's latest Audit Report was of the order or Rs 47 crores which is awaiting regularization by PAC/Parliament.

The position is, however far from satisfactory as far as the State Governments are concerned. In some of the States the Appropriation Accounts are placed in the Legislature several years after the closure of the financial year and the PAC does not meet for years together to regularize the expenditure as the Bihar situation indicates. The situation needs to be remedied. Parliament by law needs to prescribe that the Appropriation Accounts and the C&AG's Audit Report thereon be placed in the House by the end of December of the following financial year.

Most countries have prescribed the date of submission of these Reports. For example in the UK, whose parliamentary model we follow, the National Audit Act stipulates that the accounts and the C&AG's Reports thereon will be laid before the House of Commons by January 31 of the following year.

There is also the need for a provision that the Public Accounts Committee will examine the Appropriation Accounts and submit its report within a time frame, say, by February 15, so that the excess grant, if any, could be regularized before next year's Budget is presented in Parliament/State Legislature (and if the PAC in its wisdom does not find adequate justification for the "excess expenditure" it should be in a position to recommend to the Legislature and ensure that the corresponding cut in next year's grant to the delinquent department is made).

Coming back to the situation in Bihar, as matters stand today a staggering sum of Rs 5383 crores has been spent up-to March 1995 without any legal authority. (The figures of excess expenditure for 1995-96 will be available only when the C&AG submits his

Appropriation Audit Report.) it is doubtful if the Public Accounts Committee of Bihar would be in a position to recommend regularization of "excess expenditure" of the Bihar Legislature would approve the same. Should the Central Government remain a passive spectator in such a situation?

If so much money has been drawn from the State coffer without any legal authority does it not point to a failure of the constitutional machinery in the State? Does the situation not warrant imposition of financial emergency as envisaged in Article 360 of the Constitution? Let legal and constitutional experts debate the issue and suggest a way out.

The Indispensable Audit

PUBLIC enterprises were set up as part of country's development planning process. Frequently, demand is made to do away with the Comptroller and Auditor General's (CAG's) audit of these enterprises on the ground that it hinders decision-making and risk taking on their part. The latest such move has come from the Irani Committee, set up by Department of Company Affairs to suggest changes in company law. While the Committee went beyond its terms of reference and made suggestions without wider consultations, the Government it seems is giving serious consideration to its recommendation.

The issue of audit of public sector undertakings (PSUs) by the CAG was settled by Parliament in the 1950s, when government companies were being set up for the first time for carrying on commercial and industrial activities.

The then CAG, V. Narhari Rao, pointed out that it would be unconstitutional if the CAG does not have authority to audit them. Supporting him, the Public Accounts Committee observed, "The CAG should have unquestioned right to audit the expenditure of these concerns, because they are financed from the Consolidated Fund."

A solution was found by inserting a provision in the Companies Act of 1956, which stipulated that the CAG will have a right to conduct supplementary audit of a government company (defined as one where government shareholding is 51 per cent or more) and the statutory auditor of the company will be appointed on his recommendation and he can issue directions to them.

Recognizing the special character of public enterprises, a committee of the Congress party in Parliament headed by V.K. Krishna Menon (1959) recommended a separate committee.

Based on its recommendations, Parliament constituted a Committee on Public Undertakings (1964), "to examine in the context of autonomy and efficiency of the public undertakings whether their affairs are being managed in accordance with sound business principles and prudent commercial practices". The CAG's reports, after they are submitted to Parliament, are remitted to the aforesaid committee.

The role of the CAG in the context of autonomy of PSUs is often debated. During the last three decades, several high-level government committees, such as the Administrative Reforms Commission, the L. K. Jha Committee and the Arjun Sen Gupta Committee, have studied this in depth. They have all come to the conclusion that the requirement of parliamentary accountability demands that public enterprises should remain within the ambit of the CAG's audit.

However, they have suggested that the CAG should adapt his audit style suitable for a business entity.

It needs to be appreciated that the CAG's audit of balance-sheet is largely responsible for maintaining transparency in the accounts of PSUs, which can be said to represent the true and fair state of affairs of the company'. The same cannot be said about the private corporate sector, where there are numerous instances of accounts being manipulated, often with the connivance of their auditors. These companies suddenly go bust, causing immense suffering to their shareholders and loss to financial institutions, which fund them.

The unexpected collapse of Enron, World Com and a large number of companies around the world has shown that corporate greed is a universal phenomenon and an effective check on them in necessary. Australian professors Clarke-Dean-Oliver observed thus: "Corporate accounting does not do violence to the truth occasionally and trivially, but comprehensively, systematically, and universally, annually and perennially."

The CAG also conducts performance audit, whether operations are conducted with due regard to economy, efficiency and effectiveness. Statutory auditors do not have mandate to do performance audit. Every year, audit reports bring out numerous cases of loss, waste and nugatory expenditure.

Two instances from the latest 2005 audit report are illustrative. ONGC has incurred losses running into several thousand crores owing to the one sided joint venture agreement with the Enron-Reliance consortium for exploration of the Panna Mukta and Tapti Ravva oilfields. The execution of the Golden Quadrilateral project by the

National Highway Authority shows severe managerial deficiencies, resulting in huge slippage in road construction work as well as heavy loss to the exchequer.

Audit helps in exposing cases of fraud, which would otherwise never come to light—the infamous Kuo Oil deal entered into by IOC with a nonexistent firm in Hong Kong is a case in point.

PSU managers often feel irked when audit examines individual transactions and points out lapses by taking the benefit of hindsight.

Keeping these considerations in view, an Audit Board was constituted with technical experts as members, to provide commercial type audit. But things have not improved, as the office of the CAG has not changed its audit methodology and a large part of its staff lack the technical competence to do high quality investigation.

It is time it changed its style of functioning, developed professionalism and looked at the special requirement of PSUs, which face tough challenges while operating in a highly competitive global environment.

While admittedly there is considerable scope of improving the working of the of the CAG, there is no case of doing away with audit. In advanced democratic countries such as France, Italy, the US, Germany and Japan, government-owned enterprises fall within the jurisdiction of its Supreme Audit Institutions. CAG helps make operations of government institutions transparent and accountable, and is an instrument of Parliament for enforcing accountability of the Executive, a sine qua non for any democratic polity.

Balco Privatisation C&AG and Governments Accountability

The Balco privatization deal which has been subject of acrimonious debate in Budget session of Parliament has shed more head than light. The NDA government had its way by virtue of its majority and defeating an opposition sponsored motion for a Joint Committee of the House, but this is hardly the way vital economic decisions should be taken. The Minister for Disinvestment Arun Shourie's argument is that deal is transparent, that price which government has secured has nothing to do with value of the "assets" of the company but concept of a "going concern" be applied and all papers relating to sale will be placed before the Comptroller & Auditor General (C&AG) to prove that deal was fair.

While the government is trying to get a certificate of good conduct from C&AG, one should understand the manner in which the office of C&AG functions. Under Article 151 of the Constitution the Audit Report of the C&AG are placed in Parliament and get remitted to Public Accounts Committee (PAC) for further examination. Thus C&AG derives his authority solely from the PAC and the Parliament. If basic issues relating to privatization have already been discussed in Parliament and government has already made up its mind there is very little that the C&AG or the PAC's report can do. The office of C&AG at present has very little expertise in the area of valuation and does not hire experts to get technical advice, unlike its counterpart, the General Accounting Office in USA and therefore its examination will simply be a common sense exercise much of which is already in public domain. Even if C&AG's investigation brings out something startling what is the assurance that action will get taken against erring public officials. C&AG enjoys no legal power to enforce its finding unlike France and Germany which has an Audit Court system to punish public officials for their malfeasance. Bulk of C&AG's Reports are gathering dust as neither PAC is abe to examine them nor government initiates action on them on its own. The Minister for Disinvestment would not be unaware of these limitations of public audit system in India. If he has real faith in the institution of C&AG he should have got the deal preaudited by that office before the agreement for sale was entered into so that lacuna, if any, detected in the transaction could be rectified. Otherwise it will simply be a case of closing the stable after the horse has bolted.

As per media reports Balco's 51% equity has been sold to Sterlite Group for Rs. 551.5 crs. which will automatically give it ownership right. One of the issues in the controversy is whether the price is fair. The company's gross block (value of assets at the time of original purchase) as on March, 2000 was of the order of Rs. 932 crs. Assets need to be valued as per current market price or at replacement value and it is obvious to anyone whether air price has been secured. The Minister for Distinvestment says that the concept of "asset-value" should not be applied to judge whether price is fair but the concept of "going concern" be used. Let us buy this argument. This implies that in the interest of national economy this industry should be run irrespective of the fact who is the owner.

The company has proven track record of making substantive profit for the last many years. Its profit before tax was Rs. 116 cr in 1999-2000 Rs. 135 crs in 1998-99 and Rs. 135 crs in 1997-98 on an equity capital of Rs. 488.85 crs. One of the most significant things about the company is that resources to the extent of 50 percent on its capital investment have been generated internally. The company has thus sound fundamentals. What would be the fiar value the government should get for selling 51% equit worth Rs. 249.31 crs (lit'us for the time being leave aside the issue of Government converting 50% equity into debt for which there seems hardly any justification). The most acceptable and transparent method of disinvestment is offering shares at a fixed price to general public through public offering with the help of recognized market intermediaries. Though there may be difficulty in determining optimum price when shares are old first time, the problem can be overcome by offering a smaller lot of 10 to 15% in the first offer and establishing a responsible market price and off-loading balance shares in several lots over a period of say two years when market conditions are favourable. A wide ownership of shares would have helped Balco becoming a board managed company, professionalising the management and taking a major step towards establishing responsible corporate governance.

It is difficult to understand why government is not going through the normal market route of disinvestment and giving monopoly control of a s strategic industry to a private group most of whom do not have professional management and belive in dynastic control of business. Even developed countries such as U.K. and France had a provision barring single groups from acquiring monopoly control over privatized industries. The French Privatisation At of 1993 had a provision that government would acquire a 'golden share' so that it could exercise control on matters such as sale of more than 10 per cent share capital to an individual and shareholding available to foreign investor will be limited to 20 per cent.

Much of the problems of privatization arise due to the fact that government has no policy framework for privatization of PSUs and no strategy for implementing them. Each privatization is an adhoc exercise. At present Cabinet of CCEA (Cabinet Committee on Economic Affairs) approves each deal including valuation. This blurs Cabinet's policy making responsibility with implementation which is the job of permanent bureaucracy/technical experts. The Governments of the day, irrespective of which party is in power, are averse to work under a policy framework approved by Parliament. This is largely because of political executive's (Cabinet) mistrust of Parliament as well as bureaucracy and its desire to concentrate all powers in itself without any meaningful delegation to implementing authority. Whether it is the controversial ONGC Reliance Enron or NMDC Baladilla deal signed when Congress was in power, it is the same story.

Several experts question whether it is legal to privatize through executive decision making process without parliamentary senction. The Courts in India have held that PSUs are "State" within the meaning of Article 12 of the Constitution. The Delegation of Financial Power Rules of the Ministry of Finace provide that share capital for setting a new company is a "New Instrument of Service" for which specific approval of Parliament is required as expenditure is incurred from Consolidated Fund of India. Can, therefore, the status of government company changed to an ordinary corporate entity without parliamentary authority? When government is diluting its share holding it is basically shedding its property right. Can property rights of "people" inherent in a government company be shed without the authority of law? Does this not attract Article 300-A of the Constitution, which enjoins that property rights cannot be taken away without the authority of law? The Constitutional traditions of many countries abide that privatization must be approved by Parliament. In France prior legislative authorization is required to privatize majority owned enterprises. The French Constitutional Council has ruled that the Constitutional principle of equality among all citizens and declaration of human rights which mandates payment of just compensation when property is confiscated prohibit the transfer of public assets to private investors at less than real value.

For privatization to succeed it is necessary that government draws a proper policy famework and secures broad parliamentary mandate through a Privatisation Act. The Act should lay down the ground rules for privatization and provide for an independent expert body preferably a statutory Commission to handle the nitty-gritty of actual disinvestments process such as share valuation and technique of selling it. It needs to be realized that privatization is not a technical exercise but a political process and there is need to build broad political consensus based on democratic procedures. A UNDP Report points to seven sins of privatization and says that hastily conceived or executed it may achieve very little. The Balco deal hardly fulfills the canons of accountability of Executive to Parliament and may derail the entire disinvestment process.

Public Accountability of Public Sector Enterprises

Public accountability means the obligations of the persons and authorities entrusted with public resources to be answerable for the fiscal, managerial and programme responsibilities that are conferred on them and report on the management of such resources. The underlying principle is that government agencies as well as Public Enterprises are accountable or answerable to the Government, the Legislature and hence to the people.

PSEs are autonomous institutions having separate legal entity. They are incorporated as a Company under the Indian Companies Act (there are a few PSEs which are constituted under separate Acts such as Electricity Boards, food Corporation and Warehousing Corporation) and theoretically they should enjoy the same autonomy as their compeers have in the private sector. But in the interest of public accountability their autonomy is circumscribed by the Government and the Parliament through a complex control mechanism. The government has reserved for itself major areas of PSE's functioning such as appointment of Chairman and the members of the Board of Directors and other major policy matters such as investment decisions, wage policy, pricing policy etc. Parliament has also assumed an overseeing responsibility over their functioning. They are also subject to audit jurisdiction of Comptroller and Auditor General (C&AG).

The post-independence Indian economic development, as enshrined in the Industrial Policy Resolution of 1956, envisaged that the commanding heights of the economy will be under the State hand and accordingly key sectors of the economy such as power, petroleum, coal, steel, and transport were reserved for public sector. However, countries like Britain were constantly appraising the performance of their nationalised industries. In the U.K. several White Papers were presented in the Parliament and when Margaret Thatcher came to power she felt that State-run industries cannot be efficient and will be a permanent drain on the national exchequer largely due to trade unions' hold over them. She initiated a policy of large scale Privatisation. Many other advanced industrial countries realigned their economic policies and restructured public sector management by privatising them so that they become more efficient and competitive in the face of globalization as the national economies were getting integrated to the global economic network and only the fittest could survive. The Indian policy makers were too slow to respond to the realities of fast changing global economic order. It was only in July 1991, a New Industrial Policy was enunciated, which makes a departure from the policy followed since independence, limiting the role of public sector to essential infrastructure goods and services, exploration of oil and natural resources and strategic industries. The new policy also promised to make a move towards privatisation and review portfolios of the existing industries with a view to disinvest them.

Today there is worldwide movement towards privatisation and lessening the role of the State in national economic activity. Right-oriented economists claim this as a success of their philosophy as they believe in the market forces, liberalisation, lessening of barriers to trade and investment and an open door international trade regime. However, the general acceptance of the privatisation idea can only be partly attributed to the intellectual influence of economists who are backed by powerful institutions like World Bank and IMF with their considerable financial muscle. People all over the world are disillusioned with Government especially big Governments and want it to be cut to size.

This was expressed in no unmistakable terms by President Regan soon after he had taken over office when he observed "*Government is not the provider of solution to the people's problem but Government is the problem.*" As the forces of democracy take root all over the world people assert their right and want a greater say in policy making. They see in politicians an unlimited desire for power, lust and greed which they can secure by controlling directly or indirectly as much economic activity as possible.

The corruption scandals which had rocked some of the richest economies of the world like Japan, Italy and South Korea involving their Heads of State and top politicians in bribery and other unsavory deals has reinforced people's view that politicians nay governments cannot be trusted with vast economic power being controller by them. Be that as it may, we cannot wish away the Government. So long as nation States exist we have to have a Government to govern. But people have started asserting their rights and demand good governance and a responsible government.

In India Public sector is the vehicle through which the entire post-independence industrialisation process has taken place. Public sector accounts for 50 per cent of industrial assets and 25 percent of industrial production. Public sector, however, suffers from serious ills like low productivity, indifference to consumer's needs and a large part of it is a drain on the economy. For this reason there is a general realisation that role of public sector in the national economy should be reduced. However, it is difficult to visualise a situation where we can do without them.

Public sector industries will continue to enjoy key role in certain sectors of the economy particularly those concerned with infrastructure or socio-economic upliftment of people with low rate of return. This is a fact which even advanced industrial economies like USA have realised despite considerable glib talk about the virtues of private enterprise. The US Commodity Credit Corporation which supports inefficient and uneconomic farms after spending billions of dollars of taxpayers money is one such example.

France's entire banking system is in State hand and even modest attempt to privatise it has not been allowed to proceed. Public expenditure as percentage of GNP is 54% in Sweden, 53% in Italy, 46% in France, 43% in UK, 34% in German and 24% in USA as compared to developing countries average of 21%, indicating that the State has assumed a much more important role in dealing with socio-economic development of the people.

It must therefore be realised that PSEs will continue to play an important part in our national economic development and it is therefore important that they be run efficiently. As PESs are government institutions, Governments policy as well as its interface with Parliament plays a key role in its successful running. We will examine these issues in the following paragraphs.

Reconceptualising Government—PSE Relationship

It is time the government realises that its "control" mechanism over Public Enterprises is not an end in itself. What is important is that PSEs should function efficiently, contribute to national economy and serve the consumers.

This requires a reconceptualisation of paradigm of PSE-Government relationship and a change in the mind-set of the government officials. Prof James Austin of Harvard University suggests that PSE-Government relationship should be viewed as of managed interdependence instead of autonomy and control.

The reasons are (a) PSEs and central government are inextricably linked (b) their mutuality of interests far exceed their point of conflict, (c) their interaction can be viewed as a positive rather than a negative sum game, (d) the interaction is subject to a systematic management process. The reconceptualisation paradigm stresses shared interests and mutual dependence. Today with dismantling the barriers to trade and investment as a result of WTO accord and the globalisation wave sweeping the world the national governments all over the world will have to realign their policies to ensure that their interface with industry is mutually beneficial and promotes their effieiency and growth.

Public Corporation

The audit arrangement of PEs organised in the form of a corporation is laid down in the relevant Act creating the corporation. Thus, the CAG is the sole auditor (there is no provision for audit by chartered accountants) in case of statutory corporations like Air India, Indian Airlines, International Airport Authority, ONGC, Electricity Boards and State Road Transport Corporations. However, there are certain corporations like Food Corporation and Warehousing Corporation where audit arrangement is analogous to Government companies—there is a provision of audit both by CAs as well as CAG.

In case of certain public corporations, particularly in the field of banking, there is no provision for CAG's audit though they are fully owned by Government. Thus, nationalised banks, LIC, IFCI, UTI, IDBI etc. are not subject to CAG's audit jurisdiction.

The Audit Technique

The audit of PEs could be divided in two categories:

(i) Audit of annual accounts and balance sheet

(ii) Transaction audit: An examination that the transactions of a public body have been carried with due regard to wisdom, faithfulness and economy. This includes what is known as efficiency-cum-propriety audit or value for money audit.

Audit of Annual Accounts

The audit of annual accounts and balance sheet is conducted by chartered accountants (CAs) [also known as statutory auditor] who is appointed by the Central Government on the advice of the CAG. These accounts are also test-checked by the CAG (Government audit) in what is called supplementary audit. The main purpose of the audit is to ensure that the accounts reflect a true and fair state of affairs of the company.

It is sometimes argued that certification of annual accounts be left of the CAs as in case of private sector and CAG's audit under section 619 of Companies Act be dispensed with as it leads to duplication of work done by CAs and delays certification of accounts. How valid is such a viewpoint?

It may be mentioned that in private sector accounting and financial policies are laid down by the management with profit as the main criterion and the statutory auditor has to conduct his audit within the framework of this policy so long as it does not conflict with the basic legal provision. Statutory auditors generally see that a company complies with the technical requirement of Company Law and various guidelines issued by the Institute of Chartered Accountants. Thus, if the Company has made adequate 'disclosure' in the 'notes to the accounts', the legal requirements are fulfilled. On the other hand, the Government audit looks beyond the legality and whether accounting policies followed by the company as reflected in 'notes to accounts' appended to balance sheet are meant to camouflage the real financial health of the company and distort the profitability profile. Another function of Government audit is to ensure that statutory auditors have applied themselves adequately according to professional norms and their audit has been qualitative and purposive.

It may be noted that the primary responsibility for audit of annual accounts of a Government company vests with CA's who spend a great deal of time with a large contingent of auditors going through every voucher and record. Under Section 619(3) (a) of the Companies Act, the CAG has issued directions to statutory auditors, regarding the manner of conducting the audit. Due to the division of work, the CAG is required to conduct only a supplementary audit whereby a small audit team conducts a test check of selected transactions in a short span of three-four weeks to be able to independently certify that the annual accounts represent a true and fair state of affairs of the company.

Thus, it is a healthy combination of CA's and CAG's audit that helps in adequately discharging the audit responsibility of a Government company. It must, however, be admitted that there is need for greater coordination in CA's and Government audit so that there is no duplication of work and audit is organised in such a manner that the exercise of certifying the accounts and issuing the audit certificate is done well in time so that the companies are able to hold annual general meetings within the time schedule prescribed under the Companies Act.

Transaction Audit

Private sector companies are audited only by a firm of chartered accountants. There are, however, certain limitations in the working of chartered accountants as they are not expected to comment on the propriety of managerial decisions. The Public Accounts Committee had noted "whatever be the utility of such certificates in the case of private companies, it is considered that so far as Government companies are concerned it is impossible to form a judgement of the efficiency of these Government companies only from the balance sheet and profit and loss account.

The capital structure, pricing policy, production standards, labour relations etc. of Government companies differ materially from those of their counterparts in private sector. Quite often, concessions are given to these companies in the shape of interest-free loans which an ordinary commercial concern is not allowed to get.

Unlike private companies, the maximization of profits is neither the primary motive nor the only index of the success of Government companies—if the balance sheet and the profit and loss account are not a true measure of their success, there must be some other ways of satisfying Parliament that they are run efficiently. It is necessary, therefore, to prescribe some tests by which it may be possible to have a more correct appreciation of their financial working. Partly, some idea can be obtained from the efficiency-cum-propriety audit conducted by the Comptroller & Auditor General". This indeed is the justification for extending the jurisdiction of CAG on public undertakings.

Value for Money Audit

Much of the traditional audit by Supreme Audit Institutions (SAI) used to be concerned with what was known as regularity audit. Regularity audit implies checking regularity of actions taken by public officials *i.e.* while spending money or collecting revenue, public officials have followed laid down rules, regulations and procedures. A review of regularity of public administration activities is a vital function of State audit but it serves only a limited purpose as it does not go into how and why the funds were spent.

Lastly, as the activities of Government have expanded manifold, there is an universal consensus that State audit must go beyond 'regularity' and encompass 'value for money audit' and conduct a review of economy, efficiency and effectiveness of State activities and what has come to be known as '3 E's audit'. This audit is also known as performance audit.

Economy is concerned with minimising the cost of resources used for an activity having regard to appropriate quality.

Efficiency is concerned with the relationship between the output in terms of goods, services or other results and resources used to produce them. How far does the activity achieve the maximum output for a given input or use the minimum input for a given output?

Effectiveness is concerned with the relationship between the intended input and the actual input of an activity, to establish how far does output in terms of goods, services or other results help to achieve the effects that were intended and how far they achieve policy objectives? The achievement of economy, efficiency and effectiveness depends upon the existence of sound arrangements for planning, appraisal, authorisation and control of the use of resources. It is the management's responsibility to establish the necessary control and see that they are working properly. The audit objective is to undertake an independent assessment of the strength and effectiveness to consider ways in which improvements might be secured and to report results in order to enhance accountability.

Problem Areas of Audit Board Functioning

While a comprehensive examination by the Audit Board is a fairly effective method of assessing the performance of an undertaking, there are several factors which detract from its effectiveness:

(i) It takes several years for a comprehensive appraisal to be finalised from the time the study is initiated. Unless audit reports are promptly finalised, they fail to act as tool for managerial improvement. The delay occurs due to several reasons. Quite often, the company management does not produce promptly the records and documents for audit examination and delays answering audit queries. Even after the draft audit report is finalised, there is delay in holding meetings of the Audit Board with the top management of the undertakings and Secretary of the administrative Ministries to discuss the audit findings. Due to the audit procedure of thoroughness, checking facts at every stage and giving an opportunity to the auditee organisation to present its viewpoint, the finalisation of audit reviews invariably gets delayed.

(ii) The Audit Board is able to finalise its comprehensive appraisal of only four to five undertakings in one year. As there are more than 225 Central Government enterprises, some of the enterprises are not reviewed at all or reviewed only after a gap of ten years or more. The ARC had envisaged that every enterprise should be reviewed once in five to seven years.

Lack of Executive Authority

If the departmental officers take prompt action on the CAG's findings and initiate remedial action, one need not feel concerned if the Parliamentary Committees are not able to examine these reports. There is, however, a tendency on the part of departmental officers not to take action on the audit paragraphs till the Committee on Public Undertaking or the Public Accounts Committee takes up the examination. A sub-committee of the Public Accounts Committee had observed that if a departmental head finds that there has been irregularity or lapse on the part of officers concerned he should initiate departmental disciplinary action and take further remedial action.

The Committee observed, 'It is very depressing to find that in spite of audit reports revealing loss of public funds or misuse or misapplication of public funds, there is no investigating agency charged with the duty to probe these aspects and identify the culprits responsible for it'. The Committee recommended that such audit paras which *prima facie* establish loss of public funds should be registered as first information report and should be made the subject matter of investigation by concerned vigilance officers or ACB or CBI.

Unfortunately in India, the CAG enjoys no executive authority against officers who have committed misdemeanour or misappropriation or breach of trust in respect of public funds. The position is in contrast with continental countries like France. The decision of the French Court of Audit has the force of law and it has the power to recover public funds that are improperly spent or cash deficits from the concerned accounting officers.

Checking Evasion of Public Accountability

The system of Parliamentary democracy that we have adopted works through checks and balances. Our Constitution provides a mechanism through which Parliament keeps a check on an overzealous executive. The institution of CAG could thus be regarded as part of the legislative wing as it helps in exercising control to ensure that public money has been spent with due regard to the legislature's intention. It is, however, noticed that there are attempts by the executive to evade Parliamentary control. This could be illustrated by the following:

(a) Setting up of new autonomous bodies and entrusting them with functions which should normally be discharged by Government.

(b) Avoidance of audit control envisaged under Section 619(B) of the Companies Act.

(c) Excluding CAG's jurisdiction from the audit of banks and other financial institutions.

Proliferation of Government Companies

A disturbing feature that is emerging lately in our country is the tendency on the part of Central and State Governments to set up Government companies with substantial capital to take over existing functions of the Government without considering the commensurate advantages. The tendency is particularly pronounced in case of States where many companies have been set up without any real commercial activity (Ex: Police Housing Corporation and Scheduled Castes and Tribes Welfare Corporation).

The entrusting of such functions to Government companies removes them from the purview of normal legislative scrutiny and control. Where such autonomous bodies have been set up in the cooperative sector or as registered society, they do not even attract CAG's audit. A.H. Hanson a distinguished authority on the subject had noted three decades back with anguish that in some parts of the world the proliferation of public enterprises was such that they constituted a headless fourth branch of the Government. Since then, the situation had deteriorated in the developing countries.

Deemed Government Companies

There are some companies in which more than 51% of the paid-up share capital is held jointly by Central (and/or State Government), Central (and/or State) Government companies and corporations owned or controlled by Central (and/or State) Government. Such companies are not regarded strictly as Government companies in terms of Section 617 of the Companies Act. As the funds invested in these companies are either by Government or Government-owned corporations or companies, the Public Accounts Committee felt that they should not be allowed to escape public accountability. Pursuant to the recommendation of the Committee the Companies Act was amended in 1975 by inserting a new Section, 619(B).

As a result of this amendment the provisions of Section 619 were made applicable to such companies. Thus, the statutory auditors of these companies are to be appointed on the recommendation of CAG, who himself has a right to conduct a supplementary audit of their accounts in the same manner as any Government company. However, the annual accounts of these companies are not required to be placed in the Legislature nor do they fall within the purview of examination done by the Committee on Public Undertakings. There were 44 such companies on the Central side as on March, 31, 1987.

Lately, there has been an attempt on the part of some joint venture companies, where a portion of equity is held by the public financial institutions, to evade CAG's audit jurisdiction as envisaged in Section 619(B) of the Companies Act. The Department of Company Affairs has issued an administrative notification stating that investment by institutions like the Industrial Finance Corporation (IFC) or Industrial Credit and Investment Corporation (ICICI) in joint venture companies be excluded from the list of the corporations owned or controlled by the Central Government on the ground that control envisaged by the Central Government envisaged a direct control. Thus, for example, the Shipping Credit and Investment Company which is a subsidiary of ICICI has been excluded from the purview of CAG's audit. It is a moot point whether such companies should be allowed to escape CAG's audit by taking recourse to an administrative notification issued by the Department of Company Affairs, as the intention of Section 619B of the Companies Act is to bring within the purview of CAG's audit every company where the majority shareholding is held by bodies which are financed by public funds.

Nationalised Banks—Outside CAG's Jurisdiction

It may be mentioned that LIC, Nationalised Banks, IDBI, Export-Import Bank of India, National Bank of Agriculture and Rural Development, IFC, UTI etc. are not subject to CAG's audit. The reasons for not bringing these financial institutions with the purview of CAG's audit are not clear. Lately, the performance of some of the nationalised banks has been causing grave anxiety as their operations are hidden behind the veil of public scrutiny and accountability. During a discussion on a calling attention motion in Parliament (Sept. 1990) one Member of Parliament alleged that almost 30 per cent of commercial banks assets amounting to Rs. 20,000 crores was stuck in bad and sticky debts.

In the case of Bank of India, one of the largest commercial banks it is estimated that loan losses are of the order of Rs. 920 crores but its books of accounts show a provision for bad and doubtful debts of the order of Rs. 250 crores only.

In reply to a question in Parliament, the Minister of Finance observed that 'the Government and the Reserve Bank are now engaged in revising the format for balance sheet and profit and loss account for nationalised banks with a view to ensure greater transparency and accountability'. Apparently, the state of banks' keeping of financial accounts is unsatisfactory. It seems that secrecy rules relating to provisions for bad and doubtful debts and secret reserves help banks to camouflage their financial health.

The unsatisfactory state of banks' finances has led to the demand by several Parliamentary Committees and other informed fora to bring bank audit with CAG's purview so that banks become really accountable to Parliament. The *Economic and Political Weekly* observes. "The Government can make a small beginning towards making these institutions more accountable by eliminating forthwith the perverse immunity they now enjoy; it needs no stressing that ordinary commercial audit by firms of chartered accountants cannot suffice for institutions which use vast sums of public funds and claim to advance major national economic purposes.

It is also not very convincing to argue that subjecting the Government-owned financial institutions to the CAG's scrutiny will in some mysterious way undermine the confidence in the financial system when the CAG regularly looks into and publishers reports, for instance the activities of Ministry of Defence". The Comptroller and Auditor General of India has also expressed the view that if his Department were to be entrusted with this responsibility in public interest he would do full justice with the assigned task.

Audit of Public Enterprises

Public enterprises (PE) are today under great pressure to show better performance. Senior executives of public enterprises and some students of corporate behaviour complain that public enterprises are not able to 'perform' due to inadequate 'delegation' and 'authority' given to them. Government control and Parliamentary scrutiny (which includes audit by CAG) is said to be standing in the way of public enterprises better performance. Views are sometimes expressed that they should be placed on par with 'private enterprises', that CAG's audit be done away with and it would suffice if checking of their annual accounts is done by private firm of chartered accountants. Most of these views emanate from inadequate understanding of the reason behind creation of public enterprises and fail to appreciate the fact that they are basically an extended arm of the State with certain special features.

Public enterprises in India came to be created as a result of our socialistic planning model. It was felt that the traditional Government machinery was found unsuitable to manage the affairs of an enterprise which has industrial and commercial character. Creation of autonomous institutions to manage their affairs was therefore favoured. The inspiration had come largely from Britain where Herbert Morrison, the dynamic Minister in Lord Atlee's Labour Government, had propounded the thesis in his famous book 'Socialism and Transport'. W.A. Robson an authority on the subject described the concept of public corporations aptly in the following words. 'The original impetus to the movement for public corporation came from a twofold desire to secure freedom from parliamentary supervision over management on the one hand and treasury control over personnel and finance on the other".

The creation of an autonomous organisation to manage commercial activity on behalf of Government necessarily required legislative enactment as several 'waivers' from the usual budgetary and treasury controls had to be secured. The Indian Constitution prescribes an elaborate system of Parliamentary control over Government funds and specific constitutional requirements were to be met for spending money or collecting revenues, like presentation of an Annual Financial Statement (Article 112); Discussion and voting of Demands for Grants (Article 113), Consideration and passing of Appropriation and Finance Bill (Article 114 and 117). These elaborate controls over 'finances' have been dispensed with in the case of 'State Enterprises' so that they enjoy freedom consistent with their business character.

The policy-makers found that while creation of an autonomous organisation was required to manage its commercial activity, the enactment of an all-comprehensive Act of Parliament for creation of each such organisation was not feasible. During the Second and Third Five Year Plans there was great proliferation of Government business and commercial activity and a large number of autonomous public enterprises were required to be created to manage them. If for creation of each State enterprise a separate Act was to be passed by the Parliment/State Legislature, it would have been a long time consuming exercise and necessarily delayed the process of industrialisation. Therefore after initially experimenting with few statutory corporations like Air India, Indian Airlines, ONGC in the fifties, the Government found it expedient to have 'Company-form' for State-enterprises. An ingenious device was thus found: the creation of State Enterprise would be facilitated if they could be incorporated under the Indian Companies Act (with Government as the sole or atleast majority share-holder) and thus allowed to function outside Government's detailed treasury and personnel control. Accordingly, government companies were initially set up in India in terms of the Indian Companies Act, 1913.

This method of organising public enterprises in the form of a company by the Government was termed by Mr V Narahari Rao, the first Comptroller & Auditor General of India, as a fraud on the Constitution. He was of the opinion that the formation of such companies tended to whittle away Parliamentary control; the company law as existing at the time did not give Comptroller & Auditor General and automatic right to audit these enterprises; even if he was requested to do the audit, it could neither be proper nor binding as his duties and functions were to be prescribed by Parliament and could not be regulated solely by articles of association of the company; if he was appointed as Auditor, he would have to submit his report to the company and not to Parliment through the President and therefore Parliament could not watch the regularity of operation and financial results of such enterprises through Parliamentary Committees.

Taking a wider view of his own responsibility, he felt that where there had been unconstitutional diversion of money from the Consolidated Fund, he might be within his right to continue audit and report to Parliament even if the Government company was formed; he could not acquiesce his jurisdiction being ousted in the matter of audit by such unconstitutional acts. He forcefully put his views in December 1952 before a Sub-Committee of the Public Accounts Committee which eventually recommended that the Comptroller & Auditor General should have the unquestioned right to audit the expenditure of these concerns by whatever name they may be called, because they were financed from the Consolidated Fund.

Consequently, in the new Companies Act, 1956 which came into force in that year, the audit arrangements for Government companies were put on a satisfactory footing with the provisions regarding appointment of statutory auditors on the advice of the Comptroller & Auditor General, who will also have the power to direct the manner in which the audit should be conducted and who has also the right to comment on the report of the statutory auditors as well as conduct supplementary test audit (Section 619).

It may be worthwhile mentioning that the Indian Companies Act was basically meant to regulate the affairs of the private sector enterprises. The provisions for audit of companies registered under the Companies Act by an independent firm of Chartered Accountants

(CA) was meant to protect the interest of individual shareholders who are a disarate and disorganised group and could be tricked by an unscrupulous management. The same analogy cannot hold good for State enterprises which have to work in a different context and are 'accountable' to Government and Parliament for their actions. Therefore, it should be 'somebody' who understands the 'mood' and 'temper of the Parliament, who can enforce the canons of 'public accountability' and what better authority could be found than the Institution of CAG who is discharging this function with reference to Government finance any way.

The above narrative underlines the fact that 'Chartered Accountants' have come to be associated with auditing of State Enterprises through an accident of history—the accident being that State Enterprise happened to get incorporated under the Indian Companies Act (meant to regulate the activities of the private sector) where they had a role to play. It may also be worth mentioning that the present Indian Companies Act is not wholly suitable to regulate the affairs of State Enterprises, for example, holding of annual general meeting is a formality as approval for appointment of members of Board of Directors and passing of annual accounts, its two main functions are already settled in advance. Many academicians hold the view that it is time Government promulgates a separate law for regulating public enterprises.

In almost all the democratic countries of the world, be it Britain, France, the US, Australia or Canada, state enterprises have been created by specific statutory enactment. Express audit by Supreme Audit Institution has also been provided in the Act governing such state enterprises with the sole exception of great Britain. In USA, auditing is carried out by Comptroller General who is not only an auditor but a critic of policy. A Australia the audit is generally made by the Auditor General. In the systems which have continental type of administrative law, the public audit control follows as a matter of course from public law statutes of public corporations.

In France, they are audited by Court de Comptes (Court of Accounts) and in Italy by Corte di Conti an independent tribunal. It may be worthwhile dwelling briefly on British practice as we are often tempted to imitate that country.

In Britain key industries like coal, power transport were nationalised when Atlee's Labour Government Came in power after the second world war, as socialism was the by-word on which it fought elections. Conservatives were strongly opposed to Labour Government's nationalisation programme and somehow the Government of the day thought that if CAG was to critically examine their working the Conservatives will get another handle to whip the Government on this issue. Frank Tribe, the then Auditor General, was also reluctant to take up audit to nationalised industries due to shortage of qualified staff.

Against this background, auditing responsibility was given to private firms of chartered accountants. Paul Enzing, a well known authority of Parliamentary finance summed up the situation sarcastically in the following words: "Quite unintentionally the Labour Government paid a compliment to private enterprise in preferring auditing by private firms to that of Audit Department". It is, however, worth mentioning that, for some time past, the Public Accounts Committee has been urging the Government to bring nationalised industry within the purview of Auditor General but, since Britain has lately embarked on a major programme of privatisation the issue has receded into background.

In India the annual accounts of government companies are subject to the so-called dual audit-by a firm of chartered accountants (CAs) and by Comptroller & Auditor General (also called Government Audit). It is sometimes contended that certification of Annual Accounts be left to Chartered Accountants (also known as Statutory Auditors) and CAG's audit under Section 619 of the Companies Act be dispensed with (to be charitable to CAC they concede that he could conduct occasional efficiency-cum-performance audit with changed emphasis). In support, the protagonists of this view argue that CAG's audit is a mere duplication of the work done by CAs; CAG's audit makes no special contribution to improved (True & Fair) presentation of financial results of the company; CAG's audit is irksome and delays finalisation of Annual Accounts. It must be said that the above line of argument emanates largely due to inadequate understanding of the system and method of functioning of CAG which the following narrative tries to explain.

The audit of Central Public Sector Undertakings is conducted by the offices of Member, Audit Board (MAB) as representative of CAG who are stationed at various places in the country like Delhi, Calcutta and Bombay etc. (audit of State Government undertakings is conducted by the Accountant General-Commercial Audit in each State). Each MAB is responsible for audit of a group of companies based on functional requirement and geographical convenience—an attempt is made that the same MAB conducts audit of specialised group of companies in sectors such as petroleum and oil; steel; civil aviation, etc. A Member, Audit Board is required to develop a high level of specialisation about the working of the companies which fall in his audit jurisdiction.

This is achieved *inter-alia* by special training programmes, specialists' lectures, studying the minutes of the meeting of Board of Directors; monitoring discussions of the Government, Public Investment Board and the Planning Commission and maintaining guard files on the emerging trends in the industry as appear from articles in newspapers, magazines and specialised journals. This is in addition to the first-hand knowledge about the working of a company acquired by an MAB's office by being continuously associated with its audit right from the time of its inception. It is this expertise which gives the Government auditor a greater insight into the working of Government companies compared to statutory auditor have relatively limited association with them.

It may be worth mentioning that there is a basic difference in the approach of management of public sector compared to private sector while preparing profitability profile. In the case of private sector, the attempt is to depress the profits (while maintaining a high dividend rate to retain shareholders' confidence) so that the company's income tax liability is minimised.

On the other hand, in the case of Government companies the tendency is to show higher quantum of profits or to minimise losses as somehow the success or efficiency of these enterprises has come to be judged by the profitability criteria. A government-auditor has to look into areas where due to 'sharp' accounting practices profitability profile has got distorted. Because of his greater knowledge and insight into the working of public sector he is able to detect such cases which do not come to notice in the normal course. This can be illustrated by citing a few cases:

Conversion of Debt into Equity from Back Date

Many PEs have taken recourse to large borrowing from Government. Because of their poor financial health some of them do not find it possible to pay even interest on loans and press Government to convert a part of loan into equity and change the capital structure. Such decisions in Government has issued sanction for conversion of debt into equity from a back date. The companies concerned in such cases have written back the interest accounted for in the previous year and taken it as 'accrued income' for the current year, thus inflating profit of that year. Under the Companies Law the share-capital of a company cannot be increased from a back date (thus conversion of debt into equity can have only prospective effect and not retrospective). The correct procedure in such cases should be to treat the interest portion of the loan as having been written off instead of giving the company a windfall income in its books of accounts.

Subsidy from Government

Many enterprises like those in the field of shipbuilding and fertilisers get heavy subsidies from the Government because of the system of administered prices. In the case of shipbuilding, subsidy is based on a highly complicated formula of international parity prices. Some of these companies press the Government to liberalise the subsidy formula and account for 'accrued income' on the basis of proposals made by them to the Government rather than predetermined formula.

It is common in the corporate sector to camouflage their real financial health by giving qualifying notes to the balance sheet. To illustrate, often a question arises, if an Arbitration Award has gone against the company or an income-tax case is pending in the Supreme Court after having been lost in the Tribunal and the High Court or foreign loan liability, has gone up due to devaluation of the rupee, is it enough to disclose this by way of notes in the Accounts or should a corresponding liability not be provided in the Balance Sheet? The thinking amongst most professional accountants is that once adequate 'disclosures' have been made in the 'Notes to the Accounts', the 'technical' requirements of Company Law have been met. Should we be satisfied with the meeting of the "technical" requirement? Government audit does not take such a phiosophical view. It feels duty bound to bring out the impact of such practices on the profitability of the company.

It is sometimes seen that different PEs follow widely divergent accounting practices even when issues are common. Take, for instance, the question of accounting of arrears to be paid to employees as a result of Pay Commission Award (presently awaiting governmental clearance). One group of PEs has provided the entire liability in the current year (1988-89), another group of PEs has taken part of the liability this year and the balance as problem period adjustment, a third group has not provided for any liability and merely disclosed it by way of notes to Accounts. While technically it is open to these companies to adopt any one of the above practice', it is the attempt of Government audit to harmonise the practice in various PEs so that their results are available on a uniform basis.

It may be mentioned that in the private sector, accounting and financial policies are laid down by the Management with profit as the main criterion and a statutory auditor has to conduct his audit within the framework of this policy so long as it does not conflict with the basic legal provisions. On the other hand, public enterprises have to work in the larger public interest and are answerable not only for regularity but propriety of their action. The above discussion brings out the following.

(i) Because of its greater expertise and insight into the working of PEs and understanding of the Government's mind, audit by CAG's is able to focus attention on some critical policy issues which Statutory Auditors would not be able to do in the normal course.

(ii) Statutory Auditors generally see that a company audited by them complies with the technical requirements of the Company Law and the various guidelines issued by the Institute of Chartered Accountants etc. Thus, if the company has made adequate 'disclosure' in the 'Notes to the Accounts' the legal requirements are fulfilled. Government audit looks beyond the legality, into the propriety of management decisions and whether the Notes to Accounts are meant to camouflage the real financial health of the company.

(iii) Government audit attempts to harmonise the accounting practices in various PEs so that their results are presented on a uniform basis.

It may also be mentioned that since CAG is to discharge responsibilities relating to 'Value for Money' audit and report to Parliament, he cannot do full justice to his job unless he cannot do full justice to his job unless he conducts accounts audit of PEs as accounts audit is part of an integrated audit activity and cannot be compartmentalised.

The above discussion should not be interpreted to mean that CAs are not doing their job competently. There is little doubt that they are discharging their responsibility in relation to the audit of PEs in the highest traditions of their profession. The point that is being emphasised is that there is complementary relationship between CAG's audit and CA's audit. The primary responsibility for audit of Annual Accounts of most of the PEs vests with CAs who spend every year a great deal of time with a large contingent of auditors going through every voucher and record. On the other hand, CAG's audit by its very definition is 'Supplementary' and a small audit team conducts a test check of selected transactions in a short span of three four weeks. CAG's audit concentrates largely on issues of propriety and policy nature while the CA's audit concentrates on the 'regularity' aspect and it is a healthy combination of the two that helps in adequately discharging the auditing responsibilities of a Government company.

What is the Public Enterprise management's response to Government audit? What kind of relationship exists between the two institutions?

It can safely be said on the basis of experience that the relationship between the Government Auditors and PE's manager is positive and healthy. Every year, before CAG's comments on Annual Accounts are finalised, a great deal of dialogue and discussion takes place between the Members Audit Board and the Finance Directors and other senior managers of PEs. If PEs give satisfactory explanation to audit observations the points are not pursued. However, where PEs are following an apparently unsound accounting policy or there is a difference of opinion on a technical issue, 'assurances' are taken that the management will review the policy and wherever necessary consult legal and technical experts. However, in a few cases where audit finds that accounts do not reflect 'true and fair' picture, CAG's comments under Section 619(4) of the Companies Act are given. It may be noted that only a handful of companies carry CAG's qualification on the Balance Sheet and in a majority of cases Accounts are certified as presented by the Management by way of giving nil comments. Nil comments are however issued only after management has carried out the necessary rectification in Accounts or satisfied Government audit that improvement in presentation will be effected in the next year's Accounts.

It is sometimes contended that certification of accounts by CAG delays its finalisation within the time schedule laid down in the Companies Act. This is not really true. Government audit normally needs a period of four to six weeks for issuing the audit certificate and if completed accounts are made available even by end-August the certification job is invariably completed within the prescribed schedule. Most cases of delayed finalisation of accounts are due to internal problems of the company's management. As a matter of fact, a number of companies owned by State Governments have not finalised their accounts for as long as five to six years.

There is no doubt that the Supplementary audit done by CAG puts some additional 'pressure' on a Government company. Should the managment of these companies grudge it? After all, it is public money that is invested in them and therefore they should be prepared to subject themselves to some degree of public accountability. It may be claimed that due to presence of CAG's audit, the Annual Accounts of Government companies by and large reflect the 'true and fair' picture of their finances and the Parliament and the people know their real financial health. The same cannot be said for many private corporate sector companies in India where a great deal of window-dressing takes place and one discovers that a going company has suddenly turned sick. And in many such cases, when a private sector company falls sick it becomes the responsibility of the Government as very often it has to take over its management in the larger national interest. It is in this context that several Parliamentary Committees have recommended the need for CAG's audit of banks and other financial institutions so that there is greater accountability of public funds invested therein.

Besides audit of Annual Accounts, CAG also conducts transaction audit in what has come to be known as 'Value for Money' or 3Es' audit a review of economy, efficiency and effectiveness with which the activities of PEs are being carried out. Significant finding of CAG are reported to Parliament every year though his Audit Report on Commercial Undertaking. In addition, comprehensive appraisals of a select number of undertaking are also prepared and placed in Parliament.

Some critics of CAG have expressed a view that individual audit paras which appear in his Audit Report (Commercial) have an adverse effect on the morale of PE managers and undermine their confidence and should be dispensed with. Instead, they have suggested that CAG should make occasional performance reviews with changed emphasis and his reports should be patterned on the World Bank model of project appraisals. How valid is such a viewpoint?

It should be noted that audit by CAG is conducted keeping in view various accounting, financial and other policies laid down and acted upon by the corporate entities. Any shortcomings in these areas, where the ground rules have been laid down by the undertaking themselves are com-mented upon by CAG. Thus CAG's report brings out systems failure, like non-adherence to tendering and contracting norms, failure to follow purchase procedure; lack of inventory control etc. which has a vital bearing on the undertaking's performance. It is difficult to see how CAG's observations inhibit the initiative of a conscientious manager. His comments if at all should help in improving managerial performance and enforcing better financial discipline in an organisation.

A comprehensive appraisal of public enterprises is done under the Audit Board system which was introduced in 1969 as a result of the recommendations of the Administrative Reforms Commission which had taken its inspiration from the French model. Out of the five Members of the Audit Board, two are technical experts with considerable experience of the industry whose performance is being evaluated and are appointed on the recommendations of the Government. The Audit Board finalises its appraisals and tries to give a balanced picture after holding extensive discussions both with the management of PEs as well as Ministery officials and their viewpoint is fully reflected in its reports. The various Parliamentary Committees, Ministry officials, senior PE managers and informed students of public sector have appreciated the quality and content of CAG's appraisals.

It must, however, be admitted that there is consi-derable scope for improving quality of these appraisals. In USA, General Accounting Office hires engineers, economists and specialists to give better content to its reports. Most public sectors in India operate in areas of high technology and the quality of CAG's appraisals will improve if there is greater association of experts and specialists with its reviews.

A disturbing feature that is emerging lately is the tendency on the part of Central and State Governments to set up Government companies with substantial capital to take over hitherto existing functions of the Government without considering commensurate advantages. The entrustment of such functions of Government companies removes them from the purview of normal legislative scrutiny and control. Should they be allowed to escape total public accountability?

A. H. Hanson, a distinguished authority on public enterprises, has noted with anguish that in some parts of the world the proliferation of public corporations has been such that they now constitute a headless fourth branch of the Government. Basing on Latin American experience, he says. "Practically every new economic function that the Government undertakes is assigned *Ad Hoc* to a corporation with two inevitable results, (a) the economic ministries have become hollow shells, (b) the task of coordinating and directing the growing multitude of so-called independent agencies amongst which the economic responsibilities of the Government are fragmented is beyond anyone's capacity".

These dangers are no less apparent in India and there is need for a great deal of caution when unbridled 'autonomy' free from Parliamentary supervision is sought.

The well wishers of the public sector should, therefore, see in the Comptroller & Auditor General an institution which attempts to enforce integrity uniformity, 'openness in working' and public accountability in the functioning of public enterprises so that Parliament and people have full confidence in their working and they enjoy their support in marching towards the goal of socio-economic transformation of our society.

4

The Public Accounts Committee

The Public Accounts Committee (PAC) is the instrument of Parliament for enforcing the accountability of the Executive and bringing financial discipline and probity in the working of the government. The PAC examines the Audit Reports submitted by CAG to Parliament and therefore the effectiveness of audit to a large extent depends on the interest and support it receives from the PAC. During last fifty years of Indian democracy, the Public Accounts Committee, while it has been able to bring some modicum of discipline in the working of the Executive, its working has shown serious deficiencies and major reforms are needed, if it has to fulfill its assigned task.

Somnath Chatterjee, Speaker of the Lok Sabha has put the problem succinctly, while addressing a seminar on 'Legislature and Audit Interface', "Proper functioning of the process of parliamentary control over public exchequer is directly linked to the capacity of the CAG to provide high quality timely Reports to the Parliament and State Legislatures and the capacity of the Public Accounts Committee and the Committee of Public undertakings to examine them and issue their recommendations effectively and speedily. The effectiveness of the Legislative committees is not dependent only on the speed and extent of the examination of CAG's report but also on the executive's response and commitment to act upon the recommendations made in the Reports of Legislative Committees with speed and without hindrance."

The working of the PAC has been discussed by me, in Lok Sabha's publication, 50 Years of Indian Parliament, which has been reproduced as chapter XVII of this book. (Parliament and State Legislatures have constituted Committee on Public Undertakings to examine the working of public enterprises. The problems in the working of the two committees are identical and comments on the working of the PAC apply mutatis mutandis to the COPU).

Governments Response to Public Accounts Committee Recommendations

The effectiveness of the PAC depends on the government accepting its recommendations and implementing them. Normally a subject taken up by PAC for oral examination receives a great deal of attention on the part of ministries and government departments. However, attention does not mean action. While some major changes in policy have been affected as a result of PAC's recommendations, Government has also been ignoring some of its key recommendations.

A study made by GC Malhotra for 25 years period from 1980 to 2004 (7th to 13th Lok Sabha) shows that about 60 percent of the recommendations are accepted (out of a total of 6548 recommendations during this period 4016 were accepted). Another 10 percent recommendations were not pursued on receipt of governments reply. Some of the Committee's recommendations have led to major changes in governments policy, amendment in taxation laws and setting up of enquiry committees to probe into irregularities conducted by delinquent parties. However, statistics can be misleading. Often the Government has been ignoring some the key and critical recommendations.

Over years, Committee's influence has been declining largely due to its inability to examine the bulk of the material contained in the Audit Reports. Before Independence and three decades thereafter, PAC used to examine all the paras which appeared in Audit Reports. However, from 1970's onwards, PAC adopted a selective style due to large number of reviews which started appearing in audit reports, but was still able to examine about half the paras and reviews which featured in Audit Reports. A study by RK Chandrashekhar for the 1947-48 to 1987-88 revealed that about 40 percent of paras were examined by PAC (out of 13457 paras, 5409 were examined), and around 50 percent of PAC's recommendations were accepted by Government (out of 16592 recommendations, 8071 were accepted). However, during last few years the PAC is able to examine a fraction of paras which appear in Audit Reports. Every year the Audit Reports contain 700 to 1000 paragraph, while PAC is able to examine only 10 to 15 paras. For example during 2003-04, out of 759 paras and reviews which featured in Audit Reports, PAC selected 93, but could discuss only 9 paras in the 11 sittings it held. PAC is faced with huge information load. While a system of Action Taken Note to deal with paras not examined by PAC is required to be submitted by the Ministries, it has hardly served the purpose and is more of a formality. How to deal with huge volume of work is a major challenge before the PAC.

Solution lies in PAC's having more sittings and better productivity, working through sub-committee system and CAG drastically reducing the volume of its reports and improving the quality.

Public Accounts Committee in the States

The functioning of PAC in States is in total disarray. In most of the States the PAC's are not constituted in time, when constituted they meet infrequently and the consideration of Audit reports remain in heavy arrears. There were over 12000 paras pending at the end 2004, out of which State PAC's could examine only around 500 paras. In some State the CAG's Reports are pending discussion from 1983-84. In most States legislatures control over public expenditure is practically non-existent.

Financial Anarchy- Excess Expenditure over Voted Grant

One of the most serious deficiency in functioning of State PAC's is their inability to discharge even the constitutional obligation of regularizing "excess expenditure". Article 205(b) of the Constitution requires that if money has been spent on any service in excess of the amount sanctioned in the Budget it should be regularized by taking post facto sanction of the legislature. This is done on the basis of recommendations made by PAC. Appropriation audit conducted by CAG shows that State governments have been spending moneys much beyond the ceilings imposed for each department as laid down in the Annual Financial Statement (Budget). A staggering sum of Rs 179585 crs has been spent over voted Grants by various States upto March 2002. (figures after this date are not available). Excess expenditure of some of the States are as under: J&K: Rs 41321crs; West Bengal: 23412crs; UP: Rs 23248crs; Assam: 23204crs; Maharastra: Rs 10385crs; Himachal: Rs 8342crs; Bihar: Rs 6965crs; Orissa: Rs 6750crs; MP: Rs 5137crs, Tamilnadu: Rs 4374crs. In some States excess expenditure has not been regularized, which has been incurred more than ten to fifteen years back, making a mockery of constitutional provision of budgetary control over public money. Non-regularization of excess expenditure may even result in misappropriation of public funds as was the case with Animal Husbandry scam in Bihar. Commenting on the lack of financial control, Era Sezhiyan a former Chairman of PAC observes, "it is the enormity of the misuse and the monstrosity of the misappropriation that makes the entire parliamentary system and the cherished objectives of accountability and control over public purse a huge mockery."

Decentralize Account Keeping and Enforce Exchequer Control

Government should not allow any 'excess expenditure' over budgetary Grant and bring in place a system of exchequer control. In UK under the Exchequer and Audit Act, the C&AG exercises the function of exchequer control and no money can be spent beyond the budgetary appropriation. Similar is the position in New Zealand, where under the Public Finance Act `1989, no payment can be made form the Treasury unless Audit Office has certified that amount can be lawfully paid. In India the word, 'Comptroller' was specifically added to the word, 'Auditor General' by the constitutional makers, so that CAG may be able to exercise the function of exchequer control, but somehow this could not be implemented.

In the Central Government, Controller General of Accounts is responsible for keeping the Accounts and disbursing payment, and the Secretary of the Ministry is the Chief Accounting Officer. The Chief Controller of Accounts should be made personally responsible for limiting expenditure to the budgetary Grants.

The problem in the States is more complex. The accounts are compiled and kept by the Accountant General who functions under the CAG. As the account keeping is divorced from the administration, it is unable to serve the purpose of bringing sound financial management practices. The system is outdated and a legacy of colonial practice.

There is need to bring modern management practices and transfer the accounts maintenance work to the State government, on the same lines as Central government, with a Controller of Accounts attached to each department, who should be made personally responsible that expenditure is kept within budgetary ceilings. The working of the integrated financial and accounting system in Central government has demonstrated, the advantage of having internal accounting arrangements, as an integral part of each department, not only in preparation of its own accounts but also of generating information and data to facilitate better financial management in administration.

Empowering Public Accounts Committee

The Commission to Review the Working of the Constitution has observed, At the national and State levels the Public Accounts Committee are the keystone of the arch of parliamentary control of public finances. If the PAC's do not function well, financial discipline and accountability will suffer. At present, only a miniscule fraction of the reports submitted to these committees are considered and reported on. It is imperative to evolve a system whereby PAC's consider all reports submitted to them and report to the legislature within a time limit of 12 to 18 months.

At present PAC suffers from several handicaps. It is constituted every year as a result its members are unable to develop specialization and expertise. There is also delay in its constitution. The problem is particularly severe in States. If President's rule is imposed, PAC's become non- functional. There is need to restructure PAC's in such a manner that it is constituted only once during the tenure of Lok Sabha / State Legislature, and its life made co-terminus with the life of the legislature. This can be done by making its membership on the Rajya Sabha pattern with one-third members retiring every two years.

There are other limitations in PAC's working. Most of the time it has to deal with matters of past history, which does not have contemporaneous importance and too often the persons examined were not the persons who were themselves the persons who had personally handled the case being investigated. It calls for evidence only of the Secretary of the ministry under whose jurisdiction the subject falls. The Ministers who make the policy do not appear before the committee nor or public men or experts invited to give evidence or make suggestions. In USA the Congressional committees ask public men to give evidence before it and can subpoena them if they do not cooperate. Similar is the position of parliamentary committees in several other advanced countries.

One of the most severe deficiency in Committee's working is that Government can ignore its key recommendations. Several past Chairman of Parliament's financial committee have made this observation. This takes away its effectiveness. As the Committee works on non party line, free from the passions of parliamentary debate, does a very through examination of the subject under review and its reports are marked by high degree of objectivity, Government should normally accept all its recommendations. In the event of Government not accepting its recommendations it has no remedy in its hand. A convention needs to be developed that if Government does not accept its recommendations, it should place an explanatory memorandum in the House.

There is also need for greater understanding between the PAC and CAG. CAG should bring out reports on subjects in which PAC has an interest, after ascertaining its views. In USA, 80 percent of GAO's reports emanate as a result of Congressional requests. The new UK and Australia Audit Act stipulate that CAG will take into account proposals made by Committee on Public Accounts.

Epilogue Empowering Public Audit

It needs some introspection why an institution like CAG, who works on behalf of Parliament, finds itself helpless in checking the all pervasive financial mismanagement in the government and has got marginalized in the scheme of governance of the country. An answer can be found in Gunnar Myrdal's aphorism, "There is a tendency for all knowledge, like all ignorance, to deviate from the truth in an opportunistic direction." The truth is that it is opportune for government in power to have a weak audit.

A Weak Audit- Suits the Power that be

Public audit is a check on exercise of power, arbitrarily, capriciously or in disregard of public interest. Audit operates in an area of executive action in which the citizens cannot seek remedial action against extravagance or misuse of pubic funds through the Court of Law. Press cannot investigate these cases as, barring some instances, it has no access to records. The recently enacted Freedom of Information Act, while it may give relief to individuals against executive malfeasance, cannot bring to light favours shown in award of mega contracts, deliberate underassessment of tax revenue and falsification of accounts. Audit is the only safeguard against financial mal-administration and enforcing accountability of those who have the power to take decisions of vital importance to the country. This does not suit politicians in power and top echelons of bureaucracy who want unbridled power. The best recourse is to bludgeon the instrument of audit and make it ineffective.

The history of state audit under Hitler's Germany, shows how a highly professional body with tradition dating back to Bismarck's kingdom of Prussia, capitulated before a totalitarian regime and lost some of its most fundamental functions. The Rechnugshof (Federal Court of Audit) became a centralized body and its old collegiate procedure was abolished and the Audit Courts of the Lander (States) became the branches of the national audit office. The Federal auditors were barred from auditing large part of public funds which were spent through Nazi party. The reports of FCA were " for official use only" and not available to the public and lacked a basis of parliamentary support or public opinion.

The Nazis began with the proposition that many of Germany's ills were the fault of that 'talking shop', the Reichstag (Parliament), and they took pride in contravention of parliamentary principles. A post war Federal Finance Minister observed that. " Federal Court of Audit, was not suppressed, which might perhaps have caused too much scandal. It was left to atrophy quietly; it could do its work, but this was disregarded and it did not influence the state or the government in any way." A former President of FCA concludes, "The experiences of the Potsdam Rechnungshof in the time of Third Reich showed incontestably that even a state body which is still in good working order fails in its object if no Parliament stands behind it and the public hears nothing of its efforts and aspirations."

Fareed Zakaria editor of News Week International in a perceptive study, concludes that in most developing countries there is no real democracy, as except adult suffrage, other values which characterize democracy are missing. In Western democracies besides universal suffrage, the political system is marked by the rule of law, separation of powers and protection of basic liberties of speech, religion and property. Zakaria describes the political system in some of the States in India, with massive corruption and disregard for rule of law, as 'bandit democracy'. There is little doubt that in large number of States such as Bihar, UP, Tamilnadu the political system is authoritarian with little respect for law and rules. In such a situation audit inevitably gets marginalized.

The Chief Minister of Tamilnadu J Jaylalitha launched a blistering attack on Accountant General Tamilnadu and demanded his transfer, when the press highlighted the mismanagement of State finances, after AG gave a press conference following presentation of Audit Report in the Legislature. The AG Bihar in his audit report on fodder scandal, documented in graphic detail the failure of entire financial control machinery in the State with the active connivance of officials from lower rung bureaucracy to persons holding highest executive position. This invited the wrath of the then Chief Minister Laloo Prasad Yadav, who said the AG Bihar should be sent to jail for not being able to prevent the fraud! Accusations were leveled against AG

West Bengal, by West Bengal Government for pointing out severe irregularities in Personal Ledger Account when hundreds of crores of rupees were kept outside the government account and misutilized.

While political executive and higher bureaucracy have a vested interest in a weak audit so that their misdemeanors are not exposed, why the CAG, as guardian of national purse, enjoying high constitutional status, is not able to have the offenders punished and bring financial discipline in the working of public institutions?

The answer lies in the fact that it is equally opportunistic for the office of the CAG to have a soft and benign approach to financial malpractices. This helps Audit Officials to lead a cushy and comfortable life which comes when you do not confront the Government and remain on its right side. Otherwise how do you explain the office of CAG looking the other way, when so many State governments blatantly violate the constitutional requirement of keeping their expenditure within the budgetary appropriations and making a mockery of budgetary approval accorded by the Legislature (a sum of Rs 180000 crs as on March 2002 has been spent over budgetary appropriation and left to atrophy).

The issue has not featured even as an agenda item in high level AG's conference addressed by President or the Prime Minister, nor has been specifically brought to the attention of Parliament, Prime Minister or the Finance Minister with a view to find ways to put an end to the malpractice. If the office of CAG arms itself with power of exchequer control (as is the position in UK) or acquires authority to recover illegal usage of money and property from public officials, it will require painstaking investigation, doing hard work, shouldering a great deal of responsibility and coming in occasional conflict with powers that be. The general attitude of Audit Department officials is to avoid taking responsibility, toe a soft line, and lead a trouble free and comfortable life. The Audit Department's alibi for its ineffectiveness is that Government doesn't adequately respond to audit findings or the Public Accounts Committee does not take interest in its reports.

At no point of time the Audit department has made serious effort to arm itself with adequate powers to ensure that its findings get implemented or force government to devise effective means to prevent mismanagement of public funds. This happens because majority of people who work in the senior positions in Audit department are not inspired by a sense of mission, that they are working for a national cause and have a duty to safeguard public money and are prepared to confront people in power and pay the price if need be.

Attitudinal Problem

Bureaucracy in India, of which the Audit department is just one segment, is widely perceived to be wooden, static, power hungry and indifferent to the needs and aspirations of the people. Swami Ranganathananda says that most public servants are concerned with three 'p's' namely pay, promotion and prospects, and lack patriotic fervor and a spirit of service to people. He pleads for administrators to be galvanized, to work towards constructive national purpose and develop a sense of mission and become instruments of revolutionary social change and transformation. The attitudes and value system of public services in India is in contrast with advanced countries.

Public administration in developed countries is citizen friendly, responsive and deeply concerned with the welfare of common man. UK, Australia, New Zealand, USA and many other countries have adopted the philosophy of New Public Management whose main focus is on devolution of authority, customer focus and performance contracting. The emphasis is on delivering services which citizens value with a strict regimen of accountability of public servants. The Civil Services Code in UK espouses the value of integrity, honesty and treating the public with sympathy and promptness. The Ethics in Government Act of USA, says that employees hold their position as public trust, shall not use public office for private gain and act impartially.

The high ethical standards of public services in developed countries is reflected in the value system of Supreme Audit Institutions of these countries who have drawn a vision and mission statement. The Vision of NAO, UK is, " To promote the highest standards in financial management and reporting, the proper conduct of business and beneficial change in public services". Its values are: cooperative spirit; integrity; looking outwards; making a difference; open communications; professional excellence; and valuing the individuals. The American GAO's mission is, " to support the Congress in meeting its constitutional responsibilities and to help improve the performance and ensure the accountability of the federal government for the benefit of the American people". Its core Values are: Accountability; Integrity; and Reliability.

There is need for attitudinal change on the part of Indian Audit Department. It should develop a sense of mission, and realize that its primary duty is towards the citizens of this country by ensuring that best value for money is secured when tax payers money is spent and help Parliament in ensuring the accountability of the Government for benefit of the people.

A lofty ideal will help Audit to focus its energy on delivering positive results, remove road blocks in fulfilling its objective and mission and not remain content, simply by mechanically producing reports and submit them to a disinterested government. It was the spirit of service to the common man that inspired the Supreme Court to enter the arena of PIL (Public Interest Litigation) and give much needed relief to an ordinary citizen against executive inaction, omission and commission and persons in authority resorting to arbitrary exercise of power.

Similar spirit has guided the Election Commission which has been very vigilant in ensuring free and fair conduct of elections. It has been questioning misuse of official machinery by politicians in power and using its authority to see that persons fighting elections follow the laid down norms and code of conduct. A time has come for similar audit activism so that it can fulfill its mandate as a basic pillar of democracy and help fulfilling the aspirations of the people of this country.

*Public Accounts Committee—Strengthening Parliamentary Financial Control**

Parliament's control over national finance acts as a key instrument in enforcing accountability of the Executive to the Legislature, a basic ingredient of a democratic polity. Parliament's gradual control over national finance is linked with the development of democracy in Great Britain and France. In France, the struggle between monarchy and nobility over the control of tax revenues was one of the causes of the Revolution of 1789 with the cry, "no taxation without representation". In Britain, "it was through their control of the nation's purse-string that the Commons became the guardian of human rights. Control over finance enabled Parliament to secure the safety of the life, liberties and the rights of the subject against arbitrary acts by the Executive," observes Paul Enzing, a distinguished student of the subject. It took several centuries of struggle by British Parliament dating back to the Magna Carta in 1215, to assert its right to control the public purse.

The Bill of Rights of 1688 had established the House of Commons' rights to taxation and the particular purpose for which money is to be spent. But, for a long time, the House of Commons remained under the illusion that it could control expenditure by putting a check on the issue of money from the exchequer, instead of ascertaining how the money was spent. It was due to the missionary zeal Gladstone, who was Finance Minister at that time and later the Prime Minister, that the Exchequer and Audit Department Act was enacted in 1866, which "converted the nominal control by Parliament into real control".

A Public Accounts Committee was constituted for the first time in April 1861, but it became effective only when the services of a full time expert—the Comptroller and Auditor General and its staff of professional auditors—was placed at its disposal. One of the greatest achievements of the Act was that it compelled all Departments to submit to Parliament audited accounts showing whether the moneys issued by the exchequer were actually spent in accordance with parliament appropriations. The new arrangement solved the dilemma, which baffled Parliament for many years, whether expenditure should be controlled by inexpert parliamentarians or by expert non-parliamentarians.

Evolution of PAC in India

In India, Public Accounts Committee was constituted both at the Center and the Provinces in 1921 under the provision of the Government of India Act of 1919 as a result of the Montague-Chelmsford Reforms. The Chairman of the PAC was the Finance Member of the Governor General's Council. The maximum strength of the PAC was twelve and not less than two-thirds of its members were elected by the non-official members of the Assembly. During the twenty-five years of its existence upto the time we attained Independence, the Committee came to be a major force in legislative control of the expenditure and exercised increasing influence on the actions of the Government despite limitation of its constitution and restriction on its authority. The Committee continued to function under the old arrangement even after 1947, with the Finance Minister functioning as its Chairman. After the Indian Constitution came into effect on 26 January 1950, the Committee acquired its rightful place as a full-fledged Parliamentary Committee under the control of the Speaker with one of its members elected as its Chairman.

The Committee was then constituted under Rule 308 of the *Rules of Procedure and Conduct of Business in Lok Sabha.* Since 1954-55, the PAC consists of 22 members, fifteen members form the Lok Sabha who are elected by the house every year from amongst its members according to the principle of proportional representation by means of single transferable vote and seven members of the Rajya Sabha. In

1967, a convention was set to appoint a member of the Opposition party as Chairman of the Committee and Shri M.R. Masani was the first Opposition member to adorn this office. Paying tribute to the new arrangement, the Speaker, Dr. Sanjiva Reddy observed: "Shri Masani has more than vindicated his faith with his intellectual caliber, broad sweep, sense of dedication and restraint and has lent a new stature to the Committee, earning for it the respect and approbation of all those who appeared before it, and was able to carry his colleagues in the Committee who were given a full sense of participation in Committee's work." This healthy convention of appointing a member of the Opposition as Chairman has since been continuing.

Functioning of the Committee

Due to the meticulous and thorough examination of Audit Reports taken by the Committee, it has come to acquire a great deal of prestige and authority. The Committee's reports are marked by a high degree of objectivity as it invariably works on non-party lines free from the passions of debates in the House. Some of the Committee's reports have led to major changes in Government policy. In its Third Report of the First Lok Sabha on Exchequer Control on Public Expenditure, the Committee recommended separation of Audit from Accounts, which was subsequently endorsed by the Administrative Reforms commission (1968) and implemented by the Government in 1976. In its Eleventh and Fiftieth Reports (Fourth Lok Sabha), the Committee laid down guidelines for items of expenditure which would constitute New Service/New Instrument of Service under article 115 of the Constitution. The Committee's Reports on Income Tax and Central Excise issues such as Refund of Central Excise duty, Advance Licensing Scheme; and certain exemptions allowed under Wealth Tax have led to changes in taxation law to protect Government's revenue.

In its Report on Disinvestment of Pubic Enterprises' shares, in April 1994 (Seventy-fifth Report of Tenth Lok Sabha), the Committee felt that there was lack of transparency in the manner in which the exercise was undertaken and desired the Government to fix the responsibility on the officials concerned which led to the Government setting up an Enquiry Committee. The out of turn allotment of housing accommodation by the Minister for Housing was another subject of PAC's probe (1995-96) and the Committee's recommendations coupled with the Supreme Court's directive in a PIL, led to stoppage of the malpractice and formed the basis for adopting a more rational policy in this regard. Several other Reports of the Committee have also received a great deal of attention.

The effectiveness of the Committee can be judged by the response of the Government to its recommendations. The following data for the twenty-year period from 1980 to 1999 which covers the Seventh Lok Sabha to the Twelfth Lok Sabha will give an idea. The PAC gave 6112 recommendations out of which the Government accepted 3709 recommendations—thus the percentage of recommendations accepted was 61. Subsequently, about 10 per cent recommendations were dropped at the Action Taken Stage, on receipt of Governments's replies. Another 10 per cent were reiterated by PAC out of which some were accepted by the Government.

Thus, it can be said that about three-fourth of the recommendations were accepted. However, numbers may not give a correct picture. Sometimes, Government does not accept some of the major recommendations of the Committee. For example, PAC has been advising the Government for a long time to put a statutory limit on public borrowing under article 292 of the Constitution but Government had been ignoring the recommendation; it was only in December 2000 that the Fiscal Responsibility Bill has been introduced in Lok Sabha to regulate borrowing.

Public Accounts Committee of the State Governments

The functioning of Public Accounts Committee in most States is far from satisfactory. In several States, the PACs are not constituted in time, they meet infrequently and the consideration of Audit Reports is heavily in arrears. Annexure I gives an idea of the functioning of PACs in various States for three years from 1998-99 to 2000-2001. In J&K, PAC has not even been constituted.

To get an idea of the backlog of work, Audit Reports currently being discussed in some of the Sates as of January 2001, are as follows; Assam from 1991-92 onwards; Andhra Pradesh—1995-96; Punjab 1990-91 to 1997-98; Haryana—1995-96; Kerala—1986-87 to 1998-99; Maharashtra—1996-97 Karnataka—1992-93 to 1996-97; Tamil Nadu—1995-96 onwards; West Bengal—1992-93 to 1998-99. By its very nature, audit findings are reported after a lapse of considerable period from the time the event has taken place. If the consideration of report is delayed by as much as five to ten years, the value of the recommendation is lost.

Excess Expenditure over Voted Grants by States

A major problem with State PACs, unlike its counterpart at the Centre, is that they do not separately consider report on Appropriation

Accounts included in the Audit Reports of the CAG. A huge sum of excess expenditure over voted grants by various States is lying unregularised.

Articles 112 to 117 in the case of Union Government and articles 202 to 207 in the case of States lay down the procedure for presentation and approval by the Parliament and the State Legislature of the Budgets of the Central/State Governments. The Appropriation Act passed by the Legislature contains the authority to appropriate the specified sums from the Consolidated Fund of India/States for specified services. Appropriation accounts are prepared every year indicating the gross amounts on various services actually spent *vis a vis* that authorized by Appropriation Act. The CAG conducts appropriation audit under articles 149 and 151 of the Constitution to ascertain that the expenditure actually incurred under various Grants is within the authorization and the expenditure is in conformity with the law, rules and regulations. Appropriation audit conducted by CAG shows that State Governments have been spending money much beyond the ceilings imposed for each Department while passing the Annual Financial Statement (Budget) and no serious action has been taken to obtain sanction of Legislature to regularize it. A staggering sum of over Rs. 93,300 crore was spent over Voted Grant by the States as on March 1999, the latest year for which data is available (Annexure II)., Excess expenditure of Rs. 22,767 crore over Voted Grant has been incurred by J & K; Rs. 13618 crore by UP; Rs. 12569 crore by Assam; Rs. 6,058 crore by Bihar; and Rs. 5294 crore by West Bengal and has not been regularized for periods as long as ten to twenty-five years.

According to articles 113(2) and 203(2) of the Constitution, the estimates of expenditure in the form of Demands for Grants is submitted to Parliament/State Legislatures (with a view to laying down limits of expenditure for each Department such as Health, Police, Public Works, etc). The Constitution has a provision that in an exceptional case where expenditure exceeds the Grant, it should be regularized by the Legislature. Articles 115 (b) and 205 (b) states; "if any money has been spent on any service during a financial year in excess of the amount granted by that service and for that", a statement showing the amount of that expenditure and the demand of that excess should be laid before the House. The excess expenditure is regularized on the basis of the recommen-dation of the Public Accounts Committee as per procedure laid down. As per established procedure, the Ministries and Departments furnish to the PAC, explanatory notes giving reasons leading to excesses under each Grant and the PAC examines in the light of these notes the circumstances leading to such excesses and presents a report to Parliament/Legislature, recommending regularization of the excesses subject to such observations as it chooses to make.

As PACs are not functioning effectively in most States, a huge amount of *excess expenditure* remains unregularised. This is fraught with serous consequences and may result in fraud, as was the case with the Animal Husbandry scam in Bihar. There was excess expenditure in Grant of Animal Husbandry Department in Bihar, in each of the years from 1987-88 to 1995-96 (for example, for 1993-94 while the budgetary Grant was Rs. 77.14 crore, an expenditure of Rs. 199.17 crore was incurred, in 1994-95 against the Grant of Rs. 74.40 crore, a sum of Rs. 245.01 crore was spent and in 1995-96 against Grant of Rs. 82.12 crore, Rs. 22,861 crore was spent). The Bihar PAC never met to examine such serious violations of financial rules and as a result the irregularity continued for years. Much of the problem of *excess expenditure* arises as we do not have in India a system of exchequer control which ensures that no money can be drawn over budgetary grants. In UK, New Zealand and other countries, the law empowers the CAG to exercise this power and no money can be drawn from Government Treasury unless Audit Office has certified that it can be lawfully paid.

Timely Submission of Accounts

Effective control of expenditure can be exercised only if Appropriation Accounts are timely submitted to the Parliament/State Legislature and desired remedial action taken. Most countries have statutory provisions regarding date of submission of audited accounts to Parliament. In UK, under the Exchequer & Audit Department Act of 1866 the Treasury is required to submit Accounts to CAG by 30 September and the CAG is required to submit certified accounts to Parliament by January of the following year to which they relate. In New Zealand, under the Public Finance Act of 1989, the Treasury is required to forward the Annual Financial Statement to the Audit Office by 31 August, following the end of the financial year and the Audit Office is required to give its opinion within thirty days of its receipt for placing it in the House of Representatives.

In India, there is considerable delay in the submission of Appropriation Accounts even of the Union Government to the Parliament. A study for eight years from 1992-93 to 1999-2000 shows that it takes over fifteen months from the close of the financial year for the audited accounts and the audit report thereon to be placed in the Parliament. It takes another year for the PAC to examine and Parliament to approve excess expenditure (Annexure III). There is need for accelerating the time cycle for preparation of Appropriation and Finance Accounts and its audit by CAG and regularization excess expenditure by PAC. Statutory provision to the following effect needs to be made:

- The Appropriation and Finance Accounts should be prepared and finalized by the Controller General of Accounts for Union Government and Accountant General (Accounts) for the Sate Government by 30 September of the following financial year to which they relate.
- CAG should certify the accounts within two months of its receipt and submit his report to Parliament/State Legislature by November of the following year to which they relate.
- The PAC should consider the accounts and make its recommendations regarding regularization of excess expenditure by January and Parliament should approve the same by February (before presentation of next year's Budget) of the following year to which the accounts relate.

Thus, an amendment needs to be made in articles 115(b) and 205(b) of the Constitution prescribing the time limit within which excess expenditure of a particular year is to be approved by the Parliament/State Legislature.

Strengthening the PAC

There is little doubt that if parliamentary control over expenditure is to be real, the functioning of PAC has to be more effective. R.R. Morarka, former Chairman of the Committee observes; "There is no real control over Government spending. The implementation of Committee's recommendation is tardy. All this is due to inadequacy of time, both of Parliament and its Committees. The remedy, therefore, lies in strengthening of the Committee System and some effective step in this direction is the need of the hour."

The National Commission to Review the Working of the Constitution headed by Justice Venkatachaliah has released a paper on *Efficacy of Public Audit System in India* for public comments, wherein it has been suggested that PAC be made a constitutional body by amending the Constitution. The life of the Committee be made five years to be co-extensive with the life of Parliament/State Legislature with one-third of its members retiring every two years somewhat on the pattern of the Raja Sabha. It has also been suggested that PAC should examine all the reports of CAG within a time limit—say, one year from the date of presentation.

The PAC at present suffers from several limitations. Presently, the Secretary of the Ministry under whose jurisdiction the subject being taken up for examination by the Committee falls, appears for evidence before the Committee. The concerned officers who actually handled the matter do not appear before the Committee. Shri M.R. Masani, former Chairman of the Committee observed that most of the time they have to deal with matters of past history, which did not have contemporaneous importance and too often the persons examined were not themselves the persons who had personally handled the case being investigated. He suggested calling for evidence, the actual officers who were responsible for dealing with the case in question. There is considerable merit in the suggestion.

In USA, the Congressional Committees ask public men to give evidence before it and can subpoena them if they do not cooperate. The Committee investigating the recent Enron scandal in the US has asked its former Chairman to give evidence before it. In USA, Secretaries of Various Departments also give evidence before the Committee. The Public Accounts Committee in India has to find ways and means to make its functioning more effective.

Empowering Audit

It should be possible for PAC to examine all the reports of the CAG if the volume of the reports is reduced and their quality and content improved and only matters of critical importance included in the Audit Reports. It may be mentioned that in Britain, the PAC examines all the subjects contained in CAG's audit report. One reason why matters of lesser importance get included in the audit report is that the institution of CAG does not enjoy adequate powers to enforce its findings; as a result the Departments do not give adequate weight and take remedial action on its reports and these matters, therefore, have to be brought to the notice of the Legislature. A high powered Sub-Committee of the Chairman of Central PAC headed by E. Ayyapu Reddy, which had Chairmen of eight State PACs and CAG as members, expressed anguish at the lack of response of departmental officers to audit findings and observed that delayed response on the part of the Department is responsible for constant and repeated failure to enforce accountability and is just as serious as not taking up immediate investigation after lodging of First Information Report in a crime. The Committee observed:

> *It is very depressing to find that in spite of audit reports revealing loss of public funds or misuse and misapplication of public funds, there is no investigating agency charged with the duty to probe into these aspects and identify the culprits responsibly for them. Recommendations of Public Accounts Committee for investigation to enforce accountability for undisputed misuse of public funds are not yielding any tangible result for the simple reason that long lapse of time between transaction and the recommendations normally result in disappearance of incriminating evidence.*

The situation needs to be remedied by conferring quasi-judicial powers to Audit Officers so that they can summon the concerned officers before it to produce the relevant records and give evidence on oath and where loss of public money is established, require them to make good the loss. Audit Officers in countries such as New Zealand, Japan, Germany, France, South Korea, China and Thailand enjoy legal powers to take remedial action against public officials, if they find that they have caused loss of the State money or property through fraud, negligence and improper use.

There is also need for greater understanding between the PAC and the CAG regarding material to be presented in the Audit Reports so that full use of the same can be made. In USA, more than fifty per cent of the material presented in the reports of the General Accounting Office emanate as a result of Congressional request. Similar is the position in Great Britain where a good part of subjects investigated by CAG are taken up on the advice of the Public Accounts Committee. Despite many limitations, the Public Accounts Committee has been able to introduce a modicum of financial discipline in the Government. Its close working relationship with CAG has helped Audit Department to enhance its own prestige and authority and enforce some accountability of public officials at grass root level. The consciousness of the Administration that there exists a parliamentary body to scrutinize what is being done by it, acts as a deterrent against any tendency towards slackness, negligence or arbitrariness on the part of the Executive. The following points merit consideration:

- There is a strong case for making the Committee a constitutional institution with clearly defined duties, functions and responsibilities and its life made co-terminus with the life of Parliament/State Legislature.

- A statutory provision needs to be made prescribing dates for presentation of Appropriation Accounts to Parliament/State Legislature and excess expenditure over Voted Grants should be regularized by it before the end of the next year to which the Accounts relate, if the control over budgetary appropriation as prescribed in the Constitution has to have real meaning.
- Public audit and the institution of CAG be empowered and given more teeth to be able to enforce some action on its findings and check the present lackadaisical attitude on the part of public officials.

Parliament can enforce accountability of the Executive only through its control over national finance. The Public Accounts Committee is Parliament's instrument to enforce its authority. If the Committee is not able to discharge its function efficiently, it will have an adverse impact on the functioning of democratic institutions. Former British prime Minister and a great votary of parliamentary financial control, William Gladstone, observed in March 1891: "The finance of the country is ultimately associated with the liberties of the country. If the House of Commons by any possibility lose the power of the control of the grants of public money, depend upon it, your liberty will be worth very little in comparison. That powerful leverage has been what is commonly known as power of the purse—the control of the House of Commons over public expenditure." There is need for the Public Accounts Committee to function effectively if Parliament has to act as a real bulwark for democracy and liberty in our country.

Defence Deals: Comptroller Auditor General Should Play a Positive Role

Under the Indian Constitution, the CAG acts as a guardian of national finance and it is his responsibility to see that public funds are not misused. If therefore the government wants that CAG clear certain categories of defence deals, the proposal should be welcomed as a significant step towards probity and transparency in procurement. Similarly, if the CAG had adopted a more proactive role and certified the valuation of PSUs before their privatization under the NDA regime, the public would have been assured that fair returns had been secured in the sale of public assets.

Major defence deals have often been embroiled in controversy and the public has suspicions that under-handed dealings take place in most purchase transactions. This is unfortunate and affects the morale of the armed forces. We need to have a system that is transparent and in which the public reposes faith. Media reports say that the prime minister Manmohan Singh and defence minister Pranab Mukherjee have proposed that watchdog agencies, the comptroller and Auditor General of India (CAG) and the Central Vigilance commissioner (CVC) should clear defence deals before they are finalized. During the NDA regime a similar proposal was mooted and the defence secretary took up the matter formally with CAG but the latter seems to have declined. Why should CAG disown this responsibility?

Public audit is a vital instrument of maintaining probity in public finance and an institution that is as old as organized states themselves. Aristotle advocated that all public money be issued in front of the whole city to protect it from being defrauded and Kutilya, in his magnum opus *Arthashastra,* underlines the importance of audit to prevent embezzlement of money and falsification of accounts by public officials.

Public audit in its present form has developed all over the world to help the legislature in implementing programmes. The control of national finances by parliament is closely linked with the movement of democracy in countries such as England and France from where constitutional democratic institutions have emanated, for only 'representatives of the people' should have power to decide the appropriation of public funds and not the monarchy or executive. This power had two essential elements: the granting of monies by parliament and the supervision of expenditure by state audit institutions.

The supervision of expenditure by state audit was introduced for the first time in England as a result of far-reaching reforms by W.E. Gladstone, who was finance minister and then later became prime minister through the enactment of the Exchequer and Audit Department Act in 1866. The act required departments to produce annual appropriation accounts, it established the position of the CAG, obliged him to audit the accounts of all government departments and submit the report to parliament to be examined by the Committee on Public Accounts. By its very nature, audit is a post facto examination of events and transactions.

The traditional function of state audit was to conduct a regularity audit—to see that government activities were being carried on with due regard to laid down rules, regulations and guidelines. However, in recent years, the functions of government have expanded exponentially and audit has moved into the arena of 'value for money' audit—an examination of whether the government's programmes are being carried on with due regard to economy, efficiency and effectiveness. As government activities are manifold, spread over hundreds of departments and field outfits, it is simply not possible for the CAG to examine every transaction—he conducts a test check of selected departments and blocks of expenditure. However, the presence of an independent external agency which could detect an irregularity of the improper handling of public money acts as a deterrent and is the raison d'etre of state audit.

Under the Indian Constitution the CAG acts as a guardian of national finance and it is his responsibility to see that public funds are not misused. If therefore the government wants that CAG should clear certain categories of defence deals, the proposal should be welcomed as a significant step towards probity and transparency in procurement. After all, it helps nobody if lapses in purchase transactions are pointed out after deals are finalized as it is not possible to cancel or alter the terms of the contract without jeopardizing the supply of critical equipment to the armed forces. In the past, CAG's reports on Befors guns, coffin purchases during the Kargil war and numerous other cases have evoked great controversy and taken political overtones.

This has resulted in the higher echelons of bureaucracy and armed forces exercising excessive caution and playing safe, which delays decision-making processes and is largely responsible for the huge surrender of funds allocated for defence purchases every year. Delays in decisions about the purchase of vital arms and equipment may prove very costly in terms of national security. We need to change the psychology of mistrust and develop a system in which there is no witch-hunting and questioning of officials who take decisions in good faith. A preaudit by CAG, of major defence deals would clear the suspicion that hangs in the peculiar political milieu of the country today. CAG may be hesitant to take the responsibility of pre-auditing defence deals for fear of getting dragged in political controversy.

This aspect can be taken care of by building certain safeguards: (a) CAG should not be made part of the executive decision-making process—his responsibility should be limited to ensure that laid down systems and procedures have been followed and most advantageous terms have been secured for the government: (b) It should be mandatory for government to obtain CAG's clearance for all major deals, say above Rs 500 crore. This will have two advantages, the government will not be able to selectively pick and choose cases for reference as it would be required to refer all cases above a certain value and the

CAG will not be flooded with hundreds of contract cases that the defence ministry enters into every year.

If a system of pre-audit is accepted, CAG on his part will have to ensure that his clearance or reservation, as the case may be, comes speedily, say within a period of a fortnight. Prior vetting of deals by CAG will have a number of advantages. Most major deals for the purchase of arms and defence equipment are with powerful multinational firms, who carefully guard their technology and operate in secrecy and it needs a great deal of acumen on the part of Indian negotiators to drive favourable bargains. They are assisted by a battery of legal, financial and technical experts and often insert clauses in the contract in fine print, which are often missed by Indian negotiating teams. A second look by the CAG will ensure that the most advantageous terms have been secured for the government.

There is a need for CAG to come out with new techniques and methodologies of audit in view of the increasing complexity of governments operations. One such area is privatization. During the debate on the privatization of BALCO, the then minister Arun Shourie stated in parliament that CAG will audit the transaction to prove that the deal was fair. Although four years have elapsed, CAG has not yet brought out a single report on privatization. In the last session of parliament, a debate took place on the privatization of Centaur Hotel. The minister of finance P. Chidambaram observed that the deal would be looked into after receipt of CAG's report.

If CAG now points out some lapses, it will hardly serve any purpose, except some political mud-slinging, as the deal cannot by undone. Much of the controversy on privatization during the NDA's regime arose due to the selling of PSUs through the strategic sale route where valuation of the company being sold becomes a critical component. Valuation is a difficult issue with a wide divergence of opinion among experts. If CAG would have adopted a more proactive role and certified the valuation before these companies were put on sale, an assurance would have been available to the public that fair returns had been secured on these public assets.

A large part of the problem in the functioning of the office of the CAG arises due to its apathy in modernizing its method and practices in keeping with the fast pace of changes taking place in the role and responsibilities of the government. In US, the General Accounting Office acts as an umpire for government contracts or procurement when disappointed contractors appeal on the ground that adverse decisions violated a law or regulation or were unjust. GAO's procedure for such bids, which run into thousands every year, is simple, inexpensive and quick and largely resorted to by contractors as they do not like going to court. GAO is also required by law to render advance decisions on the legality of proposed payments when requested by any of the executive departments, and its decisions are binding on the aggrieved parties. Prior vetting of defence deals or certification of PSU valuation involves taking responsibility and speedy decision-making, which CAG officials avoid as they are used to working at a leisurely pace and do not have accountability. There is a need for a change in the outlook of the office of the CAG and a realization that their work should contribute to national good. The time has come for the CAG to find innovative solutions to deal with complex problems that confront the government so that it becomes an instrument for good governance and public accountability.

Jayalalitha's Intimisation of Accountant General CAG'S Functionaries Need Legal Protection

The chief Minister of Tamil Nadu, Jayalalitha's full-page press statement of August 6, published in the national dailies, faulting the conduct of the Accountant General (AG) of Tamil Nadu, raises fundamental issues regarding the institution of the Comproller and Auditor General (CAG) and his ability to function independently without fear or favour as envisaged in the Constitution. Under Article 151(2) of the Constitution, the CAG is required to place an audit Report on the State accounts in the legislature. After the audit report for 2002-03 was placed in the Tamil Nadu Legislative Assembly, the AG of Tamil Nadu issued a press note and held a press conference highlighting the important findings which featured in the Audit Report. Jayalalitha calls the action of the AG as 'constitutional impropriety', 'Central Government manipulating the AG to portray the Government of Tamil Nadu in poor light' and contends that the report cannot be dicussed unless the Public Accounts Committee has gone through the same.

The position taken by Jayalalitha is not correct and seems to be an attempt to intimidate the AG. It has been a long established convention in the Audit Department that as soon as the Audit Report is placed in the Legislature/Parliament, the Accountant General issues a press brief to highlight the significant audit findings and meets the press if the local press shows interest in the subject. It stands to reason that after the Audit Reports are placed in Parliament/State

Legislature, they come in the public domain and it is open for the press and enlightened members of the public to discuss the issues highlighted therein.

Dr. B.P. Mathur is a former member of the Indian Audit and Accounts Service (IA&AS) and has worked in the Comptroller and Auditor General's organization for over 34 years, holding the positions of Deputy Comptroller and Audits General and Chairman, Audit Board.

The audit reports of the CAG, after they are placed in Parliament/ Legislature are remitted to the Public Accounts Committee (PAC) of the Centre/State who, after detailed examination, give recommendations relating to various aspects of the functioning of administrative machinery and indicts officials if they are found to have committed misdemeanour.

The issuance of a press brief summarizing the facts mentioned in the Audit Report can by no chance be construed as an encroachment of the PAC's jurisdiction by the AG. As a matter of fact, the Public Accounts Committee regards the CAG/AG as its friend, philosopher and guide and reposes a great deal of trust and confidence in him. Lately, however, the functioning of the PACs in most States has been far from satisfactory. One of the principal duties of the PAC is to "regularise excess expenditure", incurred over the budgetary sanctions as required under Article 205 (b) of the Constitution.

In Tamil Nadu a sum of Rs 4375.76 crores incurred in excess over the budgetary grants in various years from 1991-92 to 2001-02 is still awaiting 'regularization' by the PAC/Legislature. For the year 2002-03, the government has spent Rs 2436.71 crores in excess of the budgetary grant) which includes Highways—Rs 41 crores, Public Works—Rs 145 crores and Public Debt Repayment—Rs 2096 crores) making a mockery of the exchequer control system in the State. A large part of the problem arises due to the PAC's inability to discharge the onerous responsibility entrusted to it.

It is not constituted in time, meets infrequently, has just a few sittings in a year, the consideration of Audit Reports remains heavily in arrears and most of the audit paras meet "natural death" due to efflux of time. In the UK, from where we have drawn our parliamentary conventions, the Public Accounts Committee considers all the paras in the CAG's report within a year of presentation to Parliament and acts as a powerful instrument of enforcing financial discipline on the government of the day.

Two AIADMK MPs have filed a petition in the Madras High Court, seeking quo warranto direction for removal of the AG of Tamil Nadu, on the ground that he has committed constitutional impropriety. The position taken by the MPs is unsustainable, and one hopes that the honourable Court rejects it on the ground that it is an encroachment on the CAG's authority as guaranteed under the Constitution. It needs to be realized that the Accountant General in State functions on behalf on the CAG, and should enjoy the same immunity, privilege and power as available to the CAG under the Constitution and the CAG's Act of 1971. If this de facto position (as it obtains for more than 100 years of the Indian Audit Department's existence) is not recognized, the AG will not be able to discharge his duties and act as the custodian of national finance. At the time of the framing of the Indian Constitution, the Drafting Committee, headed by Dr. B. R. Ambedkar, had proposed an office of the Auditor-in-Chief for every State, as a constitutional office in keeping with the federal character of the Constitution.

The Government of India Act of 1935 had also a provision of separate Auditor General for the Provinces. In the USA, Germany, Canada, Australia and almost every country with a federal structure, the independence of the head of audit of the provinces is guaranteed under the Constitution/law. In the UK, following the recent devolution in Scotland and Wales and the setting up of legislative assemblies, separate Auditor Generals for them have been created. The Commission to Review the Working of the Constitution, headed by Justice Venkatachaliah, has recommended that appropriate legal recognition be given to the Accountant General to enable him to perform his duties effectively.

In the absence of legal protection, the Accountant General and other top functionaries of the Audit Department find themselves in a helpless position when an attack on them is launched, if they bring out uncomfortable facts. Sometimes back, when the AG of Bihar brought out an audit report on the fodder scandal, the then Chief Minister of Bihar said that the Accountant General should be jailed for not being able to prevent the fraud! There is an imperative need for a legal enactment defining the functions, duties and privileges of the AG, Deputy CAG and other senior functionaries of the Audit Department so that they can perform their duties fearlessly. It is hoped that the CAG of India, V.N. Kaul, will take urgent steps in this regard. The Lima Declaration of the Association of Supreme Audit Institutions states that the independence of audit is inseparably linked with the independence of its members and enjoins that that should be guaranteed under the Constitution.

The three volume Audit Report on the Tamil Nadu Government, running into 336 pages, points to the poor state in which the States finances are. The action of Jayalalitha and some of her party members is simply a ploy to divert attention from the malfunctioning of the State administration, and smacks of fascist tendencies. In Hitler's Germany, the powers and jurisdiction of the Federal Court of Audit were severely abridged, its reports restricted for "official use only", were not made available to the public and lacked a basis for parliamentary support, which *inter alia* facilitated the setting up of a totalitarian state. State audit works on behalf of Parliament in enforcing the accountability of the Executive.

The Members of Parliament, State Legislature, press and enlightened members of the public should come forward and raise their voice to protect the independence of the AG/CAG, an institution designed by our Constitution makers to work towards providing an open, transparent and accountable government.

Objectivity and Transparency Should Guide Appointment of New Comptroller Audit General

The Comptroller & Auditor General of India (CAG) acts as a vital instrument in ensuring supremacy of Parliament over the Executive and enforcing public accountability so necessary for a democratic polity. For this reason, he has been granted an exalted status and independence under the Constitution—he is appointed by the President by a warrant under his hand and seal, has the same status a Supreme Court Judge, cannot be removed from office, save in an exceptional situation, his condition of service cannot be varied to his disadvantage and his salary is charged to the Consolidated Fund of India etc.

However, an office however exalted is as good as the incumbent holding it. It is, therefore, necessary that a professional of highest competence and unquestioned integrity is appointed to the post.

The six-year term of the present CAG, VK Shunglu, expires in early March. It is therefore, necessary that a suitable person is appointed to this high office. Unfortunately, the manner of appointment of the present CAG and some of his predecessors had been mired with controversy.

From the time the Constitution came into being in 1950, the four CAGs appointed to the post were professionals belonging to the Indian

Audit and Accounts Services. However, from 1978 onwards, the last four incumbents, including the present one, are from the Indian Administrative Service (IAS). The appointment of persons who do not possess the requisite background of auditing and accounting as CAG has been subject of severe criticism by public men, press, members of Parliament including chairman of the Public Accounts Committee and officers and staff associations of the audit and accounts department.

The Indian Constitution does not lay down any qualification for the post of CAG nor the manner of his selection. However, the matter was discussed during the Constituent Assembly debates in My 1949. From the debates it is evident that the intention of the framers of the Constitution was that a person who had sufficient knowledge of finance and accounting systems of the government and had practical knowledge of the work of the finance department and had worked as an accountant general would only be appointed.

However, in practice, this assurance has not been honoured. The government has not laid down any criteria for the selection of CAG. The selection is made by the Prime Minister, presumably on the basis of some advice received from his office (PMO)/ Cabinet Secretariat/ finance minister and a recommendation is made to the President. The existing system does not inspire public confidence and lacks transparency. This is in contrast with other democratic countries who have legal provision for appointment of head of Supreme Audit Authority so that it instills public confidence.

In India, we have been following British traditions of parliamentary democracy and the post of CAG has been patterned on the British model. In the UK, an act to strengthen parliamentary control and supervision of expenditure of public money was enacted in 1983 by making a new provision for appointment and status of CAG and establishing a National Audit Office. The act stipulates that the CAG shall be appointed after an address is presented to the House of Commons by the Prime Minister acting with the agreement of the chairman of the Public Accounts Committee. The act also enjoins the CAG to conduct Value for Money audit and to see that public funds are used with due regard to economy, efficiency and effectiveness.

In the US, the Budget and Accounting Act of 1921 stipulates that the President shall appoint the Comptroller General on the advice and consent of the Senate. The GAO Act of 1980 further amplifies the selection process and envisages establishing a Commission to recommended the name for the post. In Canada, under the Auditor

General act of 1997 he is appointed by the Governor General on the basis of recommendation made by the Joint Committee of Public Accounts and Audit. In Germany the Bundestag and Bundesrat (the two Houses of Parliament) elect the President of Bundersrechnuhof (Supreme Audit Authority) without debate.

In Japan, the Commissioners of the Board of Audit are appointed by the cabinet with the consent of the both Houses of the Diet. In Korea, the Chairman of the Board of Audit is appointed by the President with the consent of the National Assembly. Similar is the position in newly industrialized countries like Thailand—the appointment of the Auditor General must receive prior approval of the national assembly.

In India, the National Commission to Review the Working of the Constitution, headed by Justice M N Venkatachaliah, has deliberated over measures to bring about improvement in the public audit systems and has released a paper to elicit public comments. It seems that the Commission is in favour of appointment of CAG to be made on the basis of recommendation by the high-level independent committee, which should include the Speaker of the Lok Sabha and the Leader of the Opposition, besides the Prime Minister.

The Commission apparently wants qualification to be laid down for the post and only a person having extensive experience of government finance and public audit and accounts system should be eligible to hold the office. The submission of the Commission's recommendations are likely to take some more time and may not be available to the government when the next CAG is to be appointed.

The finances of the country are at present in doldrums, with mounting public debt and ballooning public expenditure, bulk of which is unproductive. There is hardly any money left for development work and a large section of the population is groaning under the burden of poverty. The CAG, as a custodian of national finance, can prevent waste of national resources and help optimise public expenditure. B.R. Ambedkar, the founding father of the Constitution, had observed: "I am of the opinion that this dignitary or officer is probably the most important officer of the Constitution of India....His duties, I submit are far more important than even of the judiciary."

In view of the importance of the office, will it be too much to expect from the government that it lays down an objective criteria for selection to the post of CAG, which is to be filled shortly and follows a transparent system of appointment?

5

Indian Accounting Standards

Indian Accounting Standards, abbreviated as Ind AS are a set of accounting standards notified by the Ministry of Corporate Affairs which are converged with International Financial Reporting Standards(IFRS). These accounting standards are formulated by Accounting Standards Board of Institute of Chartered Accountants of India. Now India will have two sets of accounting standards viz. existing accounting standards under Companies (Accounting Standard) Rules, 2006 and IFRS converged Indian Accounting Standards(Ind AS). The Ind AS are named and numbered in the same way as the corresponding IFRS. NACAS recommend these standards to the Ministry of Corporate Affairs. The Ministry of Corporate Affairs has to spell out the accounting standards applicable for companies in India. As on date the Ministry of Corporate Affairs notified 35 Indian Accounting Standards(Ind AS). But it has not notified the date of implementation of the same.

Convergence with IFRS

The inception of the idea of convergence of Indian GAAP with IFRS was made by the Prime Minister of India Dr. Manmohan Singh by committing in G20 to align Indian accounting standards with IFRS. Thereafter ICAI has decided to converge its Accounting Standards with IFRS for accounting periods commencing on or after 1 April 2011 in a phased manner as envisaged the Roadmap to IFRS formulated by the Ministry of Corporate Affairs. For smooth transition to IFRS, ICAI has taken up the matter of convergence with the National Advisory Committee on Accounting Standards and various regulators such as the RBI, SEBI and IRDA, CBDT. IASB, the issuer of IFRS, is also supporting the ICAI in its endeavours towards convergence. It has been decided that there shall be two sets of Accounting Standards under the Companies Act. The new set of standards which have been converged with IFRS are now known as Indian Accounting Standards or Ind AS.

The Ministry of Corporate Affairs has notified the 35 Ind AS on 25 February 2011. The text of the 35 Ind AS are now available at the Ministry of Corporate Affairs portal. At the same time The Ministry of Corporate Affairs haven't specified the date of implementation of the same. This reluctance of

The Ministry of Corporate Affairs to notify the date even when the proposed date is less than a month away is seen as rooted in the strong lobbying by the Corporates in India to defer the implementation. But the president of ICAI. CA.G.Ramaswamy expects that it will be notified soon and there wont be any deferment.

Federal Accounting Standards Advisory Board

The Federal Accounting Standards Advisory Board (FASAB) is a United States federal advisory committee whose mission is to develop generally accepted accounting principles (GAAP) for federal financial reporting entities.

The Chief Financial Officers Act of 1990 required annual, audited financial statements for the United States Government and its component entities, referred to as federal reporting entities. In order to apply the statues of the CFO Act of 1990, the Secretary of the Treasury, the Director of the Office of Management and Budget (OMB), and the Comptroller General established FASAB to develop the "applicable accounting principles" for the newly required financial statements.

The AICPA Council designated FASAB as the body that establishes accounting principles for federal entities. The AICPA's hierarchy of generally accepted accounting principles in Statement of Auditing Standards (SAS) No. 91, The Federal GAAP Hierarchy, governs what constitutes GAAP for U.S. government reporting entities. The hierarchy lists the priority sequence of sources that an entity should look to for accounting and reporting guidance.

FASAB issues the Statement of Federal Financial Accounting Standards (SFFAS).

The codification is effective for interim and annual periods ending after September 15, 2009. All existing accounting standards documents are superseded as described in FASB Statement No. 168, The FASB Accounting Standards Codification and the Hierarchy of Generally Accepted Accounting Principles. All other accounting literature not included in the Codification is nonauthoritative.

The Codification reorganises the thousands of U.S. GAAP pronouncements into roughly 90 accounting topics and displays all topics using a consistent structure. It also includes relevant U.S. Securities and Exchange Commission (SEC), guidance that follows the same topical structure in separate sections in the Codification.

To prepare constituents for the change, the FASB has provided a number of tools and training resources. While the Codification does not change GAAP, it introduces a new structure—one that is organised in an easily accessible, user-friendly online research system. The FASB expects that the new system will reduce the amount of time and effort required to research an accounting issue, mitigate the risk of noncompliance with standards through improved usability of the literature, provide accurate information with real-time updates as new standards are released, and assist the FASB with the research efforts required during the standard-setting process.

Financial Accounting Standards Board

The Financial Accounting Standards Board (FASB) is a private, not-for-profit organisation whose primary purpose is to develop generally accepted accounting principles (GAAP) within theUnited States in the public's interest. The Securities and Exchange Commission (SEC) designated the FASB as the organisation responsible for setting accounting standards for public companies in the U.S. It was created in 1973, replacing the Committee on Accounting Procedure (CAP) and the Accounting Principles Board (APB) of the American Institute of Certified Public Accountants(AICPA).

Mission Statement

The FASB's mission is "to establish and improve standards of financial accounting and reporting for the guidance and education of the public, including issuers, auditors, and users of financial information." To achieve this, FASB has five goals:

- Improve the usefulness of financial reporting by focusing on the primary characteristics of relevance and reliability, and on the qualities of comparability and consistency.
- Keep standards current to reflect changes in methods of doing business and in the economy.

- Consider promptly any significant areas of deficiency in financial reporting that might be improved through standard setting.
- Promote international convergence of accounting standards concurrent with improving the quality of financial reporting.
- Improve common understanding of the nature and purposes of information in financial reports.

Creation of the Codification

On July 1, 2009, the FASB announced the launch of its Accounting Standards Codification, declaring it to be "the single source of authoritative nongovernmental U.S. generally accepted accounting principles." The Codification organises the many pronouncements that constitute U.S. GAAP into a consistent, searchable format. The Codification is not to be confused with the FASB's Conceptual Framework, a project begun in 1973 to develop a sound theoretical basis for the development of accounting standards in the United States.

Norwalk Agreement

FASB is pursuing a convergence project with the International Accounting Standards Board (IASB) and International Financial Reporting Standards (IFRS). On Sept. 18, 2002, in Norwalk, Connecticut, FASB and IASB met and issued a *Memorandum of Understanding.* This document outlined plans to converge IFRS and US GAAP into one set of high quality and compatible standards. As part of the project, FASB has begun moving from the principle of historical cost to fair value.

Independence

In June 2009, FASB was criticized by an advisory panel of investors after making changes on mark-to-market accounting in response to political pressure. Lobbyists had obtained its permission for banks to apply a special accounting treatment for toxic assets.

FASB Pronouncements

In order to establish accounting principles, the FASB issues pronouncements publicly, each addressing general or specific accounting issues. These pronouncements are:

- Statements of Financial Accounting Standards
- Statements of Financial Accounting Concepts
- FASB Interpretations

- FASB Technical Bulletins
- EITF Abstracts.

Australian Accounting Standards Board

The Australian Accounting Standards Board (AASB) is an Australian Government agency that develops and maintains financial reporting standards applicable to entities in the private and public sectors of the Australian economy. Also, the AASB contributes to the development of global financial reporting standards and facilitates the participation of the Australian community in global standard setting. The AASB's functions and powers are set out in the *Australian Securities and Investments Commission Act 2001*. The Australian Securities and Investments Commission's (ASIC's) role is to enforce and regulate company and financial services laws to protect Australian consumers, investors and creditors. The AASB uses a conceptual framework, which includes Statements of Accounting Concepts (SAC 1 *Definition of the Reporting Entity* and SAC 2 *Objective of General Purpose Financial Reporting*) developed by the former AASB and the Public Sector Accounting Standards Board (PSASB), to evaluate proposed accounting standards.

Standard Application

The original series of Australian Accounting Standards (AASs), which was applicable to entities not regulated under the Corporations Law, was issued by the former AASB and the PSASB of the Australian Accounting Research Foundation (AARF) on behalf of the professional accounting bodies, prior to 2000. The original series of AASB Standards (AASBs), which was applicable to entities regulated under the Corporations Law, was also issued by the former AASB, prior to 2000. Most AASs were superseded by AASBs for reporting periods beginning on or after 1 January 2005. As at 1 July 2009, only AAS 25 *Financial Reporting by Superannuation Plans* was still operative. Except AAS 25, since 1991, all standards issued by the AASB have been labelled AASB Accounting Standards and are applicable to all types of entities.

Under the Australian *Corporations Act 2001*, many entities are required to apply Australian Accounting Standards when preparing their financial statements. Some public sector entities are required to apply Australian Accounting Standards under either Commonwealth, state or territory legislation, through specific instructions to preparers or reporting frameworks that set out guidelines or regulations. Members of CPA Australia, The Institute of Chartered Accountants in Australia and the Institute of Public Accountants have a professional obligation to take all reasonable steps within their power to ensure that entities with which they are involved comply with Australian Accounting Standards when preparing their general purpose financial statements.

Accountant

An accountant is a practitioner of accountancy (UK) or accounting (US), which is the measurement, disclosure or provision of assurance about financial information that helps managers, investors, tax authorities and others make decisions about allocating resources.

The Big Four auditors are the largest employers of accountants worldwide. However, most accountants are employed in commerce and industry.

British Commonwealth

In the Commonwealth of Nations, which includes the United Kingdom, Canada, Australia, New Zealand, Hong Kong pre 1997 and several dozen other states, commonly recognised accounting qualifications are Chartered Accountant (CA or ACA), Chartered Certified Accountant (ACCA), Chartered Management Accountant (ACMA) and International Accountant (AAIA). Other qualifications in particular countries include Certified Public Accountant (CPA - Ireland and CPA - Hong Kong), Certified Management Accountant (CMA - Canada), Certified General Accountant (CGA - Canada), Certified Practising Accountant (CPA - Australia) and members of the IPA (Australia), and Certified Public Practising Accountant (CPPA - New Zealand).

- A Chartered Accountant must be a member of one of the following:
  - the Institute of Chartered Accountants in England & Wales (ICAEW) (designatory letters ACA or FCA)
  - the Institute of Chartered Accountants of Scotland (ICAS) (designatory letters CA)
  - Chartered Accountants Ireland (CAI)
  - a recognised equivalent body from another Commonwealth country (designatory letters being CA (name of country) e.g. CA (Canada))
- A Chartered Certified Accountant must be a member of the Association of Chartered Certified Accountants (designatory letters ACCA or FCCA).

- A Chartered Management Accountant must be a member of the Chartered Institute of Management Accountants (designatory letters ACMA or FCMA).
- A Chartered Public Finance Accountant must be a member of the Chartered Institute of Public Finance and Accountancy (designatory letters CPFA).
- An International Accountant is a member of the Association of International Accountants (designatory letters AIAA or FAIA).
- An Incorporated Financial Accountant is a member of the Institute of Financial Accountants (designatory letters AFA or FFA).
- An Associate Professional Accountant is a member of the Institute of Professional Accountants (designatory letters APA-UK or FPA).
- A Certified Public Accountant may be a member of the Association of Certified Public Accountants (designatory letters AICPA or FCPA) or its equivalent in another country, and is usually designated as such after passing the Uniform Certified Public Accountant Examination.
- A Public Accountant may be a member of the Institute of Public Accountants (designatory letters AIPA, MIPA or FIPA).

Excepting the Association of Certified Public Accountants, each of the above bodies admits members only after passing examinations and undergoing a period of relevant work experience. Once admitted, members are expected to comply with ethical guidelines and gain appropriate professional experience.

Chartered, Chartered Certified, Chartered Public Finance, and International Accountants engaging in practice (i.e. selling services to the public rather than acting as an employee) must gain a "practising certificate" by meeting further requirements such as purchasing adequate insurance and undergoing inspections.

The ICAEW, ICAS, ICAI, ACCA, AIA and CIPFA are six statutory RQB Qualification Bodies in the UK. A member of one them may also become a *Registered Auditor* in accordance with the Companies Act, providing they can demonstrate the necessary professional ability in that area and submit to regular inspection. It is illegal for any individual or firm that is not a Registered Auditor to perform a company audit.

All six RQBs are listed under EU mutual recognition directives to practise in 27 EU member states and individually entered into agreement with the Hong Kong Institute of Certified Public Accountants (HKICPA).

Further restrictions apply to accountants who carry out insolvency work.

In addition to the bodies above, technical qualifications are offered by the Association of Accounting Technicians, ACCA and AIA, which are respectively called AAT Technician, CAT (Certified Accounting Technician) and IAT (International Accounting Technician).

Australia

In Australia, there are three recognised professional accounting bodies: the Institute of Public Accountants (IPA), CPA Australia (CPA) and the Institute of Chartered Accountants of Australia (ICAA).

Canada

In Canada, there are four recognised accounting bodies: the Canadian Institute of Chartered Accountants (CA) and the provincial and territorial CA Institutes, the Certified General Accountants Association of Canada (CGA), the Society of Management Accountants of Canada, also known as the Certified Management Accountants (CMA) and the Society of Professional Accountants of Canada (RPA). CA and CGA were created by Acts of Parliament in 1902 and 1913 respectively, CMA was established in 1920 and RPA in 1938.

The CA program is the most focused on public accounting and most candidates obtain auditing experience from public accounting firms, although recent changes allow candidates to obtain their experience requirements in industry at companies that have been accredited for training CAs; the CGA program takes a general approach allowing candidates to focus in their own financial career choices; the CMA program focuses in management accounting, but also provides a general approach to financial accounting and tax. The CA and CMA programs require a candidate to obtain a degree as a program entry requirement. The CGA program requires a degree as an exit requirement prior to certification. Auditing and Public Accounting are regulated by the provinces. In British Columbia, Ontario and Prince Edward Island, CAs and CGAs have equal status regarding public accounting and auditing;

In the rest of Canada, CAs, CMAs, and CGAs are considered equivalents pursuant to provincial and territorial legislation. However, in practice, most public accounting and auditing in Canada is performed by CAs. As of 2006, the Chartered Certified Accountant (ACCA or FCCA) is also recognised by the Canadian government as an eligible qualification to audit federal government institutions in Canada. Furthermore, The Canadian branch of ACCA is pursuing recognition for statutory audit purposes in the province of Ontario under the province's Public Accounting Act of 2004.

New Zealand

In New Zealand, there are two local accountancy bodies the New Zealand Institute of Chartered Accountants (NZICA) and the New Zealand Association of Certified Public Accountants (NZACPA) the operating name of New Zealand Association of Accountants Inc (NZAA).

To audit public companies an individual must be a member of either the NZICA or an otherwise gazetted body. Chartered Certified Accountant (Association of Chartered Certified Accountants or FCCA) qualification has also been gazetted under). An ACCA member can practice as long as they hold an ACCA public practice certificate (with audit qualification) in their country of origin.

Sri Lanka

In Sri Lanka, a Chartered Accountant must be a member of the Institute of Chartered Accountants of Sri Lanka (designatory letters ACA or FCA), therefore it is the sole local accountancy body. To audit public companies an individual must be a member of the ICASL. In Pakistan there is a big concept of doing acca, ca, acma and higher qualification about accountancy.

Austria

In Austria the accountancy profession is regulated by the Bilanzbuchhaltungsgesetz 2006 (BibuG - Management Accountancy Law).

Hong Kong

In Hong Kong, the accountancy industry is regulated by the HKICPA under the Professional Accountants Ordinance (Chapter 50, Laws of Hong Kong). The Auditing industry for limited companies is regulated under the Companies Ordinance (Chapter 32, Laws of Hong Kong), and other Ordinances such as the Securities and Futures Ordinance, the Listing Rules, etc.

HKICPA terminated all recognition of oversea bodies in 2005 for *accreditation* under Professional Accountants Ordinance. In general, all British RQBs except for CIPFA were re-accredited. Please refer to HKICPA for latest recognition.

Removal of requirement for a qualified accountant in the Listing Rules of Hong Kong.

In November 2008, the Stock Exchange of Hong Kong Limited has removed the requirement for a qualified accountant from the Listing Rules but expanded the Code Provisions in the Code on Corporate Governance Practices regarding internal controls to make specific references to the responsibility of the directors to conduct an annual review of the adequacy of staffing of the financial reporting function and the oversight role of the audit committee.

Portugal

In Portugal, there are two accountancy qualifications: the *Técnicos Oficiais de Contas* (TOC), responsible for producing accounting and tax information, and the *Revisor Oficial de Contas* (ROC), more related to auditing practices. The TOC certification is exclusively awarded by the professional organisation *Ordem dos Técnicos Oficiais de Contas* (OTOC), and the certification to become an auditor is awarded by another professional organisation, the *Ordem dos Revisores Oficiais de Contas* (OROC). In general, accountants or auditors accredited by OTOC or OROC are individuals with university graduation diplomas in business management, economics, mathematics or law who, after further studies, applied for an exam and received the certification to be a TOC or ROC. That certification is only received after a 1-year (TOC) or 3-years (ROC) internship. Any citizen having a polytechnic degree as accounting technician is also entitled to apply for the exam and certification at the OTOC.

United States

In the United States, legally practicing accountants are Certified Public Accountants (CPAs), and other non-statutory accountants are Certified Internal Auditors (CIAs), Certified Management Accountants (CMAs) and Accredited Business Accountants (ABAs). The difference between these certifications is primarily the legal status and the types of services provided, although individuals may earn more than one certification. Additionally, much accounting work is performed by uncertified individuals, who may be working under the supervision of a certified accountant. However, as noted above the majority of accountants work in the private sector or may offer their services without the need for certification. A CPA is licensed by the state of their residence to provide auditing services to the public, although most CPA firms also offer accounting, tax, litigation support, and other financial advisory services. The requirements for receiving the CPA license varies from state to state, although the passage of the Uniform Certified Public Accountant Examination is required by all states. This examination is designed and graded by the American Institute of Certified Public Accountants. A CIA is granted a certificate from the Institute of Internal Auditors (IIA), provided that the candidate passed a rigorous examination of four parts. A CIA mostly provides their services directly to their employer rather than the public.

A CMA is granted a certificate from the Institute of Management Accountants (IMA), provided that the candidate passed a rigorous examination of two parts and meet the practical experience requirement from the IMA. A CMA mostly provides their services directly to their employers rather than the public. A CMA can also provide their services to the public, but to an extent much lesser than that of a CPA.

An ABA is granted accreditation from the Accreditation Council for Accountancy and Taxation (ACAT), provided that the candidate passed the eight-hour Comprehensive Examination for Accreditation in Accounting which tests proficiency in financial accounting, reporting, statement preparation, taxation, business consulting services, business law, and ethics. An ABA specializes in the needs of small-to-mid-size businesses and in financial services to individuals and families. In states where use of the word "accountant" is not permitted by non state licensed individuals, the practitioner may use Accredited Business Adviser. Public Accountants. In certain states, state law grants State Public Accountant to practice accountancy and taxation (except for audit). The United States Department of Labour's Bureau of Labour Statistics estimates that there are about one million persons employed as accountants and auditors in the U.S. U.S. tax law grants accountants a limited form of accountant-client privilege.

Bookkeeping

Bookkeeping is the recording of financial transactions. Transactions include sales, purchases, income, receipts and payments by an individual or organisation. Bookkeeping is usually performed by a bookkeeper. Bookkeeping should not be confused with accounting. The accounting process is usually performed by an accountant. The accountant creates reports from the recorded financial transactions recorded by the bookkeeper and files forms with government agencies.

There are some common methods of bookkeeping such as the Single-entry bookkeeping system and the Double-entry bookkeeping system. But while these systems may be seen as "real" bookkeeping, any process that involves the recording of financial transactions is a bookkeeping process. A bookkeeper (or book-keeper), also known as an accounting clerk or accounting technician, is a person who records the day-to-day financial transactions of an organisation. A bookkeeper is usually responsible for writing the "daybooks." The daybooks consist of purchases, sales, receipts, and payments. The bookkeeper is responsible for ensuring all transactions are recorded in the correct day book, suppliers ledger, customer ledger and general ledger. The bookkeeper brings the books to the trial balance stage. An accountant may prepare the income statement and balance sheet using the trial balance and ledgers prepared by the bookkeeper.

Bookkeeping Process

The bookkeeping process refers primarily to recording the financial effects of financial transactions only into accounts. The variation between manual and any electronic accounting system stems from the latency between the recording of the financial transaction and its posting in the relevant account. This delay, absent in electronic accounting systems due to instantaneous posting into relevant accounts, is not replicated in manual systems, thus giving rise to primary books of accounts such as Sales Book, Cash Book, Bank Book, Purchase Book for recording the immediate effect of the financial transaction. In the normal course of business, a document is produced each time a transaction occurs. Sales and purchases usually have invoices or receipts.

Deposit slips are produced when lodgements (deposits) are made to a bank account. Cheques are written to pay money out of the account. Bookkeeping involves, first of all, recording the details of all of these *source documents* into multi-column *journals* (also known as a *books of first entry* or *daybooks*). For example, all credit sales are recorded in the Sales Journal, all Cash Payments are recorded in the Cash Payments Journal. Each column in a journal normally corresponds to an account. In the single entry system, each transaction is recorded only once. Most individuals who balance their cheque-book each month are using such a system, and most personal finance software follows this approach.

After a certain period, typically a month, the columns in each journal are each totalled to give a summary for the period. Using the rules of double entry, these journal summaries are then transferred to their respective accounts in the ledger, or *book of accounts.* For example the entries in the Sales Journal are taken and a debit entry is made in each customer's account (showing that the customer now owes us money) and a credit entry might be made in the account for "Sale of Class 2 Widgets" (showing that this activity has generated revenue for us). This process of transferring summaries or individual transactions to the ledger is called *posting.* Once the posting process is complete, accounts kept using the "T" format undergo balancing, which is simply a process to arrive at the balance of the account. As a partial check that the posting process was done correctly, a working document called an *unadjusted trial balance* is created. In its simplest form, this is a three column list. The first column contains the names of those accounts in the ledger which have a non-zero balance. If an account has a debit balance, the balance amount is copied into column two (the debit column). If an account has a credit balance, the amount is copied into column three (the credit column).

The debit column is then totalled and then the credit column is totalled. The two totals must agree - this agreement is not by chance - because under the double-entry rules, whenever there is a posting, the debits of the posting equal the credits of the posting. If the two totals do not agree, an error has been made either in the journals or during the posting process. The error must be located and rectified and the totals of debit column and credit column recalculated to check for agreement before any further processing can take place. Once the accounts balance, the accountant makes a number of adjustments and changes the balance amounts of some of the accounts. These adjustments must still obey the double-entry rule.

For example, the "inventory" account asset account might be changed to bring them into line with the actual numbers counted during a stock take. At the same time, the expense account associated with usage of inventory is adjusted by an equal and opposite amount. Other adjustments such as posting depreciation and prepayments are also done at this time. This results in a listing called the *adjusted trial balance.* It is the accounts in this list and their corresponding debit or credit balances that are used to prepare the financial statements.

Finally financial statements are drawn from the trial balance, which may include:

- the income statement, also known as the *statement of financial results, profit and loss account*, or *P&L*

- the balance sheet, also known as the *statement of financial position*
- the cash flow statement
- the statement of retained earnings, also known as the *statement of total recognised gains and losses* or *statement of changes in equity*.

Bookkeeping Systems

Two common bookkeeping systems used by businesses and other organisations are the single-entry bookkeeping system and the double-entry bookkeeping system. Single-entry bookkeeping uses only income and expense accounts, recorded primarily in a revenue and expense journal. Single-entry bookkeeping is adequate for many small businesses. Double-entry bookkeeping requires posting (recording) each transaction twice, using debits and credits.

Single-entry System

The primary bookkeeping record in single-entry bookkeeping is the cash book, which is similar to a checking (cheque) account register but allocates the income and expenses to various income and expense accounts. Separate account records are maintained for petty cash, accounts payable and receivable, and other relevant transactions such as inventory and travel expenses. These days, single entry bookkeeping can be done with DIY bookkeeping software to speed up manual calculations.

Daybooks

A daybook is a descriptive and chronological (diary-like) record of day-to-day financial transactions also called a *book of original entry*. The daybook's details must be entered formally into journals to enable posting to ledgers. Daybooks include:

- Sales daybook, for recording all the sales invoices.
- Sales credits daybook, for recording all the sales credit notes.
- Purchases daybook, for recording all the purchase invoices.
- Purchases credits daybook, for recording all the purchase credit notes.
- Cash daybook, usually known as the cash book, for recording all money received as well as money paid out. It may be split into two daybooks: receipts daybook for money received in, and payments daybook for money paid out.

Petty Cash Book

A petty cash book is a record of small value purchases usually controlled by imprest system. Items such as coffee, tea, birthday cards for employees, stationery for office working, a few dollars if you're short on postage, are listed down in thepetty cash book.

Journals

A journal is a formal and chronological record of financial transactions before their values are accounted for in the general ledger as debits and credits. A company can maintain one journal for all transactions, or keep several journals based on similar activity (i.e. sales, cash receipts, revenue, etc.) making transactions easier to summarize and reference later. For every debit journal entry recorded there must be an equivalent credit journal entry to maintain a balanced accounting equation.

Ledgers

A ledger is a record of accounts. These accounts are recorded separately showing their beginning/ending balance. A journal lists financial transactions in chronological order without showing their balance but showing how much is going to be charged in each account. A ledger takes each financial transactions from the journal and records them into the corresponding account for every transaction listed. The ledger also sums up the total of every account which is transferred into the balance sheet and income statement.

There are 3 different kinds of ledgers that deal with book-keeping. Ledgers include:

- Sales ledger, which deals mostly with the Accounts Receivable account. This ledger consists of the financial transactions made by customers to the business.
- Purchase ledger is a ledger that goes hand and hand with the Accounts Payable account. This is the purchasing transaction a company does.
- General ledger representing the original 5 main accounts: assets, liabilities, equity, income, and expenses.

Abbreviations Used in Bookkeeping

- A/C - Account
- Acc - Account
- A/R - Accounts Receivable

- A/P - Accounts Payable
- B/S - Balance Sheet
- c/d - Carried down
- b/d - Brought down
- c/f - Carried forward
- b/f - Brought forward
- Dr - Debit record
- Cr - Credit record
- G/L - General Ledger; (or N/L - Nominal Ledger)
- P&L - Profit & Loss; (or I/S - Income Statement)
- PP&E - Property, Plant and Equipment
- TB - Trial Balance
- GST - Goods and Services Tax
- VAT - Value Added Tax
- CST - Central Sale Tax
- TDS - Tax Deducted at Source
- AMT - Alternate Minimum Tax
- EBITDA - Earnings before Interest, Taxes, Depreciation and Amortisation
- EBDTA - Earnings before Depreciation, Taxes and Amortisation
- EBT - Earnings before Taxes
- EAT - Earnings after Tax
- PAT - Profit after tax
- PBT - Profit before tax
- Depr - Depreciation
- Dep'n - Depreciation.

Chart of Accounts

A chart of accounts is a list of the accounts codes that can be identified with numeric, alphabetical, or alphanumeric codes allowing the account to be located in the general ledger.

Computerised Bookkeeping

Computerised bookkeeping removes many of the paper "books" that are used to record transactions and usually enforces double entry bookkeeping.

Online Bookkeeping

Online bookkeeping, or remote bookkeeping, allows source documents and data to reside in web-based applications which allow remote access for bookkeepers and accountants. All entries made into the online software are recorded and stored in a remote location. The online software can be accessed from any location in the world and permit the bookkeeper or data entry person to work from any location with a suitable data communications link.

The two primary accounting methods of the *cash* and the *accruals* basis (the difference being primarily one of timing) are used to calculate US public debt, as well as taxable income for U.S. federal income taxes and other income taxes. According to the Internal Revenue Code, a taxpayer may compute taxable income by:

1. the cash receipts and disbursements method;
2. an accrual method;
3. any other method permitted by the chapter; or
4. any combination of the foregoing methods permitted under regulations prescribed by the Secretary of the Treasure.

6

Internal Auditing

Measuring the Internal Audit Function

The measurement of the internal audit function can involve a balanced scorecard approach. Internal audit functions are primarily evaluated based on the quality of counsel and information provided to the Audit Committee and top management. However, this is primarily qualitative and therefore difficult to measure. "Customer surveys" sent to key managers after each audit engagement or report can be used to measure performance, with an annual survey to the Audit Committee. Scoring on dimensions such as professionalism, quality of counsel, timeliness of work product, utility of meetings, and quality of status updates are typical with such surveys. Understanding the expectations of senior management and the audit committee represent important steps in developing a performance measurement process, as well as how such measures help align the audit function with organisational priorities.

Quantitative measures can also be used to measure the function's level of execution and qualifications of its personnel. Key measures include:

Plan Completion: This is a measure of the degree to which the annual plan of engagements is completed, measured at a point in time. This may be measured using the number of audit engagements completed, weighted by the planned size of each assignment, with estimates for audits in-progress. Measured throughout the year, it is compared against the percentage of the year elapsed.

Report Issuance: This is a measure of the time elapsed from completion of testing to issuance of the final audit report, including management's action plans. This can be measured in average days or percentage of reports issued within a certain standard, such as 30 days. Establishing expectations for the timing of management's response to report recommendations is critical.

In addition, the scope and degree of change involved in the report's action plans are key variables. For example, a report for a single retail store requiring only the store manager's action might take 3–5 days to issue. However, a report consolidating findings from 20 retail stores, with action plans with national implications determined by top management, may take 30–60 days in complex organisations.

Issue Closure: Reported audit findings are often called "issues" or "deficiencies." Professional standards require audit functions to track reported findings to resolution, which effectively requires the maintenance of an issues follow-up database. The number of days that reported issues remain open, or open after their agreed-upon closure date, are key measures. In addition, reporting database statistics such as the number of issues open (unresolved), closed (resolved), and issues opened/closed during a given period are useful statistics.

Staff Qualifications: This can be measured through the percentage of staff with professional certifications, graduate degrees, and overall years of experience.

Staff Utilisation Rate: This is measured as the percentage of time spent on audit engagements, as opposed to administrative time such as training or vacation. Many internal audit departments track time by audit engagement. This is typically captured in a database or spreadsheet.

Staffing Level: The number of positions filled relative to the authorised staffing level. Due to the challenge of finding qualified staff, departments may have rotational programs to bring in management to complete tours in the function or be "guest" auditors. Audit departments also "co-source," meaning they obtain contract auditors from service providers.

Developing and Retaining Staff

Developing and retaining quality professionals is a key concern in the profession. Key methods for developing and retaining internal audit staff personnel include:

- Providing challenging, varied assignments
- Ensuring quality supervision

- Ensuring staff participates in audit engagements from start to finish, to learn all phases of the audit process
- Providing opportunities to lead (in-charge) assignments, starting with more structured engagements such as Sarbanes-Oxley work
- Participating on departmental improvement task forces, such as preparation for quality assurance review
- Participating in the recruiting and interviewing process for new hires
- Rotating through various audit teams (in larger departments) or audits of various businesses
- Providing both outside training (e.g., seminars) and in-house training (e.g., company systems) for two weeks/year
- Participation in annual risk assessment activities, whether asking key questions or just taking notes

Reporting of Critical Findings

The Chief Audit Executive (CAE) typically reports the most critical issues to the Audit Committee quarterly, along with management's progress towards resolving them. Critical issues typically have a reasonable likelihood of causing substantial financial or reputational damage to the company. For particularly complex issues, the responsible manager may participate in the discussion. Such reporting is critical to ensure the function is respected, that the proper "tone at the top" exists in the organisation, and to expedite resolution of such issues. It is a matter of considerable judgment to select appropriate issues for the Audit Committee's attention and to describe them in the proper context.

Sarbanes–Oxley Act of 2002

The Sarbanes–Oxley Act of 2002 (Pub.L. 107-204, 116 Stat. 745, enacted July 30, 2002), also known as the 'Public Company Accounting Reform and Investor Protection Act' (in the Senate) and 'Corporate and Auditing Accountability and Responsibility Act' (in the House) and commonly called Sarbanes–Oxley, Sarbox or SOX, is a United States federal law enacted on July 30, 2002, which set new or enhanced standards for all U.S. public company boards, management and public accounting firms. It is named after sponsors U.S. Senator Paul Sarbanes (D-MD) and U.S. Representative Michael G. Oxley (R-OH).

The bill was enacted as a reaction to a number of major corporate and accounting scandals including those affecting Enron, Tyco International, Adelphia, Peregrine Systems and WorldCom. These scandals, which cost investors billions of dollars when the share prices of affected companies collapsed, shook public confidence in the nation's securities markets.

The act contains 11 titles, or sections, ranging from additional corporate board responsibilities to criminal penalties, and requires the Securities and Exchange Commission (SEC) to implement rulings on requirements to comply with the law. Harvey Pitt, the 26th chairman of the SEC, led the SEC in the adoption of dozens of rules to implement the Sarbanes–Oxley Act. It created a new, quasi-public agency, the Public Company Accounting Oversight Board, or PCAOB, charged with overseeing, regulating, inspecting and disciplining accounting firms in their roles as auditors of public companies. The act also covers issues such as auditor independence, corporate governance, internal control assessment, and enhanced financial disclosure.

The act was approved by the House by a vote of 423 in favour, 3 opposed, and 8 abstaining and by the Senate with a vote of 99 in favour, 1 abstaining. President George W. Bush signed it into law, stating it included "the most far-reaching reforms of American business practices since the time of Franklin D. Roosevelt."

Debate continues over the perceived benefits and costs of SOX. Opponents of the bill claim it has reduced America's international competitive edge against foreign financial service providers, saying SOX has introduced an overly complex regulatory environment into U.S. financial markets. Proponents of the measure say that SOX has been a "godsend" for improving the confidence of fund managers and other investors with regard to the veracity of corporate financial statements.

History and Context: Events Contributing to the Adoption of Sarbanes–Oxley

A variety of complex factors created the conditions and culture in which a series of large corporate frauds occurred between 2000–2002. The spectacular, highly-publicised frauds at Enron, WorldCom, and Tyco exposed significant problems with conflicts of interest and incentive compensation practices. The analysis of their complex and contentious root causes contributed to the passage of SOX in 2002. In a 2004 interview, Senator Paul Sarbanes stated:

"The Senate Banking Committee undertook a series of hearings on the problems in the markets that had led to a loss of hundreds and hundreds of billions, indeed trillions of dollars in market value. The hearings set out to lay the foundation for legislation. We scheduled 10 hearings over a six-week period, during which we brought in some of the best people in the country to testify. The hearings produced remarkable consensus on the nature of the problems: inadequate oversight of accountants, lack of auditor independence, weak corporate governance procedures, stock analysts' conflict of interests, inadequate disclosure provisions, and grossly inadequate funding of the Securities and Exchange Commission."

- Auditor conflicts of interest: Prior to SOX, auditing firms, the primary financial "watchdogs" for investors, were self-regulated. They also performed significant non-audit or consulting work for the companies they audited. Many of these consulting agreements were far more lucrative than the auditing engagement. This presented at least the appearance of a conflict of interest. For example, challenging the company's accounting approach might damage a client relationship, conceivably placing a significant consulting arrangement at risk, damaging the auditing firm's bottom line.
- Boardroom failures: Boards of Directors, specifically Audit Committees, are charged with establishing oversight mechanisms for financial reporting in U.S. corporations on the behalf of investors. These scandals identified Board members who either did not exercise their responsibilities or did not have the expertise to understand the complexities of the businesses. In many cases, Audit Committee members were not truly independent of management.
- Securities analysts' conflicts of interest: The roles of securities analysts, who make buy and sell recommendations on company stocks and bonds, and investment bankers, who help provide companies loans or handle mergers and acquisitions, provide opportunities for conflicts. Similar to the auditor conflict, issuing a buy or sell recommendation on a stock while providing lucrative investment banking services creates at least the appearance of a conflict of interest.
- Inadequate funding of the SEC: The SEC budget has steadily increased to nearly double the pre-SOX level. In the interview cited above, Sarbanes indicated that enforcement and rule-making are more effective post-SOX.

- Banking practices: Lending to a firm sends signals to investors regarding the firm's risk. In the case of Enron, several major banks provided large loans to the company without understanding, or while ignoring, the risks of the company. Investors of these banks and their clients were hurt by such bad loans, resulting in large settlement payments by the banks. Others interpreted the willingness of banks to lend money to the company as an indication of its health and integrity, and were led to invest in Enron as a result. These investors were hurt as well.
- Internet bubble: Investors had been stung in 2000 by the sharp declines in technology stocks and to a lesser extent, by declines in the overall market. Certain mutual fund managers were alleged to have advocated the purchasing of particular technology stocks, while quietly selling them. The losses sustained also helped create a general anger among investors.
- Executive compensation: Stock option and bonus practices, combined with volatility in stock prices for even small earnings "misses," resulted in pressures to manage earnings. Stock options were not treated as compensation expense by companies, encouraging this form of compensation. With a large stock-based bonus at risk, managers were pressured to meet their targets.

Timeline and Passage of Sarbanes–Oxley

The House passed Rep. Oxley's bill (H.R. 3763) on April 24, 2002, by a vote of 334 to 90. The House then referred the "Corporate and Auditing Accountability, Responsibility, and Transparency Act" or "CAARTA" to the Senate Banking Committee with the support of President George W. Bush and the SEC. At the time, however, the Chairman of that Committee, Senator Paul Sarbanes (D-MD), was preparing his own proposal, Senate Bill 2673.

Senator Sarbanes' bill passed the Senate Banking Committee on June 18, 2002, by a vote of 17 to 4. On June 25, 2002, WorldCom revealed it had overstated its earnings by more than $3.8 billion during the past five quarters (15 months), primarily by improperly accounting for its operating costs. Sen. Sarbanes introduced Senate Bill 2673 to the full Senate that same day, and it passed 97–0 less than three weeks later on July 15, 2002.

The House and the Senate formed a Conference Committee to reconcile the differences between Sen. Sarbanes's bill (S. 2673) and

Rep. Oxley's bill (H.R. 3763). The conference committee relied heavily on S. 2673 and "most changes made by the conference committee strengthened the prescriptions of S. 2673 or added new prescriptions." (John T. Bostelman, The Sarbanes–Oxley Deskbook § 2–31.)

The Committee approved the final conference bill on July 24, 2002, and gave it the name "the Sarbanes–Oxley Act of 2002." The next day, both houses of Congress voted on it without change, producing an overwhelming margin of victory: 423 to 3 in the House and 99 to 0 in the Senate.

On July 30, 2002, President George W. Bush signed it into law, stating it included "the most far-reaching reforms of American business practices since the time of Franklin D. Roosevelt."

Analysing the Cost-benefits of Sarbanes–Oxley

A significant body of academic research and opinion exists regarding the costs and benefits of SOX, with significant differences in conclusions. This is due in part to the difficulty of isolating the impact of SOX from other variables affecting the stock market and corporate earnings. Conclusions from several of these studies and related criticism are summarised below:

Compliance Costs

- FEI Survey (Annual): Finance Executives International (FEI) provides an annual survey on SOX Section 404 costs. These costs have continued to decline relative to revenues since 2004. The 2007 study indicated that, for 168 companies with average revenues of $4.7 billion, the average compliance costs were $1.7 million (0.036% of revenue). The 2006 study indicated that, for 200 companies with average revenues of $6.8 billion, the average compliance costs were $2.9 million (0.043% of revenue), down 23% from 2005. Cost for decentralised companies (i.e., those with multiple segments or divisions) were considerably more than centralised companies. Survey scores related to the positive effect of SOX on investor confidence, reliability of financial statements, and fraud prevention continue to rise. However, when asked in 2006 whether the benefits of compliance with Section 404 have exceeded costs in 2006, only 22 percent agreed.
- Foley & Lardner Survey (2007): This annual study focused on changes in the total costs of being a U.S. public company, which were significantly affected by SOX. Such costs include

external auditor fees, directors and officers (D&O) insurance, board compensation, lost productivity, and legal costs. Each of these cost categories increased significantly between FY2001-FY2006. Nearly 70% of survey respondents indicated public companies with revenues under $251 million should be exempt from SOX Section 404.

- Zhang (2005): This research paper estimated SOX compliance costs as high as $1.4 trillion, by measuring changes in market value around key SOX legislative "events." This number is based on the assumption that SOX was the cause of related short-duration market value changes, which the author acknowledges as a drawback of the study.
- Butler/Ribstein (2006): Their book proposed a comprehensive overhaul or repeal of SOX and a variety of other reforms. For example, they indicate that investors could diversify their stock investments, efficiently managing the risk of a few catastrophic corporate failures, whether due to fraud or competition. However, if each company is required to spend a significant amount of money and resources on SOX compliance, this cost is borne across all publicly traded companies and therefore cannot be diversified away by the investor.
- A 2011 SEC study found that Section 404(b) compliance costs have continued to decline, especially after 2007 accounting guidance.

Benefits to Firms and Investors

- Arping/Sautner (2010): This research paper analyses whether SOX enhanced corporate transparency. Looking at foreign firms that are cross-listed in the US, the paper indicates that, relative to a control sample of comparable firms that are not subject to SOX, cross-listed firms became significantly more transparent following SOX. Corporate transparency is measured based on the dispersion and accuracy of analyst earnings forecasts.
- Iliev (2007): This research paper indicated that SOX 404 indeed led to conservative reported earnings, but also reduced—rightly or wrongly—stock valuations of small firms. Lower earnings often cause the share price to decrease.
- Skaife/Collins/Kinney/LaFond (2006): This research paper indicates that borrowing costs are lower for companies that

improved their internal control, by between 50 and 150 basis points (.5 to 1.5 percentage points).

- Lord & Benoit Report (2006): Do the Benefits of 404 Exceed the Cost? A study of a population of nearly 2,500 companies indicated that those with no material weaknesses in their internal controls, or companies that corrected them in a timely manner, experienced much greater increases in share prices than companies that did not. The report indicated that the benefits to a compliant company in share price (10% above Russell 3000 index) were greater than their SOX Section 404 costs.
- Institute of Internal Auditors (2005): The research paper indicates that corporations have improved their internal controls and that financial statements are perceived to be more reliable.

Effects on Exchange Listing Choice of Non-US Companies

Some have asserted that Sarbanes–Oxley legislation has helped displace business from New York to London, where the Financial Services Authority regulates the financial sector with a lighter touch. In the UK, the non-statutory Combined Code of Corporate Governance plays a somewhat similar role to SOX. Howell E. Jackson & Mark J. Roe, "Public Enforcement of Securities Laws: Preliminary Evidence" (Working Paper January 16, 2007). The Alternative Investment Market claims that its spectacular growth in listings almost entirely coincided with the Sarbanes Oxley legislation. In December 2006 Michael Bloomberg, New York's mayor, and Charles Schumer, a US senator from New York, expressed their concern.

The Sarbanes–Oxley Act's effect on non-US companies cross-listed in the US is different on firms from developed and well regulated countries than on firms from less developed countries according to Kate Litvak. Companies from badly regulated countries see benefits that are higher than the costs from better credit ratings by complying to regulations in a highly regulated country (USA), but companies from developed countries only incur the costs, since transparency is adequate in their home countries as well. On the other hand, the benefit of better credit rating also comes with listing on other stock exchanges such as the London Stock Exchange.

Piotroski and Srinivasan (2008) examine a comprehensive sample of international companies that list onto U.S. and U.K. stock exchanges before and after the enactment of the Act in 2002. Using a sample of all listing events onto U.S. and U.K. exchanges from 1995–2006, they find that the listing preferences of large foreign firms choosing between U.S. exchanges and the LSE's Main Market did not change following SOX. In contrast, they find that the likelihood of a U.S. listing among small foreign firms choosing between the Nasdaq and LSE's Alternative Investment Market decreased following SOX. The negative effect among small firms is consistent with these companies being less able to absorb the incremental costs associated with SOX compliance. The screening of smaller firms with weaker governance attributes from U.S. exchanges is consistent with the heightened governance costs imposed by the Act increasing the bonding-related benefits of a U.S. listing.

Sarbanes–Oxley Section 302: Disclosure Controls

Under Sarbanes–Oxley, two separate sections came into effect—one civil and the other criminal. 15 U.S.C. § 7241 (Section 302) (civil provision); 18 U.S.C. § 1350 (Section 906) (criminal provision).

Section 302 of the Act mandates a set of internal procedures designed to ensure accurate financial disclosure. The signing officers must certify that they are "responsible for establishing and maintaining internal controls" and "have designed such internal controls to ensure that material information relating to the company and its consolidated subsidiaries is made known to such officers by others within those entities, particularly during the period in which the periodic reports are being prepared." 15 U.S.C. § 7241(a)(4). The officers must "have evaluated the effectiveness of the company's internal controls as of a date within 90 days prior to the report" and "have presented in the report their conclusions about the effectiveness of their internal controls based on their evaluation as of that date." *Id.*.

The SEC interpreted the intention of Sec. 302 in Final Rule 33–8124. In it, the SEC defines the new term "disclosure controls and procedures", which are distinct from "internal controls over financial reporting". Under both Section 302 and Section 404, Congress directed the SEC to promulgate regulations enforcing these provisions.

External auditors are required to issue an opinion on whether effective internal control over financial reporting was maintained in all material respects by management. This is in addition to the financial statement opinion regarding the accuracy of the financial statements. The requirement to issue a third opinion regarding management's assessment was removed in 2007.

Sarbanes-Oxley Section 401: Disclosures in Periodic Reports (Off-balance Sheet Items)

The bankruptcy of Enron drew attention to off-balance sheet instruments that were used fraudulently. During 2010, the court examiner's review of the Lehman Brothers bankruptcy also brought these instruments back into focus, as Lehman had used an instrument called "Repo 105" to allegedly move assets and debt off-balance sheet to make its financial position look more favourable to investors. Sarbanes-Oxley required the disclosure of all material off-balance sheet items. It also required an SEC study and report to better understand the extent of usage of such instruments and whether accounting principles adequately addressed these instruments; the SEC report was issued June 15, 2005. Interim guidance was issued in May 2006, which was later finalised. Critics argued the SEC did not take adequate steps to regulate and monitor this activity.

Sarbanes–Oxley Section 404: Assessment of Internal Control

The most contentious aspect of SOX is Section 404, which requires management and the external auditor to report on the adequacy of the company's internal control on financial reporting (ICFR). This is the most costly aspect of the legislation for companies to implement, as documenting and testing important financial manual and automated controls requires enormous effort.

Under Section 404 of the Act, management is required to produce an "internal control report" as part of each annual Exchange Act report. The report must affirm "the responsibility of management for establishing and maintaining an adequate internal control structure and procedures for financial reporting." 15 U.S.C. § 7262(a). The report must also "contain an assessment, as of the end of the most recent fiscal year of the Company, of the effectiveness of the internal control structure and procedures of the issuer for financial reporting." To do this, managers are generally adopting an internal control framework such as that described in COSO.

To help alleviate the high costs of compliance, guidance and practice have continued to evolve. The Public Company Accounting Oversight Board (PCAOB) approved Auditing Standard No. 5 for public accounting firms on July 25, 2007. This standard superseded Auditing Standard No. 2, the initial guidance provided in 2004.

The SEC also released its interpretive guidance on June 27, 2007. It is generally consistent with the PCAOB's guidance, but intended to provide guidance for management. Both management and the external auditor are responsible for performing their assessment in the context of a top-down risk assessment, which requires management to base both the scope of its assessment and evidence gathered on risk. This gives management wider discretion in its assessment approach. These two standards together require management to:

- Assess both the design and operating effectiveness of selected internal controls related to significant accounts and relevant assertions, in the context of material misstatement risks;
- Understand the flow of transactions, including IT aspects, in sufficient detail to identify points at which a misstatement could arise;
- Evaluate company-level (entity-level) controls, which correspond to the components of the COSO framework;
- Perform a fraud risk assessment;
- Evaluate controls designed to prevent or detect fraud, including management override of controls;
- Evaluate controls over the period-end financial reporting process;
- Scale the assessment based on the size and complexity of the company;
- Rely on management's work based on factors such as competency, objectivity, and risk;
- Conclude on the adequacy of internal control over financial reporting.

SOX 404 compliance costs represent a tax on inefficiency, encouraging companies to centralize and automate their financial reporting systems. This is apparent in the comparative costs of companies with decentralised operations and systems, versus those with centralised, more efficient systems. For example, the 2007 FEI survey indicated average compliance costs for decentralised companies were $1.9 million, while centralised company costs were $1.3 million. Costs of evaluating manual control procedures are dramatically reduced through automation.

Sarbanes–Oxley 404 and Smaller Public Companies

The cost of complying with SOX 404 impacts smaller companies disproportionately, as there is a significant fixed cost involved in completing the assessment. For example, during 2004 U.S. companies with revenues exceeding $5 billion spent 0.06% of revenue on SOX compliance, while companies with less than $100 million in revenue spent 2.55%. This disparity is a focal point of 2007 SEC and U.S. Senate action. The PCAOB intends to issue further guidance to help companies scale their assessment based on company size and complexity during 2007. The SEC issued their guidance to management in June, 2007.

After the SEC and PCAOB issued their guidance, the SEC required smaller public companies (non-accelerated filers) with fiscal years ending after December 15, 2007 to document a Management Assessment of their Internal Controls over Financial Reporting (ICFR). Outside auditors of non-accelerated filers however opine or test internal controls under PCAOB (Public Company Accounting Oversight Board) Auditing Standards for years ending after December 15, 2008. Another extension was granted by the SEC for the outside auditor assessment until years ending after December 15, 2009. The reason for the timing disparity was to address the House Committee on Small Business concern that the cost of complying with Section 404 of the Sarbanes–Oxley Act of 2002 was still unknown and could therefore be disproportionately high for smaller publicly held companies. On October 2, 2009, the SEC granted another extension for the outside auditor assessment until fiscal years ending after June 15, 2010. The SEC stated in their release that the extension was granted so that the SEC's Office of Economic Analysis could complete a study of whether additional guidance provided to company managers and auditors in 2007 was effective in reducing the costs of compliance. They also stated that there will be no further extensions in the future.

On September 15, 2010 the SEC issued final rule 33-9142 the permanently exempts registrants that are neither accelerated nor large accelerated filers as defined by Rule 12b-2 of the Securities and Exchange Act of 1934 from Section 404(b) internal control audit requirement.

Sarbanes–Oxley Section 802: Criminal Penalties for Violation of SOX

Section 802(a) of the SOX, 18 U.S.C. § 1519 states:

> *"Whoever knowingly alters, destroys, mutilates, conceals, covers up, falsifies, or makes a false entry in any record, document, or tangible object with the intent to impede, obstruct, or influence the investigation or proper administration of any matter within the jurisdiction of any department or agency of the United States or any*

case filed under title 11, or in relation to or contemplation of any such matter or case, shall be fined under this title, imprisoned not more than 20 years, or both."

Sarbanes–Oxley Section 1107: Criminal penalties for retaliation against whistleblowers;

Section 1107 of the SOX 18 U.S.C. § 1513(e) states:

"Whoever knowingly, with the intent to retaliate, takes any action harmful to any person, including interference with the lawful employment or livelihood of any person, for providing to a law enforcement officer any truthful information relating to the commission or possible commission of any federal offence, shall be fined under this title, imprisoned not more than 10 years, or both."

Praise

Former Federal Reserve Chairman Alan Greenspan praised the Sarbanes–Oxley Act: "I am surprised that the Sarbanes–Oxley Act, so rapidly developed and enacted, has functioned as well as it has, the act importantly reinforced the principle that shareholders own our corporations and that corporate managers should be working on behalf of shareholders to allocate business resources to their optimum use."

SOX has been praised by a cross-section of financial industry experts, citing improved investor confidence and more accurate, reliable financial statements. The CEO and CFO are now required to unequivocally take ownership for their financial statements under Section 302, which was not the case prior to SOX. Further, auditor conflicts of interest have been addressed, by prohibiting auditors from also having lucrative consulting agreements with the firms they audit under Section 201. SEC Chairman Christopher Cox stated in 2007: "Sarbanes–Oxley helped restore trust in U.S. markets by increasing accountability, speeding up reporting, and making audits more independent."

The FEI 2007 study and research by the Institute of Internal Auditors (IIA) also indicate SOX has improved investor confidence in financial reporting, a primary objective of the legislation. The IIA study also indicated improvements in board, audit committee, and senior management engagement in financial reporting and improvements in financial controls.

Financial restatements increased significantly in the wake of the SOX legislation, as companies "cleaned up" their books. Glass, Lewis

& Co. LLC is a San Francisco-based firm that tracks the volume of do-overs by public companies. Its March 2006 report, "Getting It Wrong the First Time," shows 1,295 restatements of financial earnings in 2005 for companies listed on U.S. securities markets, almost twice the number for 2004. "That's about one restatement for every 12 public companies—up from one for every 23 in 2004," says the report.

One fraud uncovered by the Securities and Exchange Commission (SEC) in November 2009 may be directly credited to Sarbanes-Oxley. The fraud which spanned nearly 20 years and involved over $24 million was committed by Value Line (NASDAQ: VALU) against its mutual fund shareholders. The fraud was first reported to the SEC in 2004 by the Value Line Fund (NASDAQ: VLIFX) portfolio manager who was asked to sign a Code of Business Ethics as part of SOX. Restitution totalling $34 million will be placed in a fair fund and returned to the affected Value Line mutual fund investors. No criminal charges have been filed.

National Accounts or National Account Systems

National accounts or national account systems (NAS) are the implementation of complete and consistent accounting techniques for measuring the economic activity of a nation. These include detailed underlying measures that rely on double-entry accounting. By construction such accounting makes the totals on both sides of an account equal even though they each measure different characteristics, for example production and the income from it. As a method, the subject may be termed national accounting or, more generally, social accounting. Stated otherwise, national accounts as *systems* may be distinguished from the data associated with those systems. While sharing many common principles with business accounting, national accounts are based on economic concepts.

Scope

National accounts broadly present output, expenditure, and income activities of the economic actors (corporations, government, households) in an economy, including their relations with other countries' economies, and their wealth (net worth). They present both flows (measured over a period) and *stocks* (measured at the end of a period), ensuring that the flows are reconciled with the stocks. As to flows, the national income and product accounts (in U.S. terminology) provide estimates for the money value of income and output per year or quarter, including GDP. As to stocks, the 'capital accounts' are a balance-sheet approach that has assets on one side (including values of land, the capital stock, and financial assets) and liabilities and net worth on the other, measured as of the end of the accounting period.

National accounts also include measures of the changes in assets, liabilities, and net worth per accounting period. These may refer to flow of funds accounts or, again, capital accounts.

There are a number of aggregate measures in the national accounts, notably including gross domestic product or GDP, perhaps the most widely cited measure of aggregate economic activity. Ways of breaking down GDP include as types of income (wages, profits, etc.) or expenditure (consumption, investment/saving, etc.). Measures of these are examples of macro-economic data. Such aggregate measures and their change over time are generally of strongest interest to economic policymakers, although the detailed national accounts contain a rich source of information for economic analysis, for example in the input-output tables which show how industries interact with each other in the production process.

National accounts can be presented in nominal or real amounts, with real amounts adjusted to remove the effects of price changes over time. A corresponding price index can also be derived from national output. Rates of change of the price level and output and the may also be of interest.

An inflation rate (growth rate of the price level) may be calculated for national output or its expenditure components. Economic growth rates (most commonly the growth rate of GDP) are generally measured in real (constant-price) terms. One use of economic-growth data from the national accounts is in growth accounting across longer periods of time for a country or across to estimate different sources of growth, whether from growth of factor inputs or technological change.

The accounts are derived from a wide variety of statistical source data including surveys, administrative and census data, and regulatory data, which are integrated and harmonised in the conceptual framework. They are usually compiled by national statistical offices and/or central banks in each country, though this is not always the case, and may be released on both an annual and (less detailed) quarterly frequency. Practical issues include inaccuracies from differences between economic and accounting methodologies, lack of controlled experiments on quality of data from diverse sources, and measurement of intangibles and services of the banking and financial sectors. Two developments relevant to the national accounts since the

1980s include the following. Generational accounting is a method for measuring redistribution of lifetime tax burdens across generations from social insurance, including social security and social health insurance.

It has been proposed as a better guide to the sustainability of a fiscal policy than budget deficits, which reflect only taxes minus spending in the current year. Environmental or green national accounting is the method of valuing environmental assets, which are usually not counted in measuring national wealth, in part due to the difficulty of valuing them. The method has been proposed as an alternative to an implied zero valuation of environmental assets and as a way of measuring the sustainability of welfare levels in the presence environmental degradation. Macroeconomic data not derived from the national accounts are also of wide interest, for example some cost-of-living indexes, the unemployment rate, and the labour force participation rate. In some cases, a national-accounts counterpart of these may be estimated, such as a price index computed from the personal consumption expenditures and the GDP gap (the difference between observed GDP and potential GDP).

Main Components

The presentation of national accounts data may vary by country (commonly, aggregate measures are given greatest prominence), however the main national accounts include the following accounts for the economy as a whole and its main economic actors.

- Current accounts:
  * production accounts which record the value of domestic output and the goods and services used up in producing that output. The balancing item of the accounts is value added, which is equal to GDP when expressed for the whole economy at market prices and in gross terms;
  * income accounts, which show primary and secondary income flows - both the income generated in production (e.g. wages and salaries) and distributive income flows (predominantly the redistributive effects of government taxes and social benefit payments). The balancing item of the accounts is disposable income ("National Income" when measured for the whole economy);
  * expenditure accounts, which show how disposable income is either consumed or saved. The balancing item of these accounts is saving.

- Capital accounts, which record the net accumulation, as the result of transactions, of non-financial assets; and the financing, by way of saving and capital transfers, of the accumulation. Net lending/borrowing is the balancing item for these accounts
- Financial accounts, which show the net acquisition of financial assets and the net incurrence of liabilities. The balance on these accounts is the net change in financial position.
- Balance sheets, which record the stock of assets, both financial and non-financial, and liabilities at a particular point in time. Net worth is the balance from the balance sheets (United Nations, 1993).

The accounts may be measured as gross or net of consumption of fixed capital (a concept in national accounts similar to depreciation in business accounts).

Chartered Accountants

Chartered Accountants were the first accountants to form a professional body, initially established in Britain in 1854. The Edinburgh Society of Accountants (formed 1854), the Glasgow Institute of Accountants and Actuaries (1854) and the Aberdeen Society of Accountants (1867) were each granted a royal charter almost from their inception. The title is an internationally recognised professional designation.

Chartered Accountants work in all fields of business and finance. Some are engaged in public practice work, others work in the private sector and some are employed by government bodies.

Chartered Accountants Institutes require members to undertake a minimum level of continuing professional development to stay ahead of their peers. They facilitate special interest groups - lead academic and professional thinking in accountancy. They provide support to members by offering advisory services, technical helplines and technical libraries. They offer opportunities for professional networking and career and business development.

In the United States the approximate equivalent is the certified public accountant.

Countries

Australia

Chartered Accountants in Australia belong to the Institute of Chartered Accountants of Australia and use the designatory letters

CA. Some senior members of the Institute may be elected Fellows and use the letters FCA.

Bangladesh

The Institute of Chartered Accountants of Bangladesh (ICAB) is the national professional accounting body of Bangladesh. Established in 1973, it is the sole organisation with the right to award the Chartered Accountant designation in Bangladesh.

Bermuda

The Institute of Chartered Accountants of Bermuda works with the Canadian Institute of Chartered Accountants and American Institute of Certified Public Accountants, and is the sole organisation in Bermuda with the right to award the Chartered Accountant designation.

Canada

In Canada, Chartered Accountants must be members of the Canadian Institute of Chartered Accountants (CICA). However, CICA membership must be held alongside membership of at least one CA institute (or *ordre* in French) of a Canadian province or territory. It is not possible to join the CICA directly.

In May 2011, Canada's Chartered Accountants have entered into discussions with Canada's Certified Management Accountants to explore the merits and feasibility of uniting Canadian national and provincial organisations. To bring two organisations together, they are considering the creation of a new designation – the Chartered Professional Accountant or CPA – and a new common qualification program.

Auditing rights are regulated by provincial governments. In British Columbia, the Business Corporations Act (which had replaced the longstanding Company Act) provides that only CAs, Certified General Accountants (CGAs), or anyone who has been granted an accounting licence by the provincial regulatory body may audit public companies. In Prince Edward Island, only qualified CAs and CGAs can perform public accounting and auditing in accordance with the Public Accounting and Auditing Act. In all other provinces, except Quebec and Ontario (detailed below), only qualified CAs, CGAs, and CMAs (Certified Management Accountants) may audit public companies.

Historically Quebec and Ontario only allowed CAs to audit public companies. In 2004, the Ontario government passed legislation that would enable CAs, CGAs and CMAs to practice public accounting under a reconstituted Public Accountants Council, and as of June 2010 Ontario CGAs are now allowed to issue audit opinions.

In August 2005, the Agreement of Internal Trade (AIT) panel issued a report recommending Quebec to change its legislation by opening public auditing to qualified accountants who are not CAs. On November 20, 2009, Quebec passed regulations granting statutory auditing rights to qualified CAs, CGAs and CMAs.

The size of the accounting bodies varies across Canada. In Ontario and Quebec, CA is larger than CGA or CMA, however CGA is the fastest growing amongst the three bodies. In Manitoba and British Columbia, CGA is the largest accounting body.

Canadian Chartered Accountants use the designatory letters CA. Some senior members may be elected Fellows and use the letters FCA. However, a Canadian CA who is a member of a different institute/order to that of the province or territory in which he or she resides may face a restriction on using designatory letters in that province or territory. It is however normally straightforward to transfer membership from one provincial institute to another.

The Canadian CA is one of the accounting designations that can be transferred to an American CPA via a reciprocity exam, although with several complications. A significant minority of US states do not offer reciprocity and the ones that do often require additional education or experience before granting a CPA license to a Canadian CA.

Qualification to become a CA requires an undergraduate degree plus articling experience and, depending on the province, additional education. Candidates in all provinces are required to pass the 3-day Uniform Evaluation (UFE).

Europe

Under the Mutual Recognition Directive, EEA and Swiss nationals holding a professional qualification can become members of the equivalent bodies in another member state. They must, however, pass an aptitude test in understanding local conditions (which for accountants will include local tax and company law variations).

The local title is however not available for use if the professional does not choose to join the local professional body. For example a holder of the French 'expert comptable' qualification could practise as an accountant in England without taking a local test but could only describe him/herself as "Expert Comptable (France)" not "Chartered

Accountant". Within the EEA, only the UK and Ireland have bodies that issue the Chartered Accountant title.

India

In India, the profession of chartered accountancy is regulated by the Institute of Chartered Accountants of India which was established by Parliament under the Chartered Accountants Act of 1949. Since then, the term Chartered Accountant has been used in place of Indian Registered Accountant. Prior to 1949, Restricted State Auditors were registered with the respective princely states and British provincial State Governments. However, now, the Restricted State Auditors have become redundant. As of April 2011, ICAI had more than 170,000 registered members. It is the second largest body of professional accountants in the world after AICPA.

Nepal

In Nepal, the profession of chartered accountancy is regulated by the Institute of Chartered Accountants of Nepal which was established by Parliament under the Chartered Accountants Act 1997.

Ireland

In Ireland, Chartered Accountants are generally members of Chartered Accountants Ireland and use the designatory letters ACA or FCA. Chartered Accountants may also be members of the Institute of Chartered Accountants in England and Wales or the Institute of Chartered Accountants of Scotland.

New Zealand

In New Zealand, Chartered Accountants belong to the New Zealand Institute of Chartered Accountants and use the designatory letters CA. Some senior members may be elected Fellows and use the letters FCA. There is also a mid-tier qualification called *Associate Chartered Accountant* with the designatory letters ACA. Associate Chartered Accountants are not eligible to hold a Certificate of Public Practice and therefore cannot offer services to the public.

South Africa

In South Africa, SAICA (South African Institute of Chartered Accountants) regulates the CA(SA) designation (Chartered Accountant (South Africa)).

People seeking to qualify as a CA(SA) normally begin with a bachelor's degree in accounting. They then complete a CTA (Certificate for Theory in Accounting), followed by part one (QE) and part two (PPE) of the qualifying exams. They must also complete three years of practical experience, working for a registered training office. Articled clerks who switch employers during this period are required to extend their training by six months.

A separate registration is needed for Chartered Accountants wishing to act as auditors in public practice, namely the RA (Registered Auditor). The RA designation is conferred by IRBA (Independent Regulatory Board For Auditors), (previously known as PAAB (Public Accountants and Auditors Board)) in terms of the Auditing Profession Act (AP Act).

Chartered Accountants who are not registered auditors may not act as or hold out to be auditors in public practice. However, the AP Act does not prohibit non-RAs from using the description 'internal auditor' or accountant' or from auditing a not-for-profit club, institution or association if he or she receives no fee for such audit.

The Training Outside Public Practice (TOPP) programme has a financial management focus; TOPP trainees can thus become chartered accountants with a more limited knowledge and experience of auditing than those who undergo the TIPP programme (Training In Public Practice), but with a more extensive financial management and business experience than the TIPP learners.

In South Africa the companies act has changed with effect July 2010, to allow companies without a public interest to choose between an audit or a review. A review is not an attest function and will be performed by Accountants whom are members of bodies, that are members of the International Federation of Accountants (IFAC). In South Africa these bodies are: ACCA, SAICA, SAIPA.

Pakistan

The Institute of Chartered Accountants of Pakistan (ICAP) was established on July 1, 1961 to regulate the profession of accountancy in Pakistan. It is a statutory autonomous body established under the Chartered Accountants Ordinance 1961.

As of July 2010, 5,078 persons were registered with the Institute as Chartered Accountants.

Sri Lanka

Chartered Accountants in Sri Lanka belong to the Institute of Chartered Accountants of Sri Lanka and use the designatory letters

ACA. Some senior members of the Institute may be elected Fellows and use the letters FCA.

United Kingdom

In the UK, there are no licence requirements for individuals to describe themselves or to practice as accountants, but to use the description "Chartered Accountant" they must be members of one of the following organisations:

- the Institute of Chartered Accountants in England & Wales (ICAEW) (designatory letters ACA or FCA);
- the Institute of Chartered Accountants of Scotland (ICAS) (designatory letters CA); or
- Chartered Accountants Ireland (CAI, which is an Irish rather than a UK body but covers Northern Ireland as well as the Republic of Ireland), designatory letters ACA or FCA).

(Although three other UK accounting bodies were also formed by Royal Charter, they grant separate designations to their members.)

The three Institutes above admit members, who become Chartered Accountants, only after passing examinations and undergoing a period of relevant work experience. The ICAEW requires that students complete 15 examinations as well as 450 days of relevant work experience. Once admitted, members are expected to comply with ethical guidelines and gain appropriate continuing professional development. Fully qualified members of the ICAEW and CAI earn the designation ACA (Associate Chartered Accountant). After 10 years membership, members are invited to apply for fellowship of their Institute and earn the designation FCA (Fellow Chartered Accountant).

Chartered Accountants who engage in public practice work (i.e. providing services to the public rather than acting as an employee) must gain a "practising certificate" by meeting further requirements such as purchasing adequate insurance and undergoing regular inspections. Chartered Accountants holding practising certificates may also become "Registered Auditors", providing they can demonstrate the necessary professional ability in that area. A Registered Auditor is able to perform statutory financial audits in accordance with the Companies Act 2006.

Certified Public Accountant

Certified Public Accountant (CPA) is the statutory title of qualified accountants in the United States who have passed the Uniform

Certified Public Accountant Examination and have met additional state education and experience requirements for certification as a CPA. Individuals who have passed the Exam but have not either accomplished the required on-the-job experience or have previously met it but in the meantime have lapsed their continuing professional education are, in many states, permitted the designation "CPA Inactive" or an equivalent phrase. In most U.S. states, only CPAs who are licensed are able to provide to the public attestation (including auditing) opinions on financial statements. The exceptions to this rule are Arizona, Kansas, North Carolina and Ohio where, although the "CPA" designation is restricted, the practice of auditing is not.

Many states have a lower tier of accountant qualification (below that of CPA), usually entitled "Public Accountant" (with designatory letters "PA"). However the majority of states have closed the designation "Public Accountant" to new entrants, with only about 10 states continuing to offer the designation. Many PAs belong to the National Society of Accountants.

Many states prohibit the use of the designations "Certified Public Accountant" or "Public Accountant" (or the abbreviations "CPA" or "PA") by a person who is not certified as a CPA or PA in that state. As a result, in many circumstances, an out-of-state CPA is restricted from using the CPA designation or designators letters until a license or certificate from that state is obtained.

Texas additionally prohibits the use of the designations "accountant" and "auditor" by a person not certified as a Texas CPA, unless that person is a CPA in another state, a nonresident of Texas, and otherwise meets the requirements for practice in Texas by out-of-state CPA firms and practitioners.

Many other countries also use the title CPA to designate local public accountants.

Services Provided by CPAs

The primary functions CPA fulfill relate to assurance services, or public accounting. In assurance services, also known as financial audit services, CPAs attest to the reasonableness of disclosures, the freedom from material misstatement, and the adherence to the applicable generally accepted accounting principles (GAAP) in financial statements. CPAs can also be employed by corporations—termed "the private sector"—in finance functions such as Chief Financial Officer (CFO) or finance manager, or as CEOs subject to their full business knowledge and practice. These CPAs do not provide services directly to the public.

Although some CPAs serve as business consultants, the consulting role is under scrutiny following the corporate climate in the aftermath of the Enron scandal. This has resulted in divestitures in the consulting divisions by many accounting firms. This trend has since reversed. In audit engagements, CPAs are (and have always been) required by professional standards and Federal and State laws to maintain independence (both in fact and in appearance) from the entity for which they are conducting an attestation (audit and review) engagement. However, most individual CPAs who work as consultants do not work as auditors.

CPAs also have a niche within the income tax preparation industry. Many small to mid-sized firms have both a tax and an auditing department.

Whether providing services directly to the public or employed by corporations or associations, CPAs can operate in virtually any area of finance including:

- Assurance and Attestation Services
- Corporate Finance (Merger & Acquisition, initial public offerings, share & debt issuings)
- Corporate Governance
- Estate Planning
- Financial Accounting
- Financial Analysis
- Financial Planning
- Forensic Accounting (preventing, detecting, and investigating financial frauds)
- Income Tax
- Information Technology, especially as applied to accounting and auditing
- Management Consulting and Performance Management
- Tax Preparation and Planning
- Venture Capital.

CPA Exam

In order to become a CPA in the United States, the candidate must sit for and pass the Uniform Certified Public Accountant

Examination (Uniform CPA Exam), which is set by the American Institute of Certified Public Accountants (AICPA) and administered by the National Association of State Boards of Accountancy (NASBA). The CPA was established in law on April 17, 1896.

Eligibility to sit for the Uniform CPA Exam is determined by individual State Boards of Accountancy. Typically the requirement is a U.S. bachelors degree which includes a minimum number of qualifying credit hours in accounting and business administration with an additional 1 year study. This requirement for 5 years study is known as the "150 hour rule" and has been adopted by the majority of state boards, although there are still some exceptions (e.g.California). This requirement mandating 150 hours of study has been adopted by 45 states. Work experience under the supervision of a practising accountant is not generally required.

The Colorado State Board of Accountancy allows Chartered Certified Accountants (ACCA), together with Chartered Accountants from eligible jurisdictions (Australia, South Africa, Canada, Ireland, New Zealand) automatic eligibility to sit for the Uniform CPA Exam as a Colorado candidate. As of December 9, 2009, ACCA members are not automatically eligible to sit for the Uniform CPA Exam.

Certain overseas qualified accountants seeking to become U.S. CPAs may be eligible to sit for the *International Qualification Examination* as an alternative to the Uniform CPA Exam.

The Uniform CPA exam tests general principles of state law such as the law of contracts and agency (questions not tailored to the variances of any particular state) and some federal law as well.

Other Licensing and Certification Requirements

Although the CPA exam is uniform, licensing and certification requirements are imposed separately by each state's laws and therefore vary from state to state.

State requirements for the CPA qualification can be summed up as the *Three Es*—Education, Examination and Experience. The Education requirement normally must be fulfilled as part of the eligibility criteria to sit for the Uniform CPA and the Examination component is the Uniform CPA itself. Some states have a two tier system whereby an individual would first become certified as a CPA—usually by passing the CPA exam. That individual would then later be eligible to be licensed once a certain amount of work experience is accomplished. Other states have a one tier system whereby an individual would be certified and licensed at the same time when both the CPA exam is passed and the work experience requirement has been met. Two-tier states include Alabama, Florida, Illinois, Montana, and Nebraska. The trend is for two-tier states to gradually move towards a one-tier system. Since 2002, the State Boards of Washington and South Dakota have ceased issuing CPA "certificates" and instead issue CPA "licenses," and Illinois plans to follow suit in 2012.

A number of states are two-tiered, but require work experience for the CPA certificate, such as Ohio.

Work Experience Requirement

The experience component varies from state to state:

- The two-tier states generally do not require work experience for a CPA certificate (it is required for a license to practice).
- Some states, such as Colorado and Massachusetts, will waive the work experience requirement for those with a higher academic qualification compared to the state's requirement to appear for the Uniform CPA
- The majority of states still require work experience to be of a *public accounting* nature. However an increasing number of states, including Oregon, Virginia, Georgia and Kentucky will accept experience of a more general nature in the accounting area. This allows persons to obtain the CPA designation while working for a corporation's finance function.
- The majority of states require work experience to be verified by a licensed CPA. This can cause difficulties for applicants based outside the United States. However, some states such as Colorado and Oregon will accept work experience certified by a Chartered Accountant as well.

Ethics

Over 40 of the state boards now require applicants for CPA status to complete a special examination on ethics, which is effectively a *fifth exam* in terms of requirements to become a CPA. The majority of these will accept the AICPA self-study *Professional Ethics for CPAs* CPE course or another course in general professional ethics. Many states, however, require that the ethics course include a review of that state's specific rules for professional practice.

Continuing Professional Education (CPE)

CPAs are required to take continuing education courses in order to renew their license. Requirements vary by state but the vast majority require 120 hours of CPE every 3 years with a minimum of 20 hours per calendar year. The requirement can be fulfilled through attending live seminars, webcast seminars, or through self-study (textbooks, videos, online courses, all of which require a test to receive credit). As part of the CPE requirement, most states require their CPAs to take an ethics course during every renewal period. Again, ethics requirements vary by state but the courses range from 2–8 hours.

Inter-state Practice

An accountant is required to meet the legal requirements of any state in which they want to practice. Also, the term "practice of public accounting" and similar terms are given definitions PA status under reciprocity to a CPA licensed in another state. CPAs from other states with less stringent educational requirements may not be able to benefit from these provisions. This does not affect those CPAs who do not plan to offer services directly to the public. Moreover, most states would grant the temporary practicing rights to a CPA of another state.

Practice Mobility

In recent years, mobility for CPAs has become a major issue of concern. Practice mobility for CPAs is the ability of a licensee to gain a practice privilege outside of their home state without getting an additional license in another state where they will be serving a client. Because the electronic age makes conducting business across state borders an everyday occurrence, there is a critical need for states to adopt a uniform mobility system that will allow licensed CPAs to provide services across state lines without unnecessary burdens that do not protect the public interest.

Currently, each state has its own rules, regulations and requirements to allow out-of-state CPAs to provide services in that state, resulting in a patchwork system that is inefficient and increasingly difficult to navigate.

The American Institute of Certified Public Accountants (AICPA) and the National Association of State Boards of Accountancy (NASBA) have analysed the current system for gaining practice privileges across state lines and have concluded it simply does not work.

Compliance and enforcement of the existing system is almost impossible, with multiple, cumbersome processes and disparities in requirements and fees. Business realities, including an increase in interstate commerce and virtual technologies require a uniform system that allows fluid practice across state lines.

Implementation of a uniform provision would allow consumers to receive timely services from the CPA best suited to the job, regardless of location, without the hindrances of unnecessary filings, forms and increased costs that do not protect the public interest.

Businesses today are often located in multiple states and have compliance responsibilities in multiple jurisdictions and a uniform process will give CPAs the flexibility to better serve these clients.

Uniform adoption of the substantial equivalency provision included in the Uniform Accountancy Act (the model bill for CPA regulation written and endorsed jointly by AICPA and NASBA) will create a system similar to the nation's driver license that will provide CPAs with mobility while retaining and strengthening state boards' ability to protect the public interest.

Prior to 2007, four states (Ohio, Missouri, Virginia and Wisconsin) had practice mobility laws in place for CPAs. In 2007, seven more states (Tennessee, Texas, Illinois, Indiana, Maine, Rhode Island and Louisiana) enacted new practice mobility laws for CPAs.

As of April 29, 2009 a total of 39 states have enacted this law. They are: Arkansas, Arizona, Colorado, Connecticut, Delaware, Florida, Georgia, Idaho, Illinois, Iowa, Indiana, Kansas, Kentucky, Louisiana, Maine, Maryland, Michigan, Minnesota, Mississippi, Missouri, Montana, Nebraska, New Jersey, New Mexico, North Dakota, Ohio, Oklahoma, Pennsylvania, Rhode Island, South Carolina, South Dakota, Tennessee, Texas, Utah, Virginia, Washington, West Virginia, Wisconsin and Wyoming. In addition, 8 other states have similar legislation pending before them (Alabama, Hawaii, Massachusetts, Nevada, New Hampshire, North Carolina, Oregon and Vermont).

AICPA Membership

The CPA designation is granted by individual state boards, not the American Institute of Certified Public Accountants (AICPA). Membership in the AICPA is not obligatory for CPAs, although some CPAs do join. To become a full member of AICPA, the applicant must hold a valid CPA certificate or license from at least one of the fifty-five U.S. state/territory boards of accountancy; some additional requirements apply.

AICPA members approved a proposed bylaw amendment to make eligible for voting membership individuals who previously held a CPA certificate/license or have met all the requirements for CPA certification in accordance with the Uniform Accountancy Act (UAA). The AICPA announced its plan to accept applications from individuals meeting these criteria, beginning no later than January 1, 2011.

Chartered Certified Accountant

Chartered Certified Accountant (designatory letters ACCA or FCCA) was historically seen as a British qualified accountant designation awarded by the Association of Chartered Certified Accountants (ACCA). However, although ACCA is UK based, it is a global body for professional accountants with 147,000 qualified members and 424,000 students globally. Support offices/centres exist in 83 countries.

The term *Chartered Certified Accountant* was introduced in 1996. Prior to that date, ACCA members were known as *Certified Accountant.* It is still permissible for an ACCA member to use this term. Members of ACCA with sufficient post-qualification experience are designated Fellows, and use the designatory letters FCCA in place of ACCA.

The term *Chartered* refers to the Royal Charter granted by Her Majesty Queen Elizabeth II of the United Kingdom.

Subjects examined include financial accounting, management accounting, auditing, taxation, financial management, performance management, strategic management and company law.

Chartered Certified Accountants work in all fields of business and finance. Some are engaged in public practice work, others work in the private sector and some are employed by government bodies.

Since *Chartered Certified Accountant* is a legally protected term, individuals who describe themselves as such must be members of ACCA. If they carry out public practice engagements, they must comply with additional regulations such as holding a practising certificate, being insured against any possible liability claims and submitting to inspections.

Certified General Accountant

Certified General Accountant (CGA) is the designation of professionals who are jointly members of the Certified General Accountants Association of Canada (CGA-Canada) and a provincial or territorial CGA association, or a CGA association overseas. Provincial, territorial and offshore CGA affiliate associations work collaboratively with CGA-Canada as part of a federation.

A CGA is an accounting professional with expertise in finance, taxation, business strategy, auditing, management and business leadership. CGAs must meet the education, experience and examination requirements established, and regularly enhanced, by CGA-Canada. CGA-Canada had 47,500 members and 25,500 students in 2009, making it the fastest growing and second largest professional accounting designation in Canada. The CGA program of professional studies is offered in Canada, Bermuda, the Caribbean, Hong Kong and mainland China. CGAs work throughout the world in industry, commerce, finance, government, public practice and the not-for-profit sector.

Certified Management Accountant

The Certified Management Accountant (CMA) designation in Canada provides a foundation in accounting, management and strategy; using both financial and non-financial information to direct tactical and operational decision-making in industry and government.

Subject matter includes strategy, management accounting, corporate finance, operations management, internal control, financial accounting, statistics and economics, and an emphasis on ethics. With 50,000 members around the world, CMA Canada grants a professional designation in strategic management accounting and is responsible for standards-setting, accreditation, and the continuing professional development of Certified Management Accountants (CMAs).

In May 2011, Canada's Certified Management Accountants have entered into discussions with Canada's Chartered Accountants to explore the merits and feasibility of uniting Canadian national and provincial organisations.

To bring two organisations together, they are considering the creation of a new designation – the Chartered Professional Accountant or CPA – and a new common qualification program.

CMA Canada is a founding member of the International Federation of Accountants.

United Kingdom & Europe

The Chartered Institute of Management Accountants (CIMA) is a United Kingdom-based professional body offering training and qualification in management accountancy and related subjects, focused on accounting for business; together with ongoing support for members.

CIMA is one of a number of professional associations for accountants in the UK and Republic of Ireland. Its particular emphasis is on developing the management accounting profession within the UK and worldwide. CIMA is the world's largest and leading professional body of management accountants, with 172,000 members and students in over 165 countries.

CIMA was founded in 1919 as "The Institute of Cost and Works Accountants" (ICWA). It specialised in the development of accounting techniques for use in the internal control of manufacturing, service and public sector operations.

It developed a position as the leading professional body in the areas of product costing, budgeting, management accounting, investment appraisal and business decision making. In October 1944 the Institute of Cost and Works Accountants organisation in Ireland was formed.

The institute changed its name from ICWA to the Institute of Cost and Management Accountants (ICMA) in 1972 and subsequently to the Chartered Institute of Management Accountants (CIMA) in 1986, after the granting of a Royal Charter. A global Accounting qualification based in the UK, which is particularly active in Commonwealth countries. Its membership has grown from 15,000 in 1970 to 79,757 members and 92,909 students in 2009.

The CIMA is a founding member of the International Federation of Accountants.

Australia

Australian Institute of Certified Management Accountants.

India

Cost and Management Accountant is the CMA designation granted by the Institute of Cost and Works Accountants of India (ICWAI).

The Institute of Cost and Works Accountants of India is the only recognised statutory professional organisation and licensing body in India specialising exclusively in Cost and Management Accountancy. ICWAI is a member of the International Federation of Accountants.

China

- Chartered Institute of Management Accountants (CIMA) China program
- Institute of Management Accountants (IMA) China program.

Pakistan

The Institute of Cost and Management Accountants of Pakistan was established in 1951 and was granted statutory status under the

Cost and Management Accountants Act, 1966 for the regulation of the profession of Cost and Management Accounting. ICMAP is the sole provider of cost and management accounting education, training and professional certification in Pakistan.

The institute has earned reputation both nationally and internationally for its high standard in imparting education and testing. The Institute has been meeting an important national human resource need through a steady flow of professional management accountants to occupy leading positions in the corporate world.

ICMAP has over 5000 members, who hold senior positions in trade, commerce, industry and government in Pakistan and abroad. The number of active registered students is around 15000, which makes ICMAP one of the largest professional institutions in Pakistan.

International Association

The Institute is member of the following international accounting bodies:

- International Federation of Accountants
- International Accounting Standards Board
- Confederation of Asian and Pacific Accountants (CAPA)
- South Asian Federation of Accountants (SAFA).

Through energetic participation in the activities of these bodies, the Institute plays a vibrant role in the development of management accounting profession both at domestic and international level.

- Institute of Cost & Management Accountants of Pakistan.

Sri Lanka

The Society of Certified Management Accountants of Sri Lanka was set up with the technical support of CMA (Canada), and Financial Sponsorship of the Canadian International Development Agency (CIDA). Approval was granted by the Ministry of Trade in the year 1999 to set up the Society of Certified Management Accountants of Sri Lanka and this was by Gazette Notification

Incorporation

The Institute of Certified Management Accountants of Sri Lanka was incorporated by Parliament Act No. 23 of 2009 under the Ministry of Trade Marketing Development Co-operatives & Consumer Services on the initiative of the Minister Hon. Bandula Gunawardhana.

CMA Admitted to Membership of International Federation of Accountants (IFAC)

CMA was admitted to Associate Membership of IFAC at the 2010 IFAC Council Meeting held during the World Congress of Accountants 2010 in Kuala Lumpur, Malaysia. IFAC is the World Accountancy Body consisting of 125 countries and 164 member bodies with a total membership of more than 2.5 million accountants in public practice, education, government service, industry and commerce.

Certified Accounting Technician

The Certified Accounting Technician (CAT) UK qualification is offered by the Association of Chartered Certified Accountants (ACCA).

Upon completion of the exams and required practical work experience the CAT graduate will be able to apply to use the letters CAT after his or her name. In addition, they will have the opportunity to join the CAT alumni.

Although CAT can be obtained as a stand-alone qualification, it is often the case that individuals study for CAT as an introductionary qualification in accountancy prior to training to become a Chartered Certified Accountant through the ACCA Professional Scheme. It usually takes one and a half years to complete the nine CAT exams.

However, there is no restriction on the number of papers that can be attempted in each sitting. CAT's rival is the Association of Accounting Technicians (AAT) qualification. ACCA was a sponsor of the AAT before breaking its links in the mid 1990s in order to form the CAT qualification. The rationale behind this move was that it wanted a technician level qualification which followed the same strategic direction of the ACCA qualification, i.e. one with an international profile.

The Certified Accounting Technician qualification (CAT) has now been placed on the Qualifications and Curriculum Authority (QCA) National Qualifications Framework, which means that publicly funded educational institutions are now eligible for grants to help them train individuals towards this qualification in the United Kingdom.

Under a recent restructure of its courses, the ACCA has placed the CAT as part of the Foundations in Accountancy suit of qualifications.

7

The Broader Meaning of Profits

The term profit (or profits) means broadly the residual share, the one noncontractual income in the business. It is what is left as a net gain to that person (or group of persons) who assumes the financial risk of the business, after paying off the claims of every one else for any uses or services rendered. Profit in this broad and popular sense is a complex of incomes from various sources and must fluctuate in nature (as well as in amount) from case to case for reasons that are accidental and personal.

We may see this in reviewing the examples above. In the small furniture shop profits includes all economic incomes in the business, whether from the investment or from the joiner's own labour. It is an inclusive term for the usances of tools, shop, materials, and land, and for the services of the owner, whether as investor, manager, or handworker. It embraces all the economic yields which by theoretical analysis can be carved out of it. As the business develops, profits, as thus used, means more or less according to circumstances which must be ascertained from the context.

If the investor owns all his buildings and land, machinery, and sources of materials, and has no borrowed capital, then profits includes all that is left of cash receipts after paying wages (and salaries), but wages may be more or less according as the investor takes a more or less active part in the management. If in the one business the buildings, water power, lands, etc., are fully owned, and in another business with exactly the same product all these things are hired, profits in the former would be much greater. While the business is owned by an individual or by partners, profits may include whatever is attributable to the owner for his management; or a fair salary may be estimated for this, and only the remainder be counted as profits. Like complications, or even more troublesome ones, are found in the case of corporations. The one company owns all its patents, the other pays royalties; the one has all its capital represented by paid-up stock and the other has more or less of outstanding bonds the interest of which is a "fixed charge" to be deducted before counting the residual share of profits. The possible variations are endless, but these illustrations suffice to show that profit in any such general sense is not a scientific term for the purpose of studying the forms of income; it has not even a precise practical significance.

Conception of Investment Profits

Is there then, no exacter conception of profits possible? Among these various meanings is there one not pre-empted by another term, one which expresses a sort of income found in practical affairs, which business men are constantly trying to estimate and of which economists must take account? Let us try to express such a conception in this definition: Investment profit is the income attributable solely to the active capital-investment in the particular enterprise. The amount and rate of investment-profit is peculiar to each business and indeed to each investment. It is never an agreed price, or a contractual payment. It is the residual after the actual contractual dues have been paid, and the estimated value of the non-contractual labour, and the factor of management (such as the services of officers, etc.) have been deducted.

The investment profit concept is most nearly exemplified in practical affairs in the bookkeeping of a corporation. Out of gross receipts must be paid all rents, interest, maintenance and depreciation of the plant, price of materials, wages, salaries of managers and officers, fees of directors, etc.; the residue is the amount which may be paid as dividends to stockholders (or added to surplus) without impairing the capital investment. § 3. Dual character of investment profit. Even investment profit usually is subjected to a comparison which divides it into two elements. We have seen that it is of the very essence of the active capital function that it takes the financial risk of the outcome.

When therefore at the end of the year (or income period) it appears that a certain profit has resulted (say $1000), this is compared with the capital invested (say $10,000) and expressed as a percentage on the investment (thus 10 percent). Now this in turn is compared with the rate of interest common on the safest loans (say 4 percent) and the remainder is the amount (or rate) by which this active-capitalist investment exceeds the current rate of passive capital investments. This merely estimated division influences further choice of investment. The rate of interest is taken to represent about what capital can do by itself (or with a negligible amount of judgment and supervision-an abstract conception) and the excess above that is attributed to the successful act of investment. Thus, however far we attempt to eliminate the personal service element of management from profits, there always remains in any active capital income this one element of investing management together with the carrying of the financial risk.

There is a dual character in investment profit; it is a capital-income and a labour-income, combined. The distinctive feature of investment profit, which fastens our attention, is precisely this excess (or deficit) of income in active-capital as compared with the normal prevailing rate of time-price, which can be secured by the most conservative passive investor. It is the hope of an income more than ordinary interest that is the inducement to active capitalists to assume the risk. We may call the amount realized more or less than the imputed yield of passive investment, pure investment profit, attributable to the exercise of the pure investment function. The amount may be expressed as a rate on the investment. This is the utmost point that has been attained in the analysis of the complex elements of "profits" as popularly used.

Enterprise and risk

To the person who exercised this function of active capital-investment various names have been applied: undertaker, its French equivalent entrepreneur, adventurer (especially used in former times of one who embarked in foreign trade), and enter priser. Each of these was meant to express the assumption of the financial risk in undertaking the ownership of the various factors and of their results embodied in the products, in paying off other claimants, and in waiting for an income indeterminable in advance, but contingent on all the various fluctuations of the market.

Enterprise is the act, or function, performed by the enter priser, and in a different but related sense is the particular business establishment, or undertaking, which is carried on by an enter priser. Business management and enterprise are functions not embodied completely in any individuals, but diffused more or less among groups of men. The active-capitalist and the passive-capitalist are not in contrast absolutely but relatively; the passive capitalist is not, and can not be, completely freed from financial risk. Enterprise is merely in this particular business the assumption of the legal financial responsibility to the extent of the enter priser's credit and resources, or in other cases to the extent of the special legal limited liability, as (in most stock companies) to the amount invested, or (often in banking) to double the amount invested.

The old English word undertaker, once so used, seems to have been driven out by a rival use; perhaps after "funeral director" displaces it there, it may be reclaimed by economics. Risk is more or less everywhere in human affairs, but among various kinds of investments there is a well-recognized gradation in the uncertainty of returns. The enter priser in a business takes the more exposed frontier of risk, and the various senior securities have prior claims. For example, if the business of a corporation goes badly the first mortgage bonds, getting a low rate of interest, are the first claim on the income and, in case of insolvency, these bonds would be paid out of any assets of the company; so in turn till we come to the common stock which gets nothing until all the other claims are satisfied but which if the business is prosperous may get dividends at any rate permitted by profits. There is thus an investment risk, an element of enterprise even in the safest investment, e.g., government bonds, but this becomes almost negligible in the case of many well-proven investments. This relativity of risk and of the enterprise function may be shown again in the interrelations of different enterprises.

Pure profit the most variable income

It is easily seen why the income to enterprise is the most variable from one establishment, and from one time, to another. It contains within it all the non-contractual elements of income. The labourer has taken a fixed wage, the passive capitalist has reduced his risk and accepted a fixed interest. Both wage workers and passive capitalists have taken the easy way, have "played safe," and have left the enter priser to bear the brunt.

The rates given are, of course, only illustrative of the proportions in which they might vary in a particular case. In fact the common stock might pay no dividends for years while dividends and interest on all the other classes of securities were regularly paid, of the financial risk. The income of each of these classes tends to conform to a general market-rate, being a medium of the gains and losses when labour and capital are applied with various degrees of risk in various undertakings. Enterprise is the most movable element. It is specialized risk-taking. Enterprise has well been called an economic buffer, Let enterprise A be tenant farming, for which are needed farm-land and buildings, borrowed money, and the uses of various rented machines. Enterprise B consists of buying land and constructing a house, shop, store-building upon it to let to enterprise A. The enter priser in this case takes the risk in deciding on the right place, kind of house, materials, etc., and runs a chance of letting it or being without a tenant. Enterprise C is private money lending, or a bank-business, lending to A.

The other enterprises receiving contractual payments from enterprise A are not free from all risk. There is a chance that the agreed payment will not be made and, if it is, that loss will result from other causes (e.g., a fire destroying the buildings). Enterprisers B to F, however, in relation to the incomes they receive from and through A, are relatively protected against risk. Enter priser A in paying a fixed rent, a fixed interest, etc., is, to the extent of his credit, putting up a margin of security against the failure of crops, of profits, etc. which takes up and distributes the strain resulting from variations in the momentum and rate of movement of industry.

The enter priser feels first the influence of changing conditions. If the prices of his products fall, the first loss comes upon him, for the goods already made must be sold. Further loss is avoided as best it can be by paying less for materials and labour. At such times the wage-earners look upon the employer as their evil genius, and usually blame him for lowering their wages, not the public for refusing to buy the product at the former high prices. "When, however, prices rise, enterprise gains through selling at higher prices the stock on hand that has been produced at low cost. Enterprise is placed between the forces of competition, between owners of resources and ultimate consumers, between labourers and the final purchasers of labour's services. The enter priser's economic survival is conditioned on vigilance, strength, and self-assertion.

Profits therefore fluctuate more from industry to industry and from man to man than do other incomes. The variations of the market may sweep away not only all "profits," but all the invested capital. As a consequence, profits may be at other times very high, for enterprise will not take the risk of great losses unless there is a chance of large gains. While the income of the salaried man is occasionally advanced, and then for long periods remains unchanged, the profits of enterprise come in waves. In seasons of prosperity profits in many enterprises swell with a dramatic swiftness while rents and wages move tardily upward. Then again for years profits fall to a level hardly exceeding a low interest on the capital invested or leave many businesses for a time with a loss. Reasons for this result will be shown more in detail under cost of production.

Profits and Costs

Meanings of Cost

The profit in enterprise results from the surplus of sales (receipts) over costs (expenses). Few words are more often heard in business than cost, or with more varied shades of meaning. In a general sense cost always means something given up, parted with, paid, to get something else. Often this outlay takes the form of pain, fatigue, or irksomeness of labour, the this is a psychic cost, better termed sacrifice. Thus it is said: he got it at the cost of tireless effort; it cost him his health. When the worker who is free to determine the length of his working day stops work, he reveals that his valuation of his labour just at that point is greater than the valuation of the product that will come from further labour-the one negative and the other positive in the balance. Psychic cost thus rises to the level of more or less conscious estimation at certain points and, like psychic income, has its part in many ways in the choices made by individuals.

It is not, however, the objective measure of cost in the transactions of trade. In another sense cost is applied to any objective good or any gratification which could have been chosen, but which was given up when another choice was made. This is alternative cost, called by some, opportunity cost. It is an option relinquished. One may stay at home and read a book or go on a picnic; the pleasure of reading a book will cost the pleasure of the picnic. A good dress may cost a vacation that must be given up for it. In this sense, each thing is a cost of every other thing that might be chosen in the place of it, the alternative cost thought of is usually the most important excluded option. Alternative cost, like psychic cost, is individual, and is significant at the moment of choice but is not the measure in which business outlay is expressed.

The sense in which cost is mostly used in business in the common phrase "cost of production" is money cost. It expresses not the pain of the labourer in doing the work, not the sacrifice of the owner of the capital in saving the money, but merely the sum of money paid out by the producer. Costs, proceeds, and profits are all in business practice reckoned in terms of money. The enterpriser invests in order to realize profits. Enterprise is investment, the putting of capital into concrete forms of wealth; and it is in turn the sale of wealth, a process which might be called divestment. The realization of profit means getting out a total sum of capital greater than was put into the business. Capital is thrown into the melting pot, and is taken out crystallized into new forms of wealth which may or may not bear a greater price than the costs. The price of the products depends on the valuations of possible purchasers. The customers may be foolish men with unwholesome desires, and profit-making may result from pandering to their vices; but in any case the enterpriser finds himself limited by this condition: to gain a profit he must produce a surplus of value (as judged by his customers) between costs and selling price.

Superficial View of Costs and Prices

It is well after this discussion of costs to consider their relation (as a more fundamental problem of theory) to prices and values. The business man, as such, is rarely interested in this question. He knows that many influences unite to determine the cost of the factors he buys, but they are distant; he cannot influence them, and in the single stage of his production his costs seem to fix the price of his products. In some purchases, however, and on the stock exchange, a remarkable power of noting and analysing the more distant influences is displayed. But in general a superficial view of value is taken in business; it does not pay to do otherwise. The active investor simply takes the price of various factors as he finds them, and seeks to combine them and to sell them when and where he can reap a profit. Yet if he is asked, "What determines the prices of goods? he probably replies, "They are fixed by cost-of-production." This is the way it appears from the enterpriser's point of view as he is deciding whether to extend or contract his production and sales, whether to raise or lower his prices.

Costs Adjusted to Prices of Products

But costs vary from one establishment to another. No matter what any particular enterpriser's costs may be, the price of the goods is determined by the bidding of buyers and sellers in the market. If any one is so situated that he can regularly get more than cost on any unit, he attributes the gain to whatever agent gives the advantage,-to his patents, his land, his own ability,-and thereafter he adds more to costs on that account. In this case we see plainly that the value (or price) of the factors (that is, the cost) is being marked up (or down) according to the price of the products, and not vice versa. Economists long took that proposition as sound, and tried to build upon it a scientific explanation of prices and values as they are. It always has been recognized that there are difficulties in such an explanation. We shall not enter into the controversy, but briefly indicate the point of view we now take.

The rule must be reversed also in the case of many large classes of goods. Some things that can not be multiplied or reproduced, such as autographs, old violins, old paintings, diamonds, bring prices that are not dependent on the cost of production. The same is true of great numbers of natural resources, including all lands taken in a state of nature, whether agricultural, mineral, residential, or commercial. That leaves still to be explained the relation of costs to the prices of the great class of goods which are grown by the art of man, e.g., grain, cotton, cattle, etc., and manufactured, e.g., tools, machines, cloth, etc. Now it is noticeable that every one of these objects has a cost just because it happens to be looked at just when it is in the enterpriser's hands at an intermediate stage of its production. The cost rule applies only to factors that have been bought at a price, and the total cost is simply the sum of the prices of the factors. But how did the factors, the various qualities of labour, the materials, use of agents, etc., get their price? That question has been answered in earlier chapters: from the value of the expected product, or uses. The business enterpriser is a middleman, buying to sell again, and his costs determine whether or not he can make a profit, but they do not determine the prices of the products. Rather they are seen to be determined by the prices, when a broad enough view of the situation is taken.

Principles of Price

Buyers' Composite Valuation Curve

We have now to examine the process by which market-price is determined where two groups of bidders are present. This fulfils the conditions of a complete market, where there is two-sided, competitive bidding. Each trader comes to the market with valuations already in his mind more or less definitely. It may be that he is disposed to buy one unit if the price is high; if it is lower he will buy two units; if still lower, three units, etc. Or he is disposed to sell one unit at a certain price, two units if the price offered is higher, three if it is still higher, etc.

The situation from the standpoint of the prospective buyers is represente. One of them (Bl) stands ready to purchase one unit at a price as high as 14 if he can do no better, but he will, of course, buy at a lower figure if possible. B 2 will, if he must, pay as high as 13 for a unit. Other buyers are willing to buy (one unit each) at prices respectively lower-12, 11, etc. At the extreme end of the scale there are certain individuals who would be induced to buy only by a price extremely low-4, 3,1, etc. The diagram, therefore, represents this situation where the individual (prospective) buyers have different mental attitudes (valuations) as cording to kinds of goods, to times, and to circumstances. A fall of a particular price by 1 percent may correspond with an increase of demand by 1 percent or 2 percent or 10 percent as the case may be. When eggs were 35 cents a dozen in Chicago (between 1909-1911) and fell to 34 cents the change in demand was hardly noticeable.

But at 30 cents (about 15 percent less) the demand rose from about 15,000 cases to 30,000 a week (100 percent),-a considerable degree of elasticity. (The standard case contains 30 dozen.) At 20 cents a dozen demand was remarkably elastic, and additional supplies to the amount of 50,000 to 100,000 cases were taken (probably used as substitutes for meat, and to put into cold-storage) with hardly noticeable decline in price. Later, in June and July, however, when the demand for cold-storage purposes falls off, and possibly because eggs are somewhat less palatable in hot weather, the price fell lower (to 18, and one year even to 15 cents). When at a given price a small reduction in price inregards the good in question, and where in the aggregate the whole body of buyers stand ready to take the various amounts indicated, according as the prevailing price is higher or lower. If it is high they will take a relatively small quantity: if it is low they will take a larger amount.

If, for example, the price should prove to be 12, it will be seen that only four units will be taken by the would-be purchasers. They will be secured, of course, by the most urgent buyers, B 1, B 2, B 3, and B 4.. There is no one else who stands ready to buy at a price as high as 12. There are others who would buy at a lower figure, but if the ruling market price is as high as 12 they are, by their own attitude of choice, necessarily excluded from the actual market transactions. Similarly for any other price in the scale there will be a definite number of included or actual buyers, and a definite amount of the good which in the aggregate will be taken by those buyers at that price. This amount, the demand, which the buyers will take at any specified price is a composite, the combined result, of course, of the bids of the various individuals concerned. This set of valuations with which a trader enters a market reflects a disposition, an attitude of choice, a provisional judgment, which is subject to change with new conditions.

Elasticity of demand. The changes of demand (and of supply) relative to a certain amount of change of price are very different accreases largely the amount that will be bought and sold, demand and supply are said to be elastic. For example, at 35 cents the demand for eggs in Chicago is relatively inelastic, and at 20 cents it is very elastic.

Sellers' Composite Valuation Curve

S1, the most urgent seller, is willing to sell one unit at a price as low as 4;3 S 7 will part with a unit at a price of 7.5 if he can do no better; S 12 will not be tempted to sell unless he can get 10 for a unit of the good, etc. Here again the diagram simply depicts the fact that at any given price there will be a certain number of actual or included sellers, and the amount offered by those sellers at that price, or the supply, will also be a definite quantity. At a low price this quantity is small; at a high price it is large.

Choice and Value

Choice; its Origin: The world of industry, as we look out upon it, appears to be alive with motion, like a beehive. In the crowded harbour, the busy railroad yard, the noisy steel mill, the bustling department store, we see a ceaseless and bewildering activity. In all this movement and apparent confusion, there is, however, a large degree of order and a pretty regular succession of events which reflects a succession of choices that men are making.

These choices are not always and entirely the result of deliberate and conscious calculation. They are determined in a very great degree by habit or by instinct. Every living creature has a nervous organization of some sort-plants as well as the lowest forms of animals. This nervous organization has a pretty definite "set" or habit of response toward its environment; that is, the nerves react in certain ways to external stimuli.

The seed in moist soil germinates; it sends rootlets into the earth in search of water and of the particular soil-elements which it by nature "chooses"; it sends stock and leaf upward into the light and air, it spreads or climbs or twines according to its nature. The chick picks its way out of the shell, and then instinctively (by its inborn nature) picks at any particle it sees. It finds some objects "good" and it eats them; it finds others "bad" and it rejects them. It thus adds to its instinctive choice the choice resulting from experience.

Development of Conscious Choice: Every human being starts on his life of choice in just this way, with a fund of natural impulses, a capacity for certain instinctive reactions. The newborn child cries when hungry or uncomfortable, and it does not know in advance (the first time) what it is crying for. It is moved by mere impulse, who we say loosely that it "knows" well enough when it gets the right thing. Some food it rejects, other food it takes; and its mere impulse has now become a vague aversion or a vague desire. Very quickly it learns to associate the presence of some object with this or with that choice, and reaches for it, cries for it, giving now a very definite direction to the impulse which it feels. Feeling directed in this way upon some particular object or action is called desire. If we speak of this as a "conscious desire," we mean not that the person is reflecting on the nature of the desire, but simply that he is conscious of the presence of the thing, and that he desires it. As the child grows older, choice becomes vastly more complex, but all human choice is the development of the first simple impulsive acts. The difference in this matter between man and the animals lies in the degree to which the original fund of impulses is strengthened or weakened by experience and training, and is modified by the greater growth of forethought, imagination, and reason. As the man attains his maturity, deliberate calculation enters more and more into the making of choice. Yet the instinctive and habitual elements of choice continue to be very potent.

Tastes change with age, are trained, are influenced by custom, by example, and by suggestions of many kinds, and are given a wider range by wealth, travel, and opportunity. But choice is ruled fundamentally by impulse and by instinct; one likes what he likes; de gustibus non disputandum est. Choice develops in this way as it is directed upon each of the great classes of things with which man is surrounded; clothing, houses, furniture, horses, automobiles, books, etc. It operates also upon the actions of the man himself. He reaches out or withdraws his hand; he seeks or he shuns; he labours to make or to destroy, to possess or to get rid of. Thus the choice among one's own acts is intertwined with one's choice of things.

The Idea of Scarcity: Now we are not likely to feel a very keen desire for a particular thing unless the supply of it at our disposal is relatively limited. The air which we breathe is essential to life. But the air is all around us, and ordinarily in boundless abundance. Moreover, we breathe by reflex or automatic action of the muscles without conscious attention. The result is that we do not ordinarily feel a desire for air. But in a crowded room where there is a real scarcity of fresh air relative to our need for it, our desire for a breath of fresh air may become very keen indeed. Under such circumstances the air takes on a very different importance as an object of choice. Our impulsive actions and our thought are directed toward getting it. The diver in his diving suit must make this his first and most constant interest; the drowning man tragically feels this need.

The scarcity which we are now discussing is such a limitation in the number or quantity of objects that not all desires can be met then and there by the amount of goods available. In the numberless cases where some desires are not met or are only partially met, we are under the necessity of making a choice as to which desires shall be met. This involves a choice-and therefore a comparison-among things.

Valuation: If we choose one thing rather than another it is plain that for us the first thing has the greater importance. For one cause or another (instinct, training, experience, imagination, judgment) it weighs more in the scale of our choice than the thing which is rejected. Now in our daily life we are constantly making comparisons of this sort. A comparison of this sort between things may take the form of a mere vague preference without any exact quantitative expression of the degree to which the one thing is more important to us than the other. We prefer one object, X, to another object, Y, without attempting to express even to ourselves the exact strength of the preference. On the other hand, our valuations may and usually do take the form of definite mathematical ratios. In the early American fur trade, for example, a beaver skin came by convention to be used as a unit in terms of which the relative importance of other things (e.g., other furs, food supplies, etc.) was expressed. The other things were measured as multiples (or fractions) of the unit.

Monopoly Profits

Difficulty of Fixing the Meaning of Monopoly

The term monopoly is used loosely and in many senses. In popular discussion monopoly means almost any wealthy corporation or the power the corporation possesses, a power which is usually thought of as oppressive. Even economists have held the vaguest ideas regarding monopoly. The recent rise of trusts and monopolies has given a large new body of facts bearing upon the subject, but all the resulting discussion by the public and by economists has not brought agreement upon a definition entirely satisfactory. When usage has not settled upon any one meaning, the selection of a definition is in a measure arbitrary, though it may be guided by logic and considerations of expediency. Let us state the various meanings and indicate the one adopted in this discussion.

Monopoly is not Merely Scarcity

Monopoly should not be used as synonymous with scarcity. Scarcity is the essential condition of all value. The simplest things-bricks, sand, the commonest unskilled labour-would have no value were there not a degree of scarcity relative to the wants that may be gratified. "Monopoly," whatever else it means, always conveys the idea of some exceptional kind of scarcity, scarcity due in part to some source or cause not ordinarily present. It is a bad practice in definition to apply two words to one idea, leaving the other idea unnamed, as is done when monopoly is made synonymous with scarcity. Both words are needed.

Such a usage unfortunately is common in economic literature. Many economic writers, for example, have called land-ownership monopoly, saying that land being the work of nature cannot be increased by men, and therefore must always be scarce. Even if it were true that in the economic sense land could be produced by man, there still would be confusion here between a general class of goods and a special thing.

The fact that a particular field cannot be duplicated does not make a monopoly of land as a whole, any more than the existence of desert land in Arizona makes land valueless or a free good. Nor is a land-owner a monopolist any more than is the owner of a valuable machine. The owner of forty acres of land worth four hundred dollars, or the owner of a village lot worth a hundred dollars, can hardly be called a monopolist. It leads to absurdity to use the word monopoly with reference to landownership indiscriminately. Neither mere scarcity nor the limitation of natural stores should be called monopoly when ownership is scattered and combination between owners does not exist.

The ability of superior material agents and of skilled workers to secure higher returns than do poor ones does not constitute monopoly. The free competition assumed in abstract discussions of value, does not mean equal capacity or efficiency, but the legal freedom and personal willingness to move a productive agent into the highest industrial place it is capable of holding. The rocky field does not compete with the fertile one in the sense that it can yield the same uses. The field fit only for potatoes does not compete with those rare and favoured localities that can raise the best wines.

The gardener earning two dollars a day does not compete with the skilled physician with, an income of twenty thousand dollars a year, for he has not the economic capacity to do so; but he is free to compete (as is the owner of the rocky field) unless law, caste, class legislation, social prejudice, or some other objective factor forbids. Anything, however, that prevents the labour or capital of buyers or sellers from application for which they are fitted, defeats free competition. To use the term monopoly of any and every limitation of economic ability is to extend it to every case of value.

To use it of the high wages of skilled workmen, where no union to suppress competition exists among them, is to make it a colourless synonym of scarcity. It should be confined to a narrower and more exclusive use. Some special kinds of limitation should be connected with the idea of monopoly.

Monopoly is not Merely Superior Economic Power

Monopoly Consists in Unified Control

The limitation connected with monopoly is not that of economic capacity but that of ownership and control. The derivation of the word from the Greek points to the general thought: monos, alone, and poleo, to sell, a single seller, the sole source of supply in a given market. The term was first used in England of special grants or patents of monopoly from the crown to make or deal in specified articles, such as soap, candles, etc. The political power of the state created and defended the monopoly. This policy is pursued in a limited degree today for the encouragement of invention, in the granting of patents and copyrights. In the current definition, “The exclusive right, power, or privilege of dealing in some article or trading in some market,” the term “ dealing in “ is well chosen, for it is broad enough to cover cases of buying as well as selling, and includes power derived from political as well as from other sources. But the term “exclusive’ is too absolute, allows of no gradations, and makes the definition applicable only in the rarest cases.

Definition of Monopoly

Monopoly is such a degree of control over the supply of goods in a given market that a net gain will result to the seller if a portion is withheld. Every producer has control over some agents and some portion of the supply of products; but ordinarily the portion controlled by any one is so small that withholding it entirely from sale would not cause the market price to rise in any appreciable degree. The producer in such a case regulates his action as if the market price were fixed beyond his control, and he uses his productive agents fully up to the point where costs equal price on the marginal unit of product. A skilled worker getting five dollars a day loses that sum every day he is idle. A landowner whose land can command a competitive rent of ten dollars an acre must take that sum or less, or nothing; he cannot get more.

How can a net gain ever result from a smaller sale? As a reduction of supply results in a higher price, it is possible, as is seen in the paradox of value, for a situation to arise in the case of some goods, where a smaller number of units yield a larger sum in the market than a larger number of units. But the seller's interest lies not in the increase of total sales, but in that of net gains. Net gains, being the product of the number of units sold multiplied by the gain on each unit, increase at a much faster rate than do total sales, The existence of monopoly power in any degree depends therefore on several factors: the effect of contraction of supply in raising prices, the effect on costs, the number of units remaining in the ownership of the one contracting supply, and the possibility of preventing others from increasing supply later to profit by the higher prices.

Kinds of Monopoly

Monopoly gets its power from political, economic, and commercial sources. A political monopoly derives its power of control from a special grant from the government, forbidding others to engage in that business. The typical political monopoly is that conferred by a crown patent bestowing the exclusive right to carry on a certain business. A second kind is that conferred by a patent for invention, or the copyright on books, the object of which is to stimulate invention,, research, and writing by giving the full control and protection of the government to the inventor and writer or their assignees.

In this case the privilege is socially earned by the monopolist; it is not gotten for nothing. Moreover, the patent is limited in time, expires and becomes a social possession. A third kind is a government monopoly for purposes of revenue. In France, the government controls the tobacco trade, and the high price charged for tobacco makes the monopoly yield a large income. A fourth kind are public franchises for public service, as street-railways, lights, gas, waterworks, etc.

These are granted to private capitalists to induce them to invest capital in something which has public utility.

Economic Monopoly

Economic monopoly arises when the ownership of scarce natural agents, as mines, land, water-power, comes under the control of one man or one group of men who agree on a price. Economic monopoly is a result of private property that is undesigned by the government or by society. It is exceptional, considering the whole range of private property, but it is important. The oil-wells embracing the main sources of the world's supply have come under one control. One corporation may control so many of the richest iron-mines of the country as to be able to fix a price different from that which would result under competition. Coalmines, especially those of some peculiar and limited kind, such as anthracite, appear to become easily an object of monopolization. Economic monopoly merges into political monopolies, such as patents and franchises. Private property is a political institution designed to further social welfare, and only rarely is any particular property a monopoly. Private control of great natural resources doubtless would have been prohibited had it been foreseen.

Commercial Monopoly

Commercial monopoly, variously called contractual, organized, or capitalistic monopoly, arises where men unite their wealth to control a market, to overpower or intimidate opposition, and to keep out or limit competition by the mere Magnitude of their wealth. These various kinds so merge into each other that they cannot always be distinguished in practice. A patent may help a capitalistic monopoly in getting control of a market; great wealth may enable a company to get control of rare natural resources.

Monopolies may, for special purposes, be classified also as selling and buying, producing and trading, lasting and temporary, general and local. The terms selling and buying monopoly explain themselves, though the latter conflicts with the etymology. Under conditions of barter the selling and the buying monopoly would be the same thing in two aspects. A selling monopoly is by far the more common, but a buying monopoly may be connected with it. A large oil-refining corporation that sells most of the product may by various methods succeed in driving out the competitors who would buy the crude oil. It thus becomes practically the only outlet for the oil product, and the owners of the land thus must share their ownership with the buying monopoly by accepting, within certain limits, the price it fixes.

The Hudson Bay Company, dealing in furs, had practically this sort of power in North America. Many instances can be found, yet, relatively to the selling monopolies, those of the buying kind are rare. A producing monopoly is one controlling the manufacture or the source of supply of an article; a trading monopoly is one controlling the avenues of commerce between the source and the consumers. Monopolies are lasting or temporary, according to the duration of control. By far the larger number are of the temporary sort, because high prices strongly stimulate efforts to develop other sources of supply. Yet the average profits of a monopoly may be large throughout a succession of periods of high and low prices. Monopolies are general or local, according to the extent of territory where their power is felt. At its maximum where transportation and other costs most effectually shut out competition, monopoly power shades off to zero on the borderline of competitive territory.

Special Classes of Monopoly

Degrees of power to affect price result from varying extent of control; monopoly is a relative term. The term monopoly by its derivation has reference to a single seller; but there are other thoughts in the concept. Monopoly has reference also to the amount of the supply controlled. The frequent use of the adjectives partial, limited, and virtual are implied but usually superfluous recognitions of the relative character of monopoly. Ownership of a particular knife, pencil, book, makes one the unique seller of it, but confers no monopoly power, as the power of substitution is practically absolute; the welfare of no one depends in any appreciable measure on that, particular pencil. Ownership of an important fraction of an entire species of goods gives more power to affect value. One owning a large part of the desirable building sites or houses in town may gain by occasionally letting one stand vacant in order to drive better bargains with tenants. A trade-union may control most of the labour-supply of one kind in a town. But the test of monopoly is that a gain results from a higher price and fewer sales. It begins at the point where there is a motive to limit the supply in accordance with the paradox of value.

The control of an entire species of goods gives price-fixing power, limited only by substitution of goods. Even though one person controlled all the coal and wood in any market, their prices still would be limited. If there were but one possible source of meat-supply, most people could live without meat. The monopoly of great species of goods can thus be seen gradually to merge from one grade into another. It is a matter of quality as well as quantity. There is more or less of it in the different industries, and, as noted in the preceding paragraph, it varies over time and territory.

The Fixing of a Monopoly Price

A competitive producer gets the highest price that will permit him to dispose of his product. The enter priser seeks to get the highest price for his product that the market will afford. His ability to continue making a profit at a lower price does not induce him to reduce the price unless the reduction is to his interest. The ordinary competing manufacturer is limited in his price by two things: first, his customers may cease to buy such articles entirely and may substitute other goods if the price is too high; secondly, they may buy of other sellers. Between his wish to keep the price up, and the customer's wish to buy as cheaply as he can, the price is fixed at a point where there is no inducement for others to come in and reduce his sales, or for him to seek a better market.

There may be under these conditions a potential but very limited monopoly power. The sole druggist in a small town might occasionally get extortionate prices from particular customers in times of dire need, but he would thus drive away much of his custom, and would tempt a fairer and less grasping competitor to come in. Thus, when men and capital are free to come and go, there results an average or normal return for ability and agents of a certain grade. Prices come to equilibrium where) each is selling his total product. Where a monopoly exists to a greater or less degree, there is less reason to fear loss of custom to competitors. The degree of control determines the fear of competitors. If the control is slight, a very small rise of price will bring in competitors. The monopoly profits in this case either must be very small or they will be very brief. Those outside, controlling a large supply, will be tempted by large profits to market it at once and to increase it as fast as possible. Even where a large part of the supply is under one control, the fear of substitution puts a limit on the price demanded.

If the control were extended to all wealth, the monopolist would be the absolute despot of the lives of his fellows. But as things are, the monopolist aims, just as the competitor does, to get the price that gives the maximum gain. The monopolist, however, is in a more or less favoured position, as he can raise his price considerably before losing the most of his customers. Much depends on whether the costs increase or decrease as output grows. Where a large increase in output greatly decreases the cost, lower price may leave a larger margin between the cost and the selling price. A general monopoly price is therefore not an unlimited price. It is higher than the competitive price if the same cost of production is maintained. It may conceivably be lower than the former competitive price if the economies of combination greatly reduce the cost and justify a large increase of the output.

Discriminating Monopoly Rates

A monopoly often seeks to avoid a general market price, and it adjusts its charge in each small market separately. This is a most important aspect of the monopoly problem and a most important modification of the principle just stated. A market price is the expression of the least urgent demand that aids in carrying off a given supply. It is a maxim that there can be but one price at a time in a given market. The baker ordinarily sells the loaf at the same price to every one buying a given quantity. If he had a monopoly of the bread-supply, however, he might deal with each customer separately, ascertain, by personal inquiry into the lives of the citizens and by the aid of a force of detectives, just how much each could or would pay rather than do without bread. The policy of varying prices is thus followed by monopolies, though usually in a less inquisitorial way, to enable them to get the highest possible returns. Under the name of "charging what the traffic will bear," it is practiced by the railroads as local and personal discrimination. The endurance of some communities and of some individuals being greater than that of others, the burden is adjusted to the back, being made not as light but as heavy as each can be forced to bear.

Low Rates to Destroy Competitors

Large monopolies dealing in commodities use an adaptation of this method to kill off small competitors who, within a certain district, sell at less than the monopoly price. Prices are suddenly reduced in that community below cost until, the small competitor being ruined, the monopoly rate is re-established perhaps higher than before. Fear of suffering a like fate prevents others from attempting competition even when prices offer a great attraction and give a high monopoly profit. The profits of monopoly can be explained by the ordinary laws of value, yet evidently they form a peculiar economic and social problem. They appear to be due not to the services of the enter priser in increasing production, but to his success in limiting it. There is, therefore, an antisocial element in them not found in the profits of ordinary industry. This deserves further and closer study.

8

Cost Accounting

Financial capital can refer to money used by entrepreneurs and businesses to buy what they need to make their products or provide their services or to that sector of the economy based on its operation, i.e. retail, corporate, investment banking, etc.

Financial Capital vs. Real Capital

Financial capital or just capital in finance and accounting, refers to the funds provided by lenders (and investors) to businesses to purchase real capital equipment for producing goods/services. Real Capital or Economic Capital comprises physical goods that assist in the production of other goods and services, e.g. shovels for gravediggers, sewing machines for tailors, or machinery and tooling for factories.

Financial capital generally refers to saved-up financial wealth, especially that used to start or maintain a business. A financial concept of capital is adopted by most entities in preparing their financial reports. Under a financial concept of capital, such as invested money or invested purchasing power, capital is synonymous with the net assets or equity of the entity.

Under a physical concept of capital, such as operating capability, capital is regarded as the productive capacity of the entity based on, for example, units of output per day. Financial capital maintenance can be measured in either nominal monetary units or units of constant purchasing power.

There are thus three concepts of capital maintenance in terms of International Financial Reporting Standards (IFRS): (1) Physical capital maintenance (2) Financial capital maintenance in nominal monetary units (3) Financial capital maintenance in units of constant purchasing power.

Financial capital is provided by lenders for a price: interest. Also see time value of money for a more detailed description of how financial capital may be analysed.

Furthermore, financial capital, is any liquid medium or mechanism that represents wealth, or other styles of capital. It is, however, usually purchasing power in the form of money available for the production or purchasing of goods, etcetera. Capital can also be obtained by producing more than what is immediately required and saving the surplus. Financial capital has been subcategorised by some academics as economic or "productive capital" necessary for operations, signalling capital which signals a company's financial strength to shareholders, and regulatory capital which fulfills capital requirements.

Historical Costs

In accounting, historical costs is the original monetary value of an economic item. Historical cost is based on the stable measuring unit assumption. In some circumstances, assets and liabilities may be shown at their historical cost, as if there had been no change in value since the date of acquisition. The balance sheet value of the item may therefore differ from the "true" value.

While historical cost is criticized for its inaccuracy (deviation from "true" value), it remains in use in most accounting systems. Various corrections to historical cost are used, many of which require the use of management judgment and may be difficult to implement or verify. The trend in most accounting standards is a move to more accurate reflection of the fair or market value, although the historical cost principle remains in use, particularly for assets of little importance.

Depreciation affects the carrying value of an asset on the balance sheet. The historical cost will equal the carrying value if there has been no change recorded in the value of the asset since acquisition. Improvements may be added to the cost basis of an asset.

Historical cost does not generally reflect current market valuation. Alternative measurement bases to the historical cost measurement basis, which may be applied for some types of assets for which market values are readily available, require that the carrying value of an asset (or liability) be updated to the market price (mark-to-market valuation) or some other estimate of value that better approximates the real value.

Accounting standards may also have different methods required or allowed (even for different types of balance sheet variable real value non-monetary assets or liabilities) as to how the resultant change in value of an asset or liability is recorded, as a part of income or as a direct change to shareholders' equity. The Constant Item Purchasing Power Accounting model is an International Accounting Standards Board approved alternative basic accounting model to the traditional Historical Cost Accounting model.

Historical Cost Basis (Original Cost)

Under the historical cost basis of accounting, assets and liabilities are recorded at their values when first acquired. They are not then generally restated for changes in values.

Costs recorded in the Income Statement are based on the historical cost of items sold or used, rather than their replacement costs.

For example –

- a company acquires an asset in year 1 for $100;
- the asset is still held at the end of year 1, when its market value is $120;
- the company sells the asset in year 2 for $115.

At the end year 1 the asset is recorded in the balance sheet at cost of $100. No account is taken of the increase in value from $100 to $120 in year 1. In year 2 the company records a sale of $115. The cost of sales is $100, being the historical cost of the asset. This gives rise to a profit of $15 which is wholly recognised in year 2.

Exceptions to the Historical Cost Basis of Accounting

Revaluation of Property, Plant and Equipment

Under IFRS it is acceptable, but not required, to restate the values of property, plant and equipment to fair value. 'Fair value' is the amount for which an asset could be exchanged, or a liability settled, between knowledgeable, willing parties in an arm's length transaction. Such a policy must be applied to all assets of a particular class. It would therefore be acceptable for an entity to revalue freehold properties every three years.

The revaluations must be made with sufficient regularity to ensure that the carrying value does not differ materially from market value in subsequent years. A surplus on revaluation would be recorded as a reserve movement, not as income.

Derivative Financial Instruments

Under IFRS and US GAAP derivative financial instruments are stated at fair value ("mark to market") with movements recorded in the income statement.

Financial Reporting in Hyperinflationary Economies

IFRS requires a separate method of accounting in currencies deemed to be hyperinflationary. The characteristics of a hyperinflation include the population keeping its wealth in nonmonetary assets or relatively stable foreign currencies, prices quoted in foreign currencies or widespread indexation of prices. This might arise if cumulative inflation reaches or exceeds 100% over three years. An entity operating in a hyperinflationary economy:-

- Records a gain or loss on its 'net monetary position' in its income statement.
- Records nonmonetary items (for example, property, plant & equipment) in the balance sheet by applying indexation to their historical cost.

Management Accounting Techniques

In management accounting there are a number of techniques used as alternatives to historical cost accounting including:-

- measuring profit on sale of inventory by reference to its replacement cost. If inventory with a historical cost of $100 is sold for $115 when it costs $110 to replace it, the profit recorded would be $5 only based on replacement cost, not $15;
- charging economic rent for assets, particularly property. If a business uses a 20-year old property which it owns, depreciation on a historical cost basis might be insignificant. However, the management accounts could show a notional rent payable, being perhaps opportunity cost - the amount the business could receive if it let the property to a third party.

IASB Approved Alternative to Historical Cost Accounting

The IASB's Framework introduced Constant Item Purchasing Power Accounting as an alternative to Historical Cost Accounting in 1989 in Par. 104 (a) where it states that financial capital maintenance - not variable real value nonmonetary items, e.g. property, plant, equipment, inventory, intangible assets, etc., - can be measured in either nominal monetary units - the traditional HCA model - or in units of constant purchasing power: the CIPPA model.

The specific choice of measuring financial capital maintenance in units of constant purchasing power (the CIPPA model) at all levels of inflation and deflation as contained in the Framework for the Preparation and Presentation of Financial Statements, was approved by the International Accounting Standards Board's predecessor body, the International Accounting Standards Committee Board, in April 1989 for publication in July 1989 and adopted by the IASB in April 2001.

"In the absence of a Standard or an Interpretation that specifically applies to a transaction, management must use its judgement in developing and applying an accounting policy that results in information that is relevant and reliable. In making that judgement, IAS 8.11 requires management to consider the definitions, recognition criteria, and measurement concepts for assets, liabilities, income, and expenses in the Framework. This elevation of the importance of the Framework was added in the 2003 revisions to IAS 8."

IAS8, 11:

> *"In making the judgement, management shall refer to, and consider the applicability of, the following sources in descending order: (a) the requirements and guidance in Standards and Interpretations dealing with similar and related issues; and (b) the definitions, recognition criteria and measurement concepts for assets, liabilities, income and expenses in the Framework."*

There is no applicable International Financial Reporting Standard or Interpretation regarding the valuation of constant real value nonmonetary items, e.g. issued share capital, retained earnings, capital reserves, all other items in Shareholders Equity, trade debtors, trade creditors, deferred tax assets and liabilities, taxes payable and receivable, all other nonmonetary receivables and payables, Profit and Loss account items such as salaries, wages, rents, etc. The Framework is thus applicable.

The CIPPA model is chosen by hardly any accountant in non-hyperinflationary economies even though it would maintain the real values of constant real value nonmonetary items - e.g. issued share capital, retained income, other shareholder equity items, trade debtors, trade creditors, etc. for an unlimited period of time. This is because the CIPPA model is generally viewed by accountants as a 1970's failed inflation accounting model that requires all nonmonetary items - variable real value nonmonetary items and constant real value nonmonetary items - to be inflation-adjusted by means of the Consumer Price Index.

The IASB did not approve CIPPA in 1989 as an inflation accounting model. CIPPA by measuring financial capital maintenance in units of constant purchasing power incorporates an alternative capital concept, financial capital maintenance concept and profit determination concept to the Historical Cost capital concept, financial capital maintenance concept and profit determination concept. CIPPA only requires all constant real value nonmonetary items, e.g. issued share capital, retained income, all other items in Shareholders Equity, trade debtors, trade creditors, deferred tax assets and liabilities, taxes payable and receivable, all items in the profit and loss account, etc. to be valued in units of constant purchasing power. Variable real value nonmonetary items, e.g. property, plant, equipment, listed and unlisted shares, inventory, etc. are valued in terms of IFRS and are not required in terms of the Framework, Par. 104 (a) to be valued in units of constant purchasing power.

The IASB requires entities to implement IAS 29 which is a Constant Purchasing Power Accounting model during hyperinflation.

Advantages and Disadvantages of Historical Cost Accounting

Advantages

- Historical cost accounts are straightforward to produce
- Historical cost accounts do not record gains until they are realised
- Historical cost accounts are still used in most accounting systems.

Disadvantages

- Historical cost accounts give no indication of current values of the assets of a business
- Historical cost accounts do not record the opportunity costs of the use of older assets, particularly property which may be recorded at a value based on costs incurred many years ago
- Historical cost accounts do not measure the loss of value of monetary assets as a result of inflation.

Constant-purchasing-power accounting (CPPA) is: A consistent method of indexing accounts by means of a general index which reflects changes in the purchasing power of money. It therefore attempts to deal with the inflation problem in the sense in which this is popularly understood, as a decline in the value of the currency. It attempts to deal with this problem by converting *all* of the currency unit measurement in accounts into units at a common date by means of the index."

International Accounting Standard IAS 29 Financial Reporting in Hyperinflationary Economies is the International Accounting Standards Board's inflation accounting model under which all nonmonetary items (variable and constant real value nonmonetary items) in historical cost or current cost period-end financial statements are restated in terms of the period-end consumer price index (CPI) only during hyperinflation which the IASB describes as an exceptional circumstance.

IAS 29 does not require valuation of nonmonetary items in units of constant purchasing power on a daily basis during the accounting period. IAS 29 does not require consistent daily indexing by means of a general index which reflects daily or even hourly changes in the purchasing power of money during hyperinflation. It simply requires restatement of HC and CC period-end financial statements.

Mark-to-market

Mark-to-market or fair value accounting refers to accounting for the fair value of an asset or liability based on the current market price of the asset or liability, or for similar assets and liabilities, or based on another objectively assessed "fair" value. Fair value accounting has been a part of Generally Accepted Accounting Principles (GAAP) in the United States since the early 1990s, and has been used increasingly since then.

Mark-to-market accounting can change values on the balance sheet frequently, as market conditions change. In contrast, historical cost accounting, based on the past transactions, is simpler, more stable, and easier to perform, but does not reflect current fair value at all.

It summarizes past transactions instead. Mark-to-market accounting can become inaccurate if market prices change unpredictably. Buyers and sellers may claim a number of specific instances when this is the case, including inability to both accurately and collectively value the future income and expenses, often due to unreliable information, over-optimistic, and over-pessimistic expectations.

FAS 115

Accounting for Certain Investments in Debt and Equity Securities (Issued May 1993):

This statement addresses the accounting and reporting for investments in equity securities that have readily determinable fair values and for all investments in debt securities. Those investments are to be classified in three categories and accounted for as follows:

- Debt securities that the enterprise has the positive intent and ability to hold to maturity are classified as "held-to-maturity" securities and reported at amortized cost less impairment. (amortization refers to spreading payments over multiple periods)
- Debt and equity securities that are bought and held principally for the purpose of selling them in the near term are classified as "trading" securities and reported at fair value, with unrealised gains and losses included in earnings.
- Debt and equity securities not classified as either held-to-maturity securities or trading securities are classified as "available-for-sale" securities and reported at fair value, with unrealised gains and losses excluded from earnings and reported in a separate component of shareholders' equity (Other Comprehensive Income).

Marking-to-market a Derivatives Position

In marking-to-market a derivatives position, at predetermined periodic intervals, each counterparty exchanges the change in the market value of their position in cash. For OTC derivatives, when one counterparty defaults, the sequence of events that follows is governed by an ISDA contract.

When using models to calculate the ongoing exposure, FAS 157 requires that the entity consider the default risk ("nonperformance risk") of the counterparty and make a necessary adjustment to its calculations.

For exchange traded derivatives, if one of the counterparties defaults in this periodic exchange, that counterparty's position is immediately closed by the exchange and the clearing house is substituted for that counterparty's position. Marking-to-market virtually eliminates credit risk, but it requires the use of monitoring systems that usually only large institutions can afford.

Use by Brokers

Stock brokers allow their clients to access credit via margin accounts. These accounts allow clients to borrow funds to buy securities. Therefore, the amount of funds available is more than the value of cash (or equivalents). The credit is provided by charging a rate of interest, in a similar way as banks provide loans. Even though the value of securities (stocks or other financial instruments such as options) fluctuates in the market, the value of accounts is not calculated in real time. Marking-to-market is performed typically at the end of the trading day, and if the account value falls below a given threshold, (typically a predefined ratio by the broker), the broker issues a margin call that requires the client to deposit more funds or liquidate his account.

Hyperinflation

In economics, hyperinflation is inflation that is very high or "out of control". While the real values of the specific economic items generally stay the same in terms of relatively stable foreign currencies, in hyperinflationary conditions the general price level within a specific economy increases rapidly as the functional or internal currency, as opposed to a foreign currency, loses its real value very quickly, normally at an accelerating rate. Definitions used vary from one provided by the International Accounting Standards Board, which describes it as "a cumulative inflation rate over three years approaching 100% (26% per annum compounded for three years in a row)", to Cagan's (1956) "inflation exceeding 50% a month." As a rule of thumb, normal monthly and annual low inflation and deflation are reported per month, while under hyperinflation the general price level could rise by 5 or 10% or even much more every day.

A vicious circle is created in which more and more inflation is created with each iteration of the ever increasing money printing cycle.

Hyperinflation becomes visible when there is an unchecked increase in the money supply usually accompanied by a widespread unwillingness on the part of the local population to hold the hyperinflationary money for more than the time needed to trade it for something nonmonetary to avoid further loss of real value. Hyperinflation is often associated with wars (or their aftermath), currency meltdowns, political or social upheavals, or aggressive bidding on currency exchanges.

Characteristics

In 1956, Phillip Cagan wrote *The Monetary Dynamics of Hyperinflation*, generally regarded as the first serious study of hyperinflation and its effects. In it, he defined hyperinflation as a monthly inflation rate of at least 50%. International Accounting Standard 1 requires a presentation currency. IAS 21 provides for translations of foreign currencies into the presentation currency. IAS 29 establishes special accounting rules for use in hyperinflationary environments, and lists four factors which can trigger application of these rules:

1. The general population prefers to keep its wealth in nonmonetary assets or in a relatively stable foreign currency. Amounts of local currency held are immediately invested to maintain purchasing power.
2. The general population regards monetary amounts not in terms of the local currency but in terms of a relatively stable foreign currency. Prices may be quoted in that foreign currency.
3. Sales and purchases on credit take place at prices that are increased by an amount that will compensate for the expected loss of purchasing power during the credit period, even if the period is short.
4. Interest rates, wages and prices are linked to a price index and the cumulative inflation rate over three years approaches, or exceeds, 100%.

In its *its Exposure Draft: Severe Hyperinflation – Proposed Amendment to IFRS 1*, the IASB has requested comment on a proposed categorisation of an economy subject to severe hyperinflation as one in which the currency has both of the following characteristics: (a) a reliable general price index is not available to all entities with transactions and balances in the currency. (b) exchangeability between the currency and a relatively stable foreign currency does not exist.

Example of Hyperinflation

Angola

Angola experienced hyperinflation from 1991 to 1995. It was a result of exchange restrictions following the introduction of the novo kwanza (AON) to replace the original kwanza (AOK) in 1990. At the first months of 1991, the highest denomination was 50 000 AON. By 1994, the highest denomination was 500 000 kwanzas. In the 1995 currency reform, the readjusted kwanza (AOR) replaced the novo kwanza at the ratio of 1 000 AON to 1 AOR, but hyperinflation continued as further denominations of up to 5 000 000 AOR were issued. In the 1999 currency reform, the kwanza (AOA) was reintroduced at the ratio of 1 million AOR to 1 AOA. Currently, the highest denomination banknote is 2 000 AOA and the overall impact of hyperinflation was 1 AOA = 1 billion AOK.

Argentina

Argentina went through steady inflation from 1975 to 1991. At the beginning of 1975, the highest denomination was 1,000 pesos. In late 1976, the highest denomination was 5,000 pesos. In early 1979, the highest denomination was 10,000 pesos. By the end of 1981, the highest denomination was 1,000,000 pesos. In the 1983 currency reform, 1 peso argentino was exchanged for 10,000 pesos. In the 1985 currency reform, 1 austral was exchanged for 1,000 pesos argentinos. In the 1992 currency reform, 1 new peso was exchanged for 10,000 australes. The overall impact of hyperinflation: 1 (1992) peso = 100,000,000,000 pre-1983 pesos.

Criticism of the Official View

Ellen Brown, author of Web of Debt, admits that the left-oriented policy that Argentina had since 1947, when Juan Peron came to power, did actually create inflation. But the inflation did not become a national crisis until during the eight years that followed Peron's death in 1974. During these years the inflation rose to 206 percent, due to a "deliberate radical devaluation of the currency of the new government, along with a 175 percent increase in oil prices". This devaluation was, as she sees it, done with the hidden purpose of destabilising the economy (to create a chaos). And it was, in any case, not caused by a sudden and massive increase in the printing of money by the government. She also cites Professor Escudé who writes that this devaluation led both to "the astronomical high inflation" and "to the spread of a speculative financial system that became a hallmark of Argentina's financial life".

Austria

In 1922, inflation in Austria reached 1426%, and from 1914 to January 1923, the consumer price index rose by a factor of 11836, with the highest banknote in denominations of 500,000 krones.

Belarus

Belarus experienced steady inflation from 1994 to 2002. In 1993, the highest denomination was 5,000 rublei. By 1999, it was 5,000,000 rublei. In the 2000 currency reform, the ruble was replaced by the new ruble at an exchange rate of 1 new ruble = 1,000 old rublei. The highest denomination in 2008 was 100,000 rublei, equal to 100,000,000 pre-2000 rublei.

Bolivia

Bolivia experienced its worst inflation between 1984 and 1986. Before 1984, the highest denomination was 1,000 pesos bolivianos. By 1985, the highest denomination was 10 Million pesos bolivianos. In 1985, a Bolivian note for 1 million pesos was worth 55 cents in US dollars, one-thousandth of its exchange value of $5,000 less than three years previously. In the 1987 currency reform, the Peso Boliviano was replaced by the Boliviano at a rate of 1,000,000 : 1.

Bosnia and Herzegovina

Bosnia and Herzegovina went through its worst inflation in 1993. In 1992, the highest denomination was 1,000 dinara. By 1993, the highest denomination was 100,000,000 dinara. In the Republika Srpska, the highest denomination was 10,000 dinara in 1992 and 10,000,000,000 dinara in 1993. 50,000,000,000 dinara notes were also printed in 1993 but never issued.

Brazil

From 1967–1994, the base currency unit was shifted seven times to adjust for inflation in the final years of the Brazilian military dictatorship era. A 1967 cruzeiro was, in 1994, worth less than one trillionth of a US cent, after adjusting for multiple devaluations and note changes. In that same year, inflation reached a record 2,075.8%. A new currency called real was adopted in 1994, and hyperinflation was eventually brought under control. The *real* was also the currency in use until 1942; 1 (current) real is the equivalent of 2,750,000,000,000,000,000 of Brazil's first currency (called *réis* in Portuguese).

Bulgaria

In 1996, the Bulgarian economy collapsed due to the slow and mismanaged economic reforms of several governments in a row, shortages of wheat, and an unstable and decentralised banking system, which led to an inflation rate of 311% and the collapse of the lev, with the exchange rate to dollars reaching 3000. When pro-reform forces came into power in the spring 1997, an ambitious economic reform package, including introduction of a currency board regime and pegging the Bulgarian Lev to the German Deutsche Mark (and consequently to the euro), was agreed to with the International Monetary Fund and the World Bank, and the economy began to stabilize.

China

As the first user of fiat currency, China has had an early history of troubles caused by hyperinflation. The Yuan Dynasty printed huge amounts of fiat paper money to fund their wars, and the resulting hyperinflation, coupled with other factors, led to its demise at the hands of a revolution. The Republic of China went through the worst inflation 1948–49. In 1947, the highest denomination was 50,000 yuan. By mid-1948, the highest denomination was 180,000,000 yuan. The 1948 currency reform replaced the yuan by the gold yuan at an exchange rate of 1 gold yuan = 3,000,000 yuan. In less than a year, the highest denomination was 10,000,000 gold yuan. In the final days of the civil war, the Silver Yuan was briefly introduced at the rate of 500,000,000 Gold Yuan. Meanwhile the highest denomination issued by a regional bank was 6,000,000,000 yuan (issued by Xinjiang Provincial Bank in 1949). After the renminbi was instituted by the new communist government, hyperinflation ceased with a revaluation of 1:10,000 old Renminbi in 1955. The overall impact of inflation was 1 Renminbi = 15,000,000,000,000,000,000 pre-1948 yuan.

Free City of Danzig

Danzig went through its worst inflation in 1923. In 1922, the highest denomination was 1,000 Mark. By 1923, the highest denomination was 10,000,000,000 Mark.

Georgia

Georgia went through its worst inflation in 1994. In 1993, the highest denomination was 100,000 coupons [kuponi]. By 1994, the highest denomination was 1,000,000 coupons. In the 1995 currency reform, a new currency, the lari, was introduced with 1 lari exchanged for 1,000,000 coupons.

Germany

Germany went through its worst inflation in 1923. In 1922, the highest denomination was 50,000 Mark. By 1923, the highest denomination was 100,000,000,000,000 Mark. In December 1923 the exchange rate was 4,200,000,000,000 Marks to 1 US dollar. In 1923, the rate of inflation hit 3.25×10^6 percent per month (prices double every two days). Beginning on 20 November 1923, 1,000,000,000,000 old Marks were exchanged for 1 Rentenmark so that 4.2 Rentenmarks were worth 1 US dollar, exactly the same rate the Mark had in 1914.

Greece

Greece went through its worst inflation in 1944. In 1942, the highest denomination was 50,000 drachmai. By 1944, the highest denomination was 100,000,000,000 drachmai. In the 1944 currency reform, 1 new drachma was exchanged for 50,000,000,000 drachmai. Another currency reform in 1953 replaced the drachma at an exchange rate of 1 new drachma = 1,000 old drachmai.

The overall impact of hyperinflation: 1 (1953) drachma = 50,000,000,000,000 pre 1944 drachmai. The Greek monthly inflation rate reached 8.5 billion percent in October 1944.

Hungary, 1922–24

The Treaty of Trianon and political instability between 1919 and 1924 led to a major inflation of Hungary's currency. Unable to tax adequately, the government resorted to printing money and by 1922 inflation in Hungary had reached 98% per month.

Hungary, 1945–46

Hungary went through the worst inflation ever recorded between the end of 1945 and July 1946. In 1944, the highest denomination was 1,000 pengõ. By the end of 1945, it was 10,000,000 pengõ. The highest denomination in mid-1946 was 100,000,000,000,000,000,000 pengõ. A special currency the adópengõ – or tax pengõ – was created for tax and postal payments. The value of the adópengõ was adjusted each day, by radio announcement. On 1 January 1946 one adópengõ equalled one pengõ.

By late July, one adópengõ equalled 2,000,000,000,000,000,000,000 or 2×10^{21} pengõ. When the pengõ was replaced in August 1946 by the forint, the total value of all Hungarian banknotes in circulation amounted to $^{1}/_{1,000}$ of one US dollar.

It is the most severe known incident of inflation recorded, peaking at 1.3×10^{16} percent per month (prices double every 15 hours). The overall impact of hyperinflation: On 18 August 1946, 400,000,000,000,000,000,000,000,000,000 or 4×10^{29} (four hundred octillion (short scale)) pengõ became 1 forint.

Some historians believe that this hyperinflation was purposely started by trained Russian Marxists in order to destroy the Hungarian middle and upper classes.

Israel

Inflation accelerated in the 1970s, rising steadily from 13% in 1971 to 111% in 1979. From 133% in 1980, it leaped to 191% in 1983 and then to 445% in 1984, threatening to become a four-digit figure within a year or two. In 1985 Israel froze most prices by law and enacted other measures as part of an economic stabilisation plan. That same year, inflation more than halved, to 185%. Within a few months, the authorities began to lift the price freeze on some items; in other cases it took almost a year. By 1986, inflation was down to 19%.

Krajina

The Republic of Serbian Krajina went through its worst inflation in 1993. In 1992, the highest denomination was 50,000 dinara. By 1993, the highest denomination was 50,000,000,000 dinara. Note that this unrecognised country was reincorporated into Croatia in 1995.

Mexico

In spite of the Oil Crisis of the late 1970s (Mexico is a producer and exporter), and due to excessive social spending, Mexico defaulted on its external debt in 1982. As a result, the country suffered a severe case of capital flight and several years of hyperinflation and peso devaluation. On 1 January 1993, Mexico created a new currency, the nuevo peso ("new peso", or MXN), which chopped 3 zeros off the old peso, an inflation rate of 10,000% over the several years of the crisis. (One new peso was equal to 1000 of the obsolete MXP pesos).

North Korea, 1947–2009

Though the North Korean Won never technically failed, and is still the official currency of the reclusive communist nation, a 2009 revaluation showed the rest of the world rare cracks in the monolithic image Pyongyang presents.

The government gave citizens seven days to turn in their old won for new won – with 1,000 of the old worth 10 of the new – but allowed a maximum exchange of 150,000 of the old won. That means each adult can exchange about US$740-worth of won. The revaluation and exchange cap wiped out the savings of many North Koreans, and reportedly caused unrest in parts of the country. According to a September 2009 BBC report, some department stores in Pyongyang even stopped accepting North Korean won, instead insisting upon payment in U.S. dollars or Japanese yen.

Nicaragua

Nicaragua went through the worst inflation from 1987 to 1990. From 1943 to April 1971, one US dollar equalled 7 córdobas. From April 1971-early 1978, one US dollar was worth 10 córdobas. In early 1986, the highest denomination was 10,000 córdobas. By 1987, it was 1,000,000 córdobas. In the 1988 currency reform, 1 new córdoba was exchanged for 10,000 old córdobas. The highest denomination in 1990 was 100,000,000 new córdobas. In the 1991 currency reform, 1 new córdoba was exchanged for 5,000,000 old córdobas. The overall impact of hyperinflation: 1 (1991) córdoba = 50,000,000,000 pre-1988 córdobas.

Peru

Peru experienced its worst inflation from 1988–1990. In the 1985 currency reform, 1 inti was exchanged for 1,000 soles. In 1986, the highest denomination was 1,000 intis. But in September 1988, monthly inflation went to 132%. In August 1990, monthly inflation was 397%. The highest denomination was 5,000,000 intis by 1991. In the 1991 currency reform, 1 nuevo sol was exchanged for 1,000,000 intis. The overall impact of hyperinflation: 1 nuevo sol = 1,000,000,000 (old) soles.

Philippines

The Japanese government occupying the Philippines during the World War II issued fiat currencies for general circulation. The Japanese-sponsored Second Philippine Republic government led by Jose P. Laurel at the same time outlawed possession of other currencies, most especially "guerilla money." The fiat money was dubbed "Mickey Mouse Money" because it is similar to play money and is next to worthless. Survivors of the war often tell tales of bringing suitcase or*bayong* (native bags made of woven coconut or buri leaf strips) overflowing with Japanese-issued bills. In the early times, 75 Mickey Mouse pesos could buy one duck egg. In 1944, a box of matches cost more than 100 Mickey Mouse pesos.

In 1942, the highest denomination available was 10 pesos. Before the end of the war, because of inflation, the Japanese government was forced to issue 100, 500 and 1000 peso notes.

Poland, 1921–1924

After Poland's independence in 1918, the country soon began experiencing extreme inflation. By 1921, prices had already risen 251 times above those of 1914, but in the following three years they rose by 988,223% with a peak rate in late 1923 of prices doubling every nineteen and a half days. At independence there was 8 marek per US dollar, but by 1923 the exchange rate was 6,375,000 marek (mkp) for 1 US dollar. The highest denomination was 10,000,000 mkp. In the 1924 currency reform there was a new currency introduced: 1 zloty = 1,800,000 mkp.

Poland, 1989–1991

Poland experienced a second hyperinflation between 1989 and 1991. The highest denomination in 1989 was 200,000 zlotych. It was 1,000,000 zlotych in 1991 and 2,000,000 zlotych in 1992; the exchange rate was 9500 zlotych for 1 US dollar in January 1990 and 19600 zlotych at the end of August 1992. In the 1994 currency reform, 1 new zloty was exchanged for 10,000 old zlotych and 1 US$ exchange rate was ca. 2.5 zlotych (new).

Republika Srpska

Republika Srpska was a breakaway region of Bosnia. As with Krajina, it pegged its currency, the Republika Srpska dinar, to that of Yugoslavia. Their bills were almost the same as Krajina's, but they issued fewer and did not issue currency after 1993.

Romania

Romania experienced hyperinflation in the 1990s. The highest denomination in 1990 was 100 lei and in 1998 was 100,000 lei. By 2000 it was 500,000 lei. In early 2005 it was 1,000,000 lei. In July 2005 the leu was replaced by the new leu at 10,000 old lei = 1 new leu. Inflation in 2005 was 9%. In July 2005 the highest denomination became 500 lei (= 5,000,000 old lei).

Soviet Union/Russian Federation

Between 1921 and 1922, inflation in the Soviet Union reached 213%. In 1992, the first year of post-Soviet economic reform, inflation was 2,520%. In 1993, the annual rate was 840%, and in 1994, 224%. The ruble devalued from about 40 r/$ in 1991 to about 5,000 r/$ in late 1997. In 1998, a denominated ruble was introduced at the exchange rate of 1 new ruble = 1,000 pre-1998 rubles. In the second half of the same year, ruble fell to about 30 r/$ as a result of financial crisis.

Taiwan

As the Chinese Civil War reached its peak, Taiwan also suffered from the hyperinflation that has ravaged China in late 1940s. Highest denomination issued was a 1,000,000 Dollar Bearer's Cheque. Inflation was finally brought under control at introduction of New Taiwan Dollar in 15 June 1949 at rate of 40,000 old Dollar = 1 New Dollar

Ukraine

Ukraine experienced its worst inflation between 1993 and 1995. In 1992, the Ukrainian karbovanets was introduced, which was exchanged with the defunct Soviet ruble at a rate of 1 UAK = 1 SUR. Before 1993, the highest denomination was 1,000 karbovantsiv. By 1995, it was 1,000,000 karbovantsiv. In 1996, during the transition to the Hryvnya and the subsequent phase out of the karbovanets, the exchange rate was 100,000 UAK = 1 UAH. This translates to a hyperinflation rate of approximately 1,400% per month. By some estimates, inflation for the entire calendar year of 1993 was 10,000% or higher, with retail prices reaching over 100 times their pre-1993 level by the end of the year.

United States

During the Revolutionary War, when the Continental Congress authorised the printing of paper currency called continental currency. The monthly inflation rate reached a peak of 47 percent in November 1779 (Bernholz 2003: 48). These notes depreciated rapidly, giving rise to the expression "not worth a continental."

A second close encounter occurred during the U.S. Civil War, between January 1861 and April 1865, the Lerner Commodity Price Index of leading cities in the eastern Confederacy states increased from 100 to over 9,000. As the Civil War dragged on, the Confederate dollar had less and less value, until it was almost worthless by the last few months of the war. Similarly, the Union government inflated its greenbacks, with the monthly rate peaking at 40 percent in March 1864 (Bernholz 2003: 107).

Yugoslavia

Yugoslavia went through a period of hyperinflation and subsequent currency reforms from 1989–1994. The highest denomination in 1988 was 50,000 dinars. By 1989 it was 2,000,000 dinars. In the 1990 currency reform, 1 new dinar was exchanged for 10,000 old dinars. In the 1992 currency reform, 1 new dinar was exchanged for 10 old dinars. The highest denomination in 1992 was 50,000 dinars. By 1993, it was 10,000,000,000 dinars. In the 1993 currency reform, 1 new dinar was exchanged for 1,000,000 old dinars. However, before the year was over, the highest denomination was 500,000,000,000 dinars. In the 1994 currency reform, 1 new dinar was exchanged for

1,000,000,000 old dinars. In another currency reform a month later, 1 novi dinar was exchanged for 13 million dinars (1 novi dinar = 1German mark at the time of exchange). The overall impact of hyperinflation: 1 novi dinar = 1×10^{27}~1.3×10^{27} pre 1990 dinars. Yugoslavia's rate of inflation hit 5×10^{15} percent cumulative inflation over the time period 1 October 1993 and 24 January 1994.

Zaire (Now the Democratic Republic of the Congo)

Zaire went through a period of inflation between 1989 and 1996. In 1988, the highest denomination was 5,000 zaires. By 1992, it was 5,000,000 zaires. In the 1993 currency reform, 1 nouveau zaire was exchanged for 3,000,000 old zaires. The highest denomination in 1996 was 1,000,000 nouveaux zaires. In 1997, Zaire was renamed the Congo Democratic Republic and changed its currency to francs. 1 franc was exchanged for 100,000 nouveaux zaires. The overall impact of hyperinflation: 1 franc = 3×10^{11} pre 1989 zaires.

Zimbabwe

Hyperinflation in Zimbabwe was one of the few instances that resulted in the abandonment of the local currency. At independence in 1980, the Zimbabwe dollar (ZWD) was worth about USD 1.25. Afterwards, however, rampant inflation and the collapse of the economy severely devalued the currency.

Inflation was steady before Robert Mugabe in 1998 began a program of land reforms that primarily focused on taking land from white farmers and redistributing those properties and assets to black farmers, which sent food production and revenues from export of food plummeting. The result was that to pay its expenditures Mugabe's government and Gideon Gono's Reserve Bank printed more and more notes with higher face values.

Hyperinflation began early in the twenty-first century, reaching 624% in 2004. It fell back to low triple digits before surging to a new high of 1,730% in 2006. The Reserve Bank of Zimbabwe revalued on 1 August 2006 at a ratio of 1 000 ZWD to each second dollar (ZWN), but year-to-year inflation rose by June 2007 to 11,000% (versus an earlier estimate of 9,000%). Larger denominations were progressively issued:

1. 5 May: banknotes or "bearer cheques" for the value of ZWN 100 million and ZWN 250 million.
2. 15 May: new bearer cheques with a value of ZWN 500 million (then equivalent to about USD 2.50).

3. 20 May: a new series of notes ("agro cheques") in denominations of \$5 billion, \$25 billion and \$50 billion.
4. 21 July: "agro cheque" for \$100 billion.

Inflation by 16 July officially surged to 2,200,000% with some analysts estimating figures surpassing 9,000,000 percent. As of 22 July 2008 the value of the ZWN fell to approximately 688 billion per 1 USD, or 688 trillion pre-August 2006 Zimbabwean dollars.

Date of redenomination	*Currencycode*	*Value*
1 Aug 2006	ZWN	1 000 ZWD
1 Aug 2008	ZWR	10^{10} ZWN= 10^{13} ZWD
2 Feb 2009	ZWL	10^{12} ZWR= 10^{22} ZWN= 10^{25} ZWD

On 1 August 2008, the Zimbabwe dollar was redenominated at the ratio of 10^{10} ZWN to each third dollar (ZWR). On 19 August 2008, official figures announced for June estimated the inflation over 11,250,000%. Zimbabwe's annual inflation was 231,000,000% in July (prices doubling every 17.3 days).

For periods after July 2008, no official inflation statistics were released. Prof. Steve H. Hanke overcame the problem by estimating inflation rates after July 2008 and publishing the Hanke Hyperinflation Index for Zimbabwe.

Prof. Hanke's HHIZ measure indicated that the inflation peaked at an annual rate of 89.7 sextillion percent (89,700,000,000,000,000,000,000%) in mid-November 2008. The peak monthly rate was 79.6 billion percent, which is equivalent to a 98% daily rate, or around 7×10^{108} percent yearly rate. At that rate, prices were doubling every 24.7 hours. Note that many of these figures should be considered mostly theoretic, since the hyperinflation did not proceed at that rate a whole year.

At its November 2008 peak, Zimbabwe's rate of inflation approached, but failed to surpass, Hungary's July 1946 world record.

On 2 February 2009, the dollar was redenominated for the fourth time at the ratio of 10^{12} ZWR to 1 ZWL, only three weeks after the \$100 trillion banknote was issued on 16 January, but hyperinflation waned by then as official inflation rates in USD were announced and foreign transactions were legalised, and on 12 April the dollar was abandoned in favour of using only foreign currencies.

The overall impact of hyperinflation was 1 ZWL = 10^{25} ZWD.

Computerised Transaction Issues

Western Europe, North America and many parts of Asia and Australasia have economies that depend heavily on computerised transaction procession of money transfers. However, most nations that are subject to hyperinflation risk have not done assessments as to the ability of the electronic part of the finance system to remain intact under hyperinflation.

It is assumed (based upon IT practices for transnational processing that have evolved since the 1970s) that most money held by banks is not represented by 64 bit floating numbers. Under hyperinflation conditions most bank processing systems could fail due to overflow conditions.

Chronic Inflation

Chronic inflation occurs when a country experiences high inflation for a prolonged period of time (several years or decades) due to undue expansion or increase of the money supply. In countries with chronic inflation, inflation expectations become 'built-in', and it becomes extremely difficult to reduce the inflation rate.

Occurrence and Causes

Even more so than hyperinflation, chronic inflation is a twentieth-century phenomenon, being first observed by Felipe Pazos in 1972. High inflation can only be sustained with unbacked paper currencies over long periods, and before World War II unbacked paper currencies were rare except in countries affected by war - which often produced extremely high inflation but never for more than a few years. Most economists believe chronic inflation first emerged in Latin America following World War II, with the result that it was originally called "Latin inflation". Some economists, however, argue that the experience of France in the 1920s was the first case of chronic inflation. Japan in the years surrounding World War II is another case with characteristics very akin to well-studied cases of chronic inflation.

Early observers from the 1960s and 1970s attributed the ultimate political cause of chronic inflation as powerful group interests with radically divergent policy demands, arguing that the power of labour unions to demand high wages for workers in frequently outdated economic sectors conflicted with the basically feudal political structures of affected countries. Under these conditions, a return to a commodity money that would curb inflation quickly is politically suicidal, with the result that governments affected by chronic inflation have invariably had to resort to more subtle methods of reducing inflation, such as central bank reforms or indexing price and wage levels to the future value of money. This, however, leads to *inflation inertia* and ultimately to a public that becomes sceptical of attempts to reduce inflation: unlike hyperinflation, history has shown that it is possible for communities to live with chronic inflation relatively easily.

Other sources have argued that chronic inflation is caused by governments seeking to optimise seignorage taxes in order to pay most efficiently for public programmes, or because the societies in which it developed have consistently imported more than they can export and their currencies have had to devalue consistently to make their imports more expensive without elasticity being sufficient to reduce demand. There have on this line also been arguments for demographic causes of chronic inflation as resulting from populations growing more rapidly than production in developing nations from the 1950s to the 1980s, and until today in sub-Saharan Africa.

War, Invasion and National Emergency

When dollars were fully convertible into gold via the gold standard, both were regarded as money. However, most people preferred to carry around paper banknotes rather than the somewhat heavier and less divisible gold coins.

If people feared their bank would fail, a bank run might result. This happened in the USA during the Great Depression of the 1930s, leading President Roosevelt to impose a national emergency and issue Executive Order 6102 outlawing the "hoarding" of gold by US citizens.

There was only one prosecution under the order, and in that case the order was ruled invalid by federal judge John M. Woolsey, on the technical grounds that the order was signed by the President, not the Secretary of the Treasury as required.

In times of war people fear that their assets may be seized and that the currency may become worthless. They see gold as a solid asset which will always buy food or transportation. Thus in times of great uncertainty, particularly when war is feared, the demand for gold rises.

Investment Vehicles

Bars

The most traditional way of investing in gold is by buying bullion gold bars. In some countries, like Canada, Argentina, Austria,

Liechtenstein and Switzerland, these can easily be bought or sold at the major banks. Alternatively, there are bullion dealers that provide the same service. Bars are available in various sizes. For example in Europe, Good Delivery bars are approximately 400 troy ounces (12 kg). 1 kilogram (32 ozt) are also popular, although many other weights exist, such as the 10oz, 1oz, 10 g, 100 g, 1 kg, 1 Tael, and 1 Tola.

Bars generally carry lower price premiums than gold bullion coins. However larger bars carry an increased risk of forgery due to their less stringent parameters for appearance. While bullion coins can be easily weighed and measured against known values, most bars cannot, and gold buyers often have bars re-assayed. Larger bars also have a greater volume in which to create a partial forgery using a tungsten-filled cavity, which may not be revealed by an assay.

One way of avoiding such a scam is to buy and hold gold bars that are held within the LBMA "chain of custody" and store the gold in a LBMA recognised vault. The gold bullion held within the LBMA recognised vaults can be bought and sold easily. If it is removed from the vaults and stored outside of the chain of integrity, for example stored at home or in a private vault, the bar will have to be re-assayed before it can be returned to the LBMA chain. This process is described under the LBMA's "Good Delivery Rules".

The LBMA includes in this "traceable chain of custody" refiners as well as vaults. Both have to meet their strict guidelines. Bullion products from these trusted refiners are traded at face value by LBMA members without assay testing. By buying bullion from an LBMA member dealer and storing it in an LBMA recognised vault, customers avoid the need of re-assaying or the inconvenience in time and expense it would cost.

Efforts to combat gold bar counterfeiting include kinebars which employ a unique holographic technology and are manufactured by the Argor-Heraeus refinery in Switzerland.

Coins

Gold coins are a common way of owning gold. Bullion coins are priced according to their fine weight, plus a small premium based on supply and demand (as opposed to numismatic gold coins which are priced mainly by supply and demand based on rarity and condition).

The Krugerrand is the most widely-held gold bullion coin, with 46,000,000 troy ounces (1,400 tonnes) in circulation. Other common gold bullion coins include the Australian Gold Nugget (Kangaroo),

Austrian Philharmoniker (Philharmonic), Austrian 100 Corona, Canadian Gold Maple Leaf, Chinese Gold Panda, Malaysian Kijang Emas, French Napoleon or Louis d'Or, Mexican Gold 50 Peso, British Sovereign, American Gold Eagle, and American Buffalo.

Coins may be purchased from a variety of dealers both large and small. Fake gold coins are not uncommon, and are usually made of gold-plated lead.

Exchange-traded Products (ETPs)

Gold exchange-traded products may include ETFs, ETNs, and CEFs which are traded like shares on the major stock exchanges. The first gold ETF, Gold Bullion Securities (ticker symbol "GOLD"), was launched in March 2003 on the Australian Stock Exchange, and originally represented exactly 0.1 troy ounces (3.1 g) of gold. As of November 2010, SPDR Gold Shares is the second-largest exchange-traded fund (ETF) in the world bymarket capitalisation.

Gold ETPs represent an easy way to gain exposure to the gold price, without the inconvenience of storing physical bars. However exchange-traded gold instruments, even those which hold physical gold for the benefit of the investor, carry risks beyond those inherent in the precious metal itself. For example the most popular gold ETP (GLD) has been widely criticized, and even compared with mortgage-backed securities, due to features of its complex structure.

Typically a small commission is charged for trading in gold ETPs and a small annual storage fee is charged. The annual expenses of the fund such as storage, insurance, and management fees are charged by selling a small amount of gold represented by each certificate, so the amount of gold in each certificate will gradually decline over time.

Exchange-traded funds, or ETFs, are investment companies that are legally classified as open-end companies or Unit Investment Trusts (UITs), but that differ from traditional open-end companies and UITs. The main differences are that ETFs do not sell directly to investors and they issue their shares in what are called "Creation Units" (large blocks such as blocks of 50,000 shares). Also, the Creation Units may not be purchased with cash but a basket of securities that mirrors the ETF's portfolio. Usually, the Creation Units are split up and resold on a secondary market.

ETF shares can be sold in basically two ways. The investors can sell the individual shares to other investors, or they can sell the Creation Units back to the ETF. In addition, ETFs generally redeem

Creation Units by giving investors the securities that comprise the portfolio instead of cash. Because of the limited redeemability of ETF shares, ETFs are not considered to be and may not call themselves mutual funds.

Derivatives, CFDs and Spread Betting

Derivatives, such as gold forwards, futures and options, currently trade on various exchanges around the world and over-the-counter (OTC) directly in the private market. In the U.S., gold futures are primarily traded on the New York Commodities Exchange (COMEX) and Euronext liffe. In India, gold futures are traded on the National Commodity and Derivatives Exchange (NCDEX) and Multi Commodity Exchange (MCX).

The product symbol for gold futures is GC, and it is traded in a standard contract size of 100 troy ounces. CME Globex, CME ClearPort (CME Group) and Open Outcry (New York) are the primary futures exchange venues through which it is traded. The minimum fluctuation allowed in price is $0.10 per troy ounce, and it is held to a minimum of 995 fineness quality specification.

As of 2009 holders of COMEX gold futures have experienced problems taking delivery of their metal. Along with chronic delivery delays, some investors have received delivery of bars not matching their contract in serial number and weight. The delays cannot be easily explained by slow warehouse movements, as the daily reports of these movements show little activity. Because of these problems, there are concerns that COMEX may not have the gold inventory to back its existing warehouse receipts.

Firms such as Cantor Index, CMC Markets, IG Index and City Index, all from the UK, provide contract for difference (CFD) or spread bets on the price of gold.

Investment Strategies

Fundamental Analysis

Investors using fundamental analysis analyse the macroeconomic situation, which includes international economic indicators, such as GDP growth rates, inflation, interest rates, productivity and energy prices. They would also analyse the yearly global gold supply versus demand. Over 2005 the World Gold Council estimated yearly global gold supply to be 3,859 tonnes and demand to be 3,754 tonnes, giving a surplus of 105 tonnes. While gold production is unlikely to change in the near future, supply and demand due to private ownership is highly liquid and subject to rapid changes. This makes gold very different from almost every other commodity. Identifiable investment demand for gold, which includes gold exchange-traded funds, bars and coins, was up 64 percent in 2008 over the year before.

Gold versus Stocks

In the last century major economic crises (such as the Great Depression, World War II, the first and second oil crisis) lowered the Dow/gold ratio, an indicator of how bad a recession is and whether the outlook is deteriorating or improving, to a value well below 4. The ratio fell on February 18, 2009 to below 8. During these difficult times, many investors tried to preserve their assets by investing in precious metals, most notably gold and silver.

The performance of gold bullion is often compared to stocks due to their fundamental differences. Gold is regarded by some as a store of value (without growth) whereas stocks are regarded as a return on value (i.e., growth from anticipated real price increase plus dividends). Stocks and bonds perform best in a stable political climate with strong property rights and little turmoil. The attached graph shows the value of Dow Jones Industrial Average divided by the price of an ounce of gold. Since 1800, stocks have consistently gained value in comparison to gold in part because of the stability of the American political system. This appreciation has been cyclical with long periods of stock-out performance followed by long periods of gold-out performance. The Dow Industrials bottomed out a ratio of 1:1 with gold during 1980 (the end of the 1970s bear market) and proceeded to post gains throughout the 1980s and 1990s. The gold price peak of 1980 also coincided with the Soviet Union's invasion of Afghanistan and the threat of the global expansion of communism. The ratio peaked on January 14, 2000 a value of 41.3 and has fallen sharply since.

On November 30, 2005 Rick Munarriz of The Motley Fool posed the question of which represented a better investment: a share of Google or an ounce of gold. The specific comparison between these two very different investments seems to have captured the imagination of many in the investment community and is serving to crystallize the broader debate. At the time of writing, a share of Google's stock was $405 and an ounce of gold was one day from breaking the $500 barrier, which it did December 1. On January 4, 2008 23:58 New York Times, it was reported that an ounce of gold outpaced the share price of Google by 30.77%, with gold closing at $859.19 per ounce and a share of Google closing at $657 on U.S. market exchanges. On January 24, 2008, the gold price broke the $900 mark per ounce for the first time. The price of gold topped $1,000 an ounce for the first time ever on March 13, 2008 amid recession fears in the United States. Google closed 2008 at $307.65 while gold closed the year at $866. Leading into 2010, Google had doubled off that (100%), whereas gold had risen 40%.

The analysis of log-linear oscillations in the gold price dynamics for 2003–2010 conducted recently by Askar Akayev's research group has allowed them to forecast a collapse in gold prices in May – July 2011. As of 18 July 2011, this collapse had not yet occurred, with gold at record prices of over $1600 per ounce.

In his book *Basic Economics*, Thomas Sowell argued that, in the long-term, gold does not hold its value compared to stocks and bonds: To take an extreme example, while a dollar invested in bonds in 1801 would be worth nearly a thousand dollars by 1998, a dollar invested in stocks that same year would be worth more than half a million dollars. All this is in real terms, taking inflation into account. Meanwhile, a dollar invested in gold in 1801 would by 1998 be worth just 78 cents.

Technical Analysis

As with stocks, gold investors may base their investment decision partly on, or solely on, technical analysis. Typically, this involves analysing chart patterns, moving averages, market trends and/or the economic cycle in order to speculate on the future price.

Using Leverage

Bullish investors may choose to leverage their position by borrowing money against their existing assets and then purchasing gold on account with the loaned funds. Leverage is also an integral part of buying gold derivatives and unhedgedgold mining company shares. Leverage or derivatives may increase investment gains but also increases the corresponding risk of capital loss if/when the trend reverses.

Taxation

Gold maintains a special position in the market with many tax regimes. For example, in the European Union the trading of recognised gold coins and bullion products are free of VAT. Silver, and other precious metals or commodities, do not have the same allowance. Other taxes such as capital gains tax may also apply for individuals depending on their tax residency. U.S. citizens may be taxed on their gold profits at 15, 23, 28 or 35 percent, depending on the investment vehicle used.

Inflation Accounting

Inflation accounting is a term describing a range of accounting systems designed to correct problems arising from historical cost accounting in the presence of inflation. Inflation accounting is used in countries experiencing high inflation or hyperinflation. For example, in countries experiencing hyperinflation the International Accounting Standards Board requires corporate financial statements to be adjusted for changes in purchasing power using a price index.

Misleading Reporting under Historical Cost Accounting

"In most countries, primary financial statements are prepared on the historical cost basis of accounting without regard either to changes in the general level of prices or to increases in specific prices of assets held, except to the extent that property, plant and equipment and investments may be revalued."

Ignoring general price level changes in financial reporting creates distortions in financial statements such as

- reported profits may exceed the earnings that could be distributed to shareholders without impairing the company's ongoing operations
- the asset values for inventory, equipment and plant do not reflect their economic value to the business
- future earnings are not easily projected from historical earnings
- the impact of price changes on monetary assets and liabilities is not clear
- future capital needs are difficult to forecast and may lead to increased leverage, which increases the business's risk
- when real economic performance is distorted, these distortions lead to social and political consequenses that damage businesses (examples: poor tax policies and public misconceptions regarding corporate behaviour)

Inflation Accounting Inflation Accounting is a system of accounting which, unlike historical cost accounting, takes into account changing prices.

Income Statement General Price-level Adjustment Example

On the income statement, depreciation is adjusted for changes in general price levels based on a general price index.

	2001	*2002*	*2003*	*Total*
Revenue	33,000	36,302	39,931	109,233
Depreciation	30,000	31,500 (a)	33,000 (b)	94,500
Operating income	3,000	4,802	6,931	14,733
Purchasing power loss	-	1,500 (c)	3,000 (d)	4,500
Net income	3,000	3,302	3,931	10,233

(a) 30,000 x 105/100 = 31,500

(b) 30,000 x 110/100 = 33,000

(c) (30,000 x 105/100) - 30,000 = 1,500

(d) (63,000 x 110/105) - 63,000 = 3,000

Constant Dollar Accounting

Constant dollar accounting is an accounting model that converts nonmonetary assets and equities from historical dollars to current dollars using a general price index. This is similar to a currency conversion from old dollars to new dollars. Monetary items are not adjusted, so they gain or lose purchasing power. There are no holding gains or losses recognised in converting values.

International Standard for Hyperinflationary Accounting

The International Accounting Standards Board defines hyperinflation in IAS 29 as: "the cumulative inflation rate over three years is approaching, or exceeds, 100%."

Companies are required to restate their historical cost financial reports in terms of the period end hyperinflation rate in order to make these financial reports more meaningful.

The restatement of historical cost financial statements in terms of IAS 29 does not signify the abolishment of the historical cost model. This is confirmed by Pricewaterhouse Coopers: "Inflation-adjusted financial statements are an extension to, not a departure from, historical cost accounting."

9

Generally Accepted Auditing Standards (GAAS)

In 1947, the American Institute of Certified Public Accountants (AICPA) adopted GAAS to establish standards for audits. The standards cover the following three categories:

- General Standards – relates to professional and technical competence, independence, and professional due care.
- Field Work Standards – relates to the planning of an audit, evaluation of internal control, and obtaining sufficient evidential matter upon which an opinion is based.
- Reporting Standards – relates to the compliance of all auditing standards and adequacy of disclosure of opinion in the audit reports. If an opinion cannot be reached, the auditor is required to explicitly state their assertions.

Information Technology Audit Process Overview

The auditor must plan and conduct the audit to ensure their audit risk (the risk of reaching an incorrect conclusion based on the audit findings) will be limited to an acceptable level. To eliminate the possibility of assessing audit risk too low the auditor should perform the following steps:

1. Obtain an Understanding of the Organisation and its Environment: The understanding of the organisation and its environment is used to assess the risk of material misstatement/ weakness and to set the scope of the audit. The auditor's understanding should include information on the nature of the entity, management, governance, objectives and strategies, and business processes.

2. Identify Risks that May Result in Material Misstatements: The auditor must evaluate an organisation's business risks (threats to the organisation's ability to achieve its objectives). An organisation's business risks can arise or change due to new personnel, new or restructured information systems, corporate restructuring, and rapid growth to name a few.
3. Evaluate the Organisation's Response to those Risks: Once the auditor has evaluated the organisation's response to the assessed risks, the auditor should then obtain evidence of management's actions toward those risks. The organisation's response (or lack thereof) to any business risks will impact the auditor's assessed level of audit risk.
4. Assess the Risk of Material Misstatement: Based on the knowledge obtained in evaluating the organisation's responses to business risks, the auditor then assesses the risk of material misstatements and determines specific audit procedures that are necessary based on that risk assessment.
5. Evaluate Results and Issue Audit Report: At this level, the auditor should determine if the assessments of risks were appropriate and whether sufficient evidence was obtained. The auditor will issue either an unqualified or qualified audit report based on their findings.

Phases of an IT Audit

The audit process can be broken down into the following audit phases:

Establish the Terms of the Engagement

This will allow the auditor to set the scope and objectives of the relationship between the auditor and the organisation. The engagement letter should address the responsibility (scope, independence, deliverables), authority (right of access to information), and accountability (auditees' rights, agreed completion date) of the auditor.

Preliminary Review

This phase of the audit allows the auditor to gather organisational information as a basis for creating their audit plan. The preliminary review will identify an organisation's strategy and responsibilities for managing and controlling computer applications. An auditor can provide an in depth overview of an organisation's accounting system to establish which applications are financially significant at this phase.

Obtaining general data about the company, identifying financial application areas, and preparing an audit plan can achieve this.

Establish Materiality and Assess Risks

In order to plan the audit, a preliminary judgment about materiality and assessment of the client's business risks are made to set the scope of the audit.

Plan the Audit

Proper planning of the audit will ensure the audit is conducted in an effective and efficient manner. When developing the audit plan, the auditor sinto consideration the results of their understanding of the organisation and the results of the risk assessment process.

Consider Internal Control

To develop their understanding of internal controls, the auditor should consider information from previous audits, the assessment of inherent risk, judgments about materiality, and the complexity of the organisation's operations and systems.

Once the auditor develops their understanding of an organisation's internal controls, they will be able to assess the level of their control risk (the risk a material weakness will not be prevented or detected by internal controls).

Perform Audit Procedures

Audit procedures are developed based on the auditor's understanding of the organisation and its environment. A substantive audit approach is used when auditing an organisation's information system.

Issue the Audit Report

Once audit procedures have been performed and results have been evaluated, the auditor will issue either an unqualified or qualified audit report based on their findings.

Planning the Audit

IS Standard 050 (Planning) states, "The IT auditor should plan the information systems audit coverage to address the audit objectives and comply with applicable laws and professional auditing standards." One of the first tasks an auditor must do when planning the audit is to develop a working budget. The IT audit manager must know the capabilities of the audit staff assigned to the project. In addition to

budgeted time needed to perform the audit, the IT audit manager should also budget time needed to train the audit staff (if needed) and allow time for any error correction purposes.

While planning the audit, the auditor decides what level of audit risk (the risk of reaching an incorrect conclusion based on the audit findings) he or she is willing to accept. The more effective and extensive the audit work is, the less the risk that a weakness will go undetected and the auditor will issue an inappropriate report. Audit risk is dependent on the auditors assessed levels of inherent risk (the susceptibility of an audit area to error which could be material, assuming there are no related internal controls), control risk (the risk a material weakness will not be prevented or detected by internal controls), and detection risk (the risk substantive tests will not detect an error which could be material). These risks are determined when the auditor performs a risk assessment of the organisation.

Additionally, in order to evaluate whether an IT audit has been successful, the auditor must first identify the intended scope and objectives of the audit to test management's assertions on their information systems. To meet the audit objectives, and to ensure that audit resources will be used efficiently, the auditor will need to establish levels of materiality.

The auditor should consider both qualitative and quantitative aspects in determining materiality. An assessment of risk should be made to provide reasonable assurance that all material items will be adequately covered during the audit work. This assessment should identify areas with relatively high risk of existence of material problems.

Materiality

In assessing materiality, the IT auditor should consider:

- The aggregate level of error acceptable to management, the IT auditor, and appropriate regulatory agencies.
- The potential for the cumulative effect of small errors or weaknesses to become material.

While establishing materiality, the auditor may audit non-financial items such as physical access controls, logical access controls, and systems for personnel management, manufacturing control, design, quality control, and password generation. While planning the audit work to meet the audit objectives, the auditor should identify relevant control objectives and determine, based on materiality, which controls should be examined. Internal control objectives are placed by

management and identifies what the management strives to achieve through their internal controls.

Where financial transactions are not processed, the following identifies some measures the auditor should consider when assessing materiality:

- Criticality of the business processes supported by the system or operation.
- Cost of the system or operation (hardware, software, third-party services)
- Potential cost of errors.
- Number of accesses/transactions/inquiries processed per period.
- Penalties for failure to comply with legal and contractual requirements.

Risk Assessment

A risk is any event or action, generated internally or externally, which prevents an organisation from achieving its goals and/or objectives. Risks affect control objectives in the areas of data integrity and accuracy, timeliness of the information for decision making, ability to access the system, and confidentiality/privacy of information, to name a few.

Risk assessment allows the auditor to determine the scope of the audit and assess the level of audit risk and error risk (the risk of errors occurring in the area being audited). Additionally, risk assessment will aid in planning decisions such as:

- The nature, extent, and timing of audit procedures.
- The areas or business functions to be audited.
- The amount of time and resources to be allocated to an audit.

Audit Procedures

Audit Sampling

Audit sampling is the application of an audit procedure to less than 100% of the population to enable the IT auditor to evaluate audit evidence within a class of transactions for the purpose of forming a conclusion concerning the population.

When designing the size and structure of an audit sample, the IT auditor should consider the audit objectives determined when planning the audit, the nature of the population, and the sampling and selection methods.

Selecting the Sample

The auditor should select the sample items in such a way that they are representative of the population. The most commonly used sampling selection methods are:

- *Statistical Sampling Methods*
- Random Sampling – ensures that all combinations of sampling units in the population have an equal chance of selection.
- Systematic Sampling – involves selecting sampling units using a fixed interval between selections with the first interval having a random start.
- *Non-Statistical Sampling Methods*
- Haphazard Sampling – the auditor selects the sample without following a structured technique.
- Judgmental Sampling – the auditor places a bias on the sample. For example, selecting only sampling units over a certain value.

The selection of the sample size is affected by the level of sampling risk that the IT auditor is willing to accept. Sampling risk is the risk the auditor's conclusion may be different from the conclusion that would be reached if the entire population were subjected to the same audit procedure. The two types of sampling risk are:

1. The Risk of Incorrect Acceptance – the risk that a material misstatement is assessed as unlikely, when in fact the population is materially misstated.
2. The Risk of Incorrect Rejection – the risk that a material misstatement is assessed as likely, when in fact the population is not materially misstated.

Once the sample items have been selected to be tested, the auditor can begin audit tests using Computer Assisted Auditing Techniques (CAATs), which will be discussed shortly.

Evaluation and Documentation of Samples

The performance and evaluation of a sample must address the following issues:

- The effect of not being able to apply a planned procedure to a sample item.
- A projection of the sample results to the population being tested, then comparing those results with the planned amounts.
- Appropriate consideration to the assessed level of sampling risk must be performed.

- SAS 39 requires the auditor to adequately consider qualitative aspects of misstatements, such as the nature and cause of the misstatement and the possible relationship of the misstatements to other phases of the audit.

The auditor must document in their work papers the sampling objectives and the sampling process used. The work papers should include the source of the population, the sampling method used, sampling parameters, items selected, details of audit tests performed, and conclusions reached.

Completing the Audit

Before choosing the appropriate audit report, the auditor must consider the following issues:

- Review for Subsequent Events – two types of subsequent events require an evaluation by the auditor. They include:
  1. Type I events – events that provide additional evidence about the conditions that existed at the date of the balance sheet.
  2. Type II events – events that provide evidence about conditions that did not exist at the date of the balance sheet, but arose after that date.

Audit procedures used to review for subsequent events include asking management whether any unusual adjustments to their information systems have been made during the subsequent events period (after the completion of the audit, but before the audit report is issued), or obtaining a representation letter from management.

- Final Evidential Evaluation Processes – audit steps performed by the auditor in this phase to determine the most appropriate audit report includes obtaining a representation letter, reviewing work papers, final assessment of audit results and obtaining an independent review of the engagement.
- Communications with the Audit Committee and Management – communications should include significant audit adjustments, the auditor's judgments about the quality of the entity's accounting principles, disagreements with management, major issues discussed with management before the auditor was retained, difficulties encountered during the audit, and fraud involving senior management. Also, the auditor should discuss the draft of the audit report with management to give management the chance to correct any weaknesses or deficiencies

before they are reported and released to the public. The auditor may decide to do this in the form of a Management Comment Letter.

- Subsequent Discovery of Facts Existing at the Date of the Auditor's Report – Auditing standards 561 provides guidance for auditors when facts have come to the auditor's attention about the organisation's processes that might have affected the report had they known about them.

The auditor's conclusion and findings, which are based on documented evidence, must be objective, measurable, complete, and relevant. The findings are disclosed to management in formal statements, typically an audit report. Any recommendations must be provided for each audit finding for the report to be useful to management.

Reporting

IS Auditing Standard 070 (Reporting) states, "The IT auditor should provide a report in an appropriate form, upon the completion of the audit. The report should state the scope, objectives, period of coverage, and the nature, timing, and extent of the audit work performed. The report should state the findings, conclusions, and recommendations and any reservations, qualifications or limitations of scope that IT auditor has with respect to the audit."

Types of Reports

- Unqualified Audit Report
- Unqualified Audit Report with Explanation
- Qualified Report
- Qualified Report with Disclaimer
- Qualified Report with an Adverse Opinion.

Audit Documentation

Working papers (audit documentation) is the formal collection of auditors notes, documents, flowcharts, correspondence, results of observations, plans and results of tests, the audit plan, minutes of meetings, computerised records, data files or application results

House of Commons

The House of Commons is the lower house of the Parliament of the United Kingdom, which also comprises the Sovereign and the House of Lords (the upper house). Both Commons and Lords meet in the Palace of Westminster. The Commons is a democratically elected body, consisting of 650 members (since 2010 General Election), who are known as Members of Parliament (MPs). Members are elected through the first-past-the-post system by electoral districts known as constituencies. They hold their seats until Parliament is dissolved (a maximum of five years after the preceding election).

A House of Commons of England evolved at some point in England during the 14th century and, in practice, has been in continuous existence since, becoming the House of Commons of Great Britain after the political union with Scotland, and also, during the nineteenth century, of the United Kingdom of Great Britain and Ireland after the political union with Ireland, finally reaching its current title after independence was given to the Irish Free State in 1922.

The House of Commons was originally far less powerful than the House of Lords, but today its legislative powers greatly exceed those of the Lords. Under the Parliament Act 1911, the Lords' power to reject most legislative bills was reduced to a delaying power. Moreover, the Government is primarily responsible to the House of Commons; the prime minister stays in office only as long as he or she retains its support. Almost all government ministers are drawn from the House of Commons and, with one brief exception, all prime ministers since 1902. The full, formal style and title of the House of Commons is *The Honourable the Commons of the United Kingdom of Great Britain and Northern Ireland in Parliament assembled.*

Legislative Functions

Bills may be introduced in either house, though controversial bills normally originate in the House of Commons. The supremacy of the Commons in legislative matters is assured by the Parliament Acts, under which certain types of bills may be presented for the Royal Assent without the consent of the House of Lords. The Lords may not delay a money bill (a bill that, in the view of the Speaker of the House of Commons, solely concerns national taxation or public funds) for more than one month. Moreover, the Lords may not delay most other public bills for more than two parliamentary sessions, or one calendar year. These provisions, however, only apply to public bills that originate in the House of Commons. Moreover, a bill that seeks to extend a parliamentary term beyond five years requires the consent of the House of Lords.

By a custom that prevailed even before the Parliament Acts, only the House of Commons may originate bills concerning taxation or

Supply. Furthermore, supply bills passed by the House of Commons are immune to amendments in the House of Lords. In addition, the House of Lords is barred from amending a bill so as to insert a taxation or supply-related provision, but the House of Commons often waives its privileges and allows the Lords to make amendments with financial implications. Under a separate convention, known as the Salisbury Convention, the House of Lords does not seek to oppose legislation promised in the Government's election manifesto. Hence, as the power of the House of Lords has been severely curtailed by statute and by practice, the House of Commons is clearly the more powerful branch of Parliament.

Layout and Design

The current Commons' layout is influenced by the use of the original St. Stephen's Chapel in the Palace of Westminster. The rectangular shape is derived from the shape of the chapel. Benches were arranged using the configuration of the chapel's choir stalls whereby they were facing across from one another. This arrangement facilitated an adversarial atmosphere that is representative of the British parliamentary approach.

19th Century

The House of Commons experienced an important period of reform during the nineteenth century. Over the years, several anomalies had developed in borough representation. The constituency boundaries had not been changed since 1660, so many towns that were once important but had declined by the nineteenth century still retained their ancient right of electing two members.

The most notorious of these "rotten boroughs" were Old Sarum, which had only six voters for two MPs, and Dunwich which had fallen into the sea. At the same time, large cities such as Manchester received no separate representation (although their eligible residents were able to vote in the corresponding county seat). Also notable were the pocket boroughs, small constituencies controlled by wealthy landowners and aristocrats, whose "nominees" were invariably elected. The Commons attempted to address these anomalies by passing a Reform Bill in 1831. At first, the House of Lords proved unwilling to pass the bill, but were forced to relent when the prime minister, Lord Grey, advised King William IV to flood the House of Lords by creating pro-Reform peers. To avoid this the Lords relented and passed the bill in 1832. The Reform Act 1832, also known as the "Great Reform Act," abolished the rotten boroughs, established uniform voting requirements for the boroughs, and granted representation to populous cities, but still retained many pocket boroughs.

In the ensuing years, the Commons grew more assertive, the influence of the House of Lords having been reduced by the Reform Bill Crisis, and the power of the patrons reduced. The Lords became more reluctant to reject bills that the Commons passed with large majorities, and it became an accepted political principle that the confidence of the House of Commons alone was necessary for a government to remain in office.

Many more reforms were introduced in the latter half of the nineteenth century. The Reform Act 1867 lowered property requirements for voting in the boroughs, reduced the representation of the less populous boroughs, and granted parliamentary seats to several growing industrial towns. The electorate was further expanded by the Representation of the People Act 1884, under which property qualifications in the counties were lowered. The Redistribution of Seats Act of the following year replaced almost all multi-member constituencies with single-member constituencies.

20th Century

In 1908, the Liberal Government under Asquith introduced a number of social welfare programmes, which, together with an expensive arms race, forced the Government to seek higher taxes. In 1909, the Chancellor of the Exchequer, David Lloyd George, introduced the "People's Budget", which proposed a new tax targeting wealthy landowners. The unpopular measure, however, failed in the heavily Conservative House of Lords—and the government resigned.

The resulting general election returned a hung parliament, but Asquith remained prime minister with the support of the smaller parties. Asquith then proposed that the powers of the Lords be severely curtailed. After a further election in December 1910, the Asquith Government secured the passage of a bill to curtail the powers of the House of Lords after threatening to flood the House with 500 new Liberal peers to ensure the passage of the bill.

Thus, the Parliament Act 1911 came into effect, destroying the legislative equality of the two Houses of Parliament. The House of Lords was permitted only to delay most legislation, for a maximum of three parliamentary sessions or two calendar years (reduced to two sessions or one year by the Parliament Act 1949). Since the passage of these Acts, the House of Commons has become the dominant branch of Parliament, both in theory and in practice.

In 1918, women over 30 were given the right to vote, quickly followed by the passage of a law enabling women to be eligible for election as Members of Parliament at the younger age of 21. The only woman to be elected that year was an Irish Sinn Féin candidate, Constance Markievicz, who therefore became the first woman MP.

However, due to Sinn Féin's policy of abstention from Westminster, she never took her seat. Since the 17th century, MPs had been unpaid. Most of the men elected to the Commons had private incomes, while a few relied on financial support from a wealthy patron. Early Labour MPs were often provided with a salary by a trade union, but this was declared illegal by a House of Lords judgment of 1909. Consequently a resolution was passed in the House of Commons in 1911 introducing salaries for MPs. Government ministers had always been paid.

21st Century

Expenses Scandal

In May and June 2009 revelations of MP's expenses claims caused a major scandal and loss of confidence by the public in the integrity of MPs, as well as causing the forced resignation of the Speaker.

Members and Elections

Since 1950 each Member of Parliament represents a single constituency. There remains a technical distinction between county constituencies and borough constituencies, but the only effect of this difference is the amount of money candidates are allowed to spend during campaigns. The boundaries of the constituencies are determined by four permanent and independent Boundary Commissions, one each for England, Wales, Scotland, and Northern Ireland. The Commissions conduct general reviews of electoral boundaries once every 8 to 12 years, as well as a number of interim reviews.

In drawing boundaries, they are required to take into account local government boundaries, but may deviate from this requirement in order to prevent great disparities in the populations of the various constituencies. The proposals of the Boundary Commissions are subject to parliamentary approval, but may not be amended. After the next general review of constituencies, the Boundary Commissions will be absorbed into the Electoral Commission, which was established in 2000. Currently the United Kingdom is divided into 650 constituencies, with 533 in England, 40 in Wales, 59 in Scotland, and 18 in Northern Ireland.

General elections occur whenever Parliament is dissolved by the Sovereign. The timing of the dissolution is normally chosen by the prime minister. However, a parliamentary term may not last for more than five years, unless a Bill extending the life of Parliament passes both Houses and receives Royal Assent. The House of Lords, exceptionally, retains its power of veto over such a Bill. Conventionally, all elections in the United Kingdom are held on a Thursday. The Electoral Commission is unsure where this convention arose, but dates it to 1931, with the suggestion that it was made to coincide with market day; this would ease voting for those who had to travel to the towns to cast their ballot.

A candidate for a constituency must submit nomination papers signed by ten registered voters from that constituency, and pay a deposit of £500, which is refunded only if the candidate wins at least five per cent of the vote. The deposit seeks to discourage frivolous candidates. Each constituency returns one Member, using the first-past-the-post electoral system, under which the candidate with a plurality of votes wins. Minors, Members of the House of Lords, prisoners, and insane persons are not qualified to become Members of the House of Commons. In order to vote, one must be a resident of the United Kingdom as well as a citizen of the United Kingdom, of a British overseas territory, of the Republic of Ireland, or of a member of the Commonwealth of Nations. British citizens living abroad are allowed to vote for 15 years after moving from the United Kingdom. No person may vote in more than one constituency.

Once elected, Members of Parliament normally continue to serve until the next dissolution of Parliament. If a Member, however, dies or ceases to be qualified, his or her seat falls vacant. It is also possible for the House of Commons to expel a Member, but this power is exercised only in cases of serious misconduct or criminal activity. In each case, a vacancy may be filled by a by-election in the appropriate constituency, with the same electoral system as in general elections. The term "Member of Parliament" is normally used only to refer to Members of the House of Commons, even though the House of Lords is also a part of Parliament. Members of the House of Commons may use the post-nominal letters "MP". The annual salary of each Member is currently £63,291. Members may also receive additional salaries in right of other offices they hold (for instance, the Speakership). Most Members also claim between £100,000 and £150,000 for various office expenses (staff costs, postage, travelling, etc.) and, in the case of non-London Members, for the costs of maintaining a home in the capital.

Officers

At the beginning of each new parliamentary term, the House of Commons elects one of its members as a presiding officer, known as the Speaker. If the incumbent Speaker seeks a new term, then the House may reelect him or her merely by passing a motion; otherwise, a secret ballot is held. A Speaker-elect cannot take office until he or she has been approved by the Sovereign; the granting of the royal approbation, however, is a formality.

The Speaker is assisted by three Deputy Speakers, the most senior of which holds the title of Chairman of Ways and Means. The two other Deputy Speakers are known as the First and Second Deputy Chairman of Ways and Means. These titles derive from the Committee of Ways and Means, a body over which the Chairman once used to preside; even though the Committee was abolished in 1967, the traditional titles of the Deputy Speakers are still retained. The Speaker and the Deputy Speakers are always Members of the House of Commons.

Whilst presiding, the Speaker or Deputy Speaker wears ceremonial dress. The presiding officer may also wear a wig, but this tradition was abandoned by a former Speaker, Betty Boothroyd. Michael Martin, who succeeded the office also did not wear a wig whilst in the chamber. The current speaker, John Bercow, has chosen to wear a gown over a lounge suit, a decision which has sparked much debate and opposition. The Speaker or deputy presides from a chair at the front of the House.

This chair was designed by Augustus Pugin who initially built a prototype of the chair at King Edward's School, Birmingham, the chair is called Sapientia, and is where the Chief master sits. The Speaker is also chairman of the House of Commons Commission, which oversees the running of the House, and he or she controls debates by calling on members to speak. If a member believes that a rule (or Standing Order) has been breached, he or she may raise a "point of order", on which the Speaker makes a ruling that is not subject to any appeal. The Speaker may discipline members who fail to observe the rules of the House.

Thus, the Speaker is far more powerful than his Lords counterpart, the Lord Speaker, who has no disciplinary powers. Customarily, the Speaker and the deputies are non-partisan; they do not vote, or participate in the affairs of any political party. By convention, a Speaker seeking reelection to parliament is not opposed in his or her constituency by any of the major parties. The lack of partisanship continues even after the Speaker leaves the House of Commons. The Clerk of the House is both the House's chief adviser on matters of procedure and Chief Executive of the House of Commons. He or she is a permanent official, not a Member of the House itself. The Clerk advises the Speaker on the rules and procedure of the House, signs orders and official communications, and signs and endorses bills. He or she chairs the Board of Management, which consists of the heads of the six departments of the House.

The Clerk's deputy is known as the Clerk Assistant. Another officer of the House is the Serjeant-at-Arms, whose duties include the maintenance of law, order, and security on the House's premises. The Serjeant-at-Arms carries the ceremonial Mace, a symbol of the authority of the Crown and of the House of Commons, into the House each day in front of the Speaker, and the Mace is laid upon the Table of the House during sittings. The Librarian is head of the House of Commons Library, the House's research and information arm.

Committees

The Parliament of the United Kingdom uses committees for a variety of purposes, e.g. for the review of bills. Committees consider bills in detail, and may make amendments. Bills of great constitutional importance, as well as some important financial measures, are usually sent to the "Committee of the Whole House", a body that includes all members of the Commons. Instead of the Speaker, the Chairman or a Deputy Chairman of Ways and Means presides. The Committee meets in the House of Commons Chamber.

Most bills were until 2006 considered by Standing Committees, which consisted of between 16 and 50 members. The membership of each Standing Committee roughly reflected the strength of the parties in the House. The membership of Standing Committees changed constantly; new Members were assigned each time the committee considered a new bill. There was no formal limit on the number of Standing Committees, but usually only ten existed. Rarely, a bill was committed to a Special Standing Committee, which investigated and held hearings on the issues raised. In November 2006, Standing Committees were replaced by Public Bill Committees.

The House of Commons also has several Departmental Select Committees. The membership of these bodies, like that of the Standing Committees, reflects the strength of the parties. Each committee elects its own Chairman. The primary function of a Departmental Select Committee is to scrutinise and investigate the activities of a particular government department. To fulfil these aims, it is permitted to hold hearings and collect evidence. Bills may be referred to Departmental Select Committees, but such a procedure is seldom used. A separate type of Select Committee is the Domestic Committee. Domestic Committees oversee the administration of the House and the services provided to Members. Other committees of the House of Commons include Joint Committees (which also include members of the House of Lords), the Committee on Standards and Privileges (which considers questions of parliamentary privilege, as well as matters relating to the conduct of the members), and the Committee of Selection (which determines the membership of other committees).

The Chamber in Film and Television

In 1986, the British television production company Granada Television created a near-full size replica of the post-1950 House of Commons debating chamber at its studios in Manchester for use in its adaptation of the Jeffrey Archer novel *First Among Equals*. The set was highly convincing, and was retained after the production—since then, it has been used in nearly every British film and television production that has featured scenes set in the chamber. From 1988 until 1999 it was also one of the prominent attractions on the Granada Studios Tour, where visitors could watch actors performing mock political debates on the set. In 2002, the set was purchased by the scriptwriter Paul Abbott so that it could be used in his BBC drama serial *State of Play*. Abbott, a former Granada Television staff writer, bought it personally as the set would otherwise have been destroyed and he feared it would take too long to get the necessary money from the BBC. He currently keeps it in storage in Oxford.

The post-1941 Commons Chamber was used in the film *Ali G Indahouse*, the political satire *Restart* by Komedy Kollective, about a British prime minister seeking reelection, and was mentioned in the Robin Williams stand-up special *Robin Williams Live on Broadway* in which he describes it as "like Congress, but with a two drink minimum". The pre-1941 Chamber was recreated in Shepperton Studios for the Ridley Scott/Richard Loncraine 2002 biopic on Churchill, *The Gathering Storm*.

Patient Protection and Affordable Care Act

The Patient Protection and Affordable Care Act (PPACA) is a United States federal statute signed into law by President Barack Obama on March 23, 2010. The law (along with the Health Care and

Education Reconciliation Act of 2010) is the principal health care reform legislation of the 111th United States Congress. PPACA reforms certain aspects of the private health insurance industry and public health insurance programs, increases insurance coverage of preexisting conditions, expands access to insurance to over 30 million Americans, and increases projected national medical spending despite lowering projected Medicare spending under previous law.

PPACA passed the Senate on December 24, 2009, by a vote of 60–39 with all Democrats and two Independents voting for, and all Republicans voting against. It passed the House of Representatives on March 21, 2010, by a vote of 219–212, with 34 Democrats and all 178 Republicans voting against the bill.

A majority of the states, and numerous organisations and individual persons, have filed actions in federal court challenging the constitutionality of PPACA. As of October 2011, federalappellate courts are almost evenly divided on the constitutionality of PPACA's health insurance mandate; at the district court level, three judges upheld the constitutionality of PPACA and three declared it at least partly unconstitutional. Several other challenges were dismissed on technical grounds such as jurisdiction and plaintiffs lacking standing. The Supreme Court may review the matter as early as the end of 2011. The only part of the law to that has been challenged within appeals courts with some success has been the individual mandate to purchase health insurance.

Effect on National Spending

The United States Department of Health and Human Services reported that the bill would increase "total national health expenditures" by more than $200 billion from 2010-2019. Looking at the federal budget implications, in a May 2010 presentation on "Health Costs and the Federal Budget," CBO stated: Rising health costs will put tremendous pressure on the federal budget during the next few decades and beyond. In CBO's judgment, the health legislation enacted earlier this year does not substantially diminish that pressure. CBO further observed that "a substantial share of current spending on health care contributes little if anything to people's health" and concluded, "Putting the federal budget on a sustainable path would almost certainly require a significant reduction in the growth of federal health spending relative to current law (including this year's health legislation)."

For the effect on health insurance premiums, the CBO referred to its November 2009 analysis and stated that the effects would "probably be quite similar" to that earlier analysis. That analysis forecasted that by 2016: for the non-group market comprising 17% of the market, premiums per person would increase by 10 to 13% but that over half of these insureds would receive subsidies which would decrease the premium paid to "well below" premiums charged under current law; for the small group market 13% of the market, premiums would be impacted 1 to "3% and "8 to "11% for those receiving subsidies; for the large group market comprising 70% of the market, premiums would be impacted 0 to "3%, with insureds under high premium plans subject to excise taxes being charged "9 to "12%.

The analysis was affected by various factors including increased benefits particularly for the nongroup markets, more healthy insureds due to the mandate, administrative efficiencies related to the health exchanges, and insureds under high premium plans reducing benefits in response to the tax. Surgeon Atul Gawande has noted that bill contains a variety of pilot programs that may have a significant impact on cost and quality over the long-run, although these have not been factored into CBO cost estimates. He stated these pilot programs cover nearly every idea healthcare experts advocate, except malpractice/tort reform. He argued that a trial and error strategy, combined with industry and government partnership, is how the U.S. overcame a similar challenge in the agriculture industry in the early 20th century.

The Business Roundtable, an association of CEOs, commissioned a report from the consulting company Hewitt Associates that found that the legislation "could potentially reduce that trend line by more than $3,000 per employee, to $25,435" with respect to insurance premiums. It also stated that the legislation "could potentially reduce the rate of future health care cost increases by 15% to 20% when fully phased in by 2019". The group cautioned that this is all assuming that the cost-saving government pilot programs both succeed and then are wholly copied by the private market, which is uncertain.

The Office of the Actuary at the Centres for Medicare and Medicaid Services released a report in April 2010 saying that the PPACA would increase the number of Americans with health insurance coverage but would also increase projected spending by approximately 1% over 10 years. The report also cautioned that the increases could be larger, because the Medicare cuts in the law may be unrealistic and unsustainable, forcing lawmakers to roll them back. The report projected that Medicare cuts could put nearly 15% of hospitals and other institutional providers into debt, "possibly jeopardizing access" to care for seniors. The Bill was described as "the federal government's biggest attack on economic inequality since inequality began rising more than three decades ago".

After the bill was signed, AT&T, Caterpillar, Verizon, and John Deere issued financial reports showing large current charges against earnings, up to US$1 billion in the case of AT&T, attributing the additional expenses to tax changes in the new health care law. Under the new law as of 2013 companies can no longer deduct a subsidy for prescription drug benefits granted under Medicare Part D.

Political Impact

Public Opinion

Public opinion supported healthcare reform proposals in 2008, but turned negative when the plan changed in 2009, and remains opposed to the final version that was signed in 2010. Though in 2008 then-Senators Barack Obama and Joseph Biden campaigned against requiring adults to buy insurance; in 2009 President Obama reportedly "changed his mind" and agreed with insurance industry and Democratic Congressional proposals to include an individual mandate. Public opinion of the legislation turned negative when the individual mandate proposal was announced, and remains opposed by a margin of 10 percentage points. Specific ideas that showed majority support, such as purchasing drugs from Canada, limiting malpractice awards, and reducing the age to qualify for Medicare, were not enacted.

In March 2010, pollsters probed the reasons for opposition. In a CNN poll, 62% of respondents said the Act would "increase the amount of money they personally spend on health care," 56% said the bill "gives the government too much involvement in health care," and only 19% said they and their families would be better off with the legislation. In The Wall Street Journal, pollsters Scott Rasmussen and Doug Schoen wrote, "One of the more amazing aspects of the health-care debate is how steady public opinion has remained... 81% of voters say it's likely the plan will end up costing more than projected [and 59%] say that the biggest problem with the health-care system is the cost: They want reform that will bring down the cost of care. For these voters, the notion that you need to spend an additional trillion dollars doesn't make sense." USA Today found opinions were starkly divided by age, with a solid majority of seniors opposing the bill and a solid majority of those younger than 40 in favour. In the November 2010 midterm election, Democrats lost more seats in Congress than any party in any midterm in more than 70 years.

Politico reported that five House Democrats had run political ads highlighting their "no" votes on the bill, while there had not been any political ads highlighting a "yes" vote since April, when Harry Reid ran one. The Act is often referred to by the nickname "Obamacare", which has been characterised as pejorative but continues to be widely used to refer to the legislation, largely by its opponents. Use of the term in a positive sense has however been suggested by Democratic politicians such as John Conyers (D-MI). President Obama said subsequently, "I have no problem with people saying Obama cares. I do care." Because of the number of "Obamacare" search engine queries, the Department of Health and Human Services purchased Google advertisements, triggered by the term, to direct people to the official HHS site.

Impact on Child-only Policies

In September 2010, some insurance companies announced that in response to the law, they would end the issuance of new child-only policies. Kentucky Insurance Commissioner Sharon Clark said the decision by insurers to stop offering such policies was a violation of state law and ordered insurers to offer an open enrollment period in January 2011 for Kentuckians under 19. An August 2011 Congressional report found that passage of the health care law prompted health insurance carriers to stop selling new child-only health plans in many states. Of the 50 states, 17 reported that there were currently no carriers selling child only health plans to new enrollees. Thirty-nine states indicated at least one insurance carrier exited the child-only market following enactment of the health care laws.

Constitutional Challenges

Challenges by States

Organisations and lawmakers who opposed the passage of the bill threatened to take legal action against it upon its passage and several court challenges are currently at various stages of development. The target of the threatened lawsuits were several key provisions of the bill. Some claimed that fining individuals for failing to buy insurance is not within the scope of Congress's taxing powers. Idaho legislators passed a law that directed its attorney general to sue if mandatory insurance becomes federal law, which he duly did. A total of 28 states have filed joint or individual lawsuits (including 26 states engaged in a joint action) to overturn the individual mandate portions of the law. In a press release, the Attorneys General for several states indicated their primary basis for the challenge was a violation of state sovereignty. Their release repeated the claim challenging the federal requirement under threat of penalty, that all citizens and legal residents have qualifying health care coverage. It also claimed that the law puts an unfair financial burden on state governments. The lawsuit states the following legal rationale:

Regulation of non-economic activity under the Commerce Clause is possible only through the Necessary and Proper Clause. The Necessary and Proper Clause confers supplemental authority only when the means adopted to accomplish an enumerated power are 'appropriate', are 'plainly adapted to that end', and are 'consistent with the letter and spirit of the constitution.' Requiring citizen-to-citizen subsidy or redistribution is contrary to the foundational assumptions of the constitutional compact. Other states were either expected to join the multi-state lawsuit or are considering filing additional independent suits. Members of several state legislatures are attempting to counteract and prevent elements of the bill within their states. Legislators in 29 states have introduced measures to amend their constitutions to nullify portions of the health care reform law. Thirteen state statutes have been introduced to prohibit portions of the law; two states have already enacted statutory bans. Six legislatures had attempts to enact bans, but the measures were unsuccessful. In August 2010, a ballot initiative passed overwhelmingly in Missouri that would exempt the state from some provisions of the bill. Most legal analysts expect that the measure will be struck down if challenged in Federal court.

Reactions from Legal Experts

In February 2011, Alexander Bolton wrote in *The Hill* that consensus among legal experts largely changed following Judge Roger Vinson's decision in *Florida et al v. United States Department of Health and Human Services*. He said that prior to the ruling, it was widely felt that the Supreme Court would uphold the law by a comfortable margin, but now legal scholars generally feel it would be a 5–4 decision. Georgetown University Law Centre professor Randy Barnett said, "There's been a big change in the conventional wisdom ... the temperature of law professors has changed considerably," and describing the *Florida* decision as "extremely deep in its discussion of principles and constitutional doctrine".

Federal Court Rulings

Federal District Court ruling from United States District Court for the Northern District of Florida

On January 31, 2011, Judge Roger Vinson in State of Florida et. al. v. US Dept of Health and Human Services declared the law unconstitutional in an action brought by 26 states, on the grounds that the individual mandate to purchase insurance exceeds the authority of Congress to regulate interstate commerce. Vinson further ruled the clause was not severable, which had the effect of striking down the entire law. On August 12, 2011, a divided three-judge panel of the 11th Circuit Court of Appeals affirmed Judge Vinson's decision in part: the court agreed that the mandate was unconstitutional, but held that it could be severed, allowing the rest of the PPACA to remain. In September 2011, the Department of Justice decided not to ask for an en banc review by the 11th Circuit, and instead asked the U.S. Supreme Court to hear the case.

Commonwealth of Virginia v. Kathleen Sebelius

The first federal court ruling in the legal challenges to the health care act came on August 2, 2010, in response to the suit brought by Virginia's attorney general. U.S. District Judge Henry E. Hudson denied the Justice Department's request to have the suit dismissed, citing the complex constitutional questions the law raises and writing that the PPACA "radically changes the landscape of health insurance coverage in America."

On December 12, 2010, in the first case rejecting the law's constitutionality, Judge Hudson ruled that the individual mandate was unconstitutional, and that the "tax" imposed on people who choose not to have a "minimum essential coverage plan" was in practice a "penalty" outside the federal government's constitutional authority to raise revenues. Judge Hudson stated he could find no precedent for extending either Commerce Clause or the General Welfare Clause to encompass regulation of a person's decision *not* to purchase a product. He ruled the provision to be beyond the power given to Congress under the Commerce Clause.

His ruling covered only Section 1501 of the Act, and severed that requirement without discussing the rest of the law. A three-judge panel from the 4th Circuit Court of Appeals unanimously ruled on September 8, 2011, that the state did not have the authority to challenge the law, saying "... we vacate the judgment of the district court and remand with instructions to dismiss the case for lack of subject-matter jurisdiction." The state's attorney general said they planned to appeal the decision.

Appeals Court ruling from DC Court of Appeals

The US Court of Appeals for the District of Columbia ruled that the law is Constitutional.

The Constitutional Accountability Centre remarked that this court consists of many conservative judges and they found the law constitutional.The case was Susan Seven-Sky, et al. v. Eric Holder Jr., et al.,. Specifically, Senior Judge Lawrence Silberman, well known in conservative circles as a conservative intellectual, and who ruled that the District of Columbia's handgun law was unconstitutional, ruled that the law is constituional. Silberman said,

> *"The right to be free from federal regulation is not absolute and yields to the imperative that Congress be free to forge national solutions to national problems."*

Federal District Court ruling from United States District Court for the Western District of Virginia

On November 30, 2010, U.S. District Court Judge Norman K. Moon in Liberty University v. Timothy Geithner who sits in Virginia also declared the individual mandate constitutional.

He also declared the employer mandate constitutional. He rejected two other arguments that government lawyers have made in cases across the country in defending the new law: first, that no one has legal standing to bring challenges at this point to the 2014 mandates, and second that any such challenge is premature. He rejected the challengers' basic argument that Congress had no authority to order someone to give up their own desire not to buy a commercial product and force them into a market they do not want to enter.

He said, "Regardless of whether one relies on an insurance policy, one's savings, or the backstop of free or reduced-cost emergency room services, one has made a choice regarding the method of payment for the health care services one expects to receive.

Far from 'inactivity,' by choosing to forgo insurance, [individuals] are making an economic decision to try to pay for health care services later, out of pocket, rather than now, through the purchase of insurance....As Congress found, the total incidence of these economic decisions has a substantial impact on the national market for health care by collectively shifting billions of dollars on to other market participants and driving up the prices of insurance policies."

Federal District Court ruling from the United States District of Columbia

On February 22, 2011, Judge Gladys Kessler in Margaret Meade v. Eric Holder of the U.S. District Court for the District of Columbia, rejected a challenge to the law by 5 individuals who argued, among other things, that the Affordable Care Act violated the Religious Freedom Restoration Act and that the individual mandate exceeded Congress's power under the Interstate Commerce Clause. Kessler rejected as "pure semantics" plaintiffs' argument that failing to acquire insurance was the regulation of inactivity, noting that "those who choose not to purchase health insurance will ultimately get a "free ride" on the backs of those Americans who have made responsible choices to provide for the illness we all must face at some point in our lives." Kessler ruled that individual mandate was a valid exercise of Congress's power to regulate interstate commerce.

Federal District Court ruling by the United States District Court for the Eastern District of Michigan

On October 8, 2010, U.S. District Court Judge George Caram Steeh in Thomas More Law Centre v. Barack Obama wrote that in his view the PPACA including the individual mandate was constitutional. He rejected a private suit filed by Michigan's Thomas More Law Centre and several state residents that focused on the Commerce Clause, deciding that Congress had the power to pass the law because it affected interstate commerce and was part of a broader regulatory scheme.

On June 29, 2011, a divided three-judge panel of the Sixth Circuit Court of Appeals affirmed the decision. Judge Jeffrey Sutton, a member of the three judge panel appointed by George W. Bush, was the first Republican-appointed judge to rule that the law is constitutional.

Repeal efforts

111th Congress

Reps. Steve King of Iowa and Michele Bachmann of Minnesota, both Republicans, introduced bills in the House to repeal the Act shortly after it was passed, as did Sen. Jim DeMint in the Senate. None of the three bills was considered by either body.

112th Congress

In 2011, the Republican-controlled House of Representatives voted 245–189 to approve a bill entitled "Repealing the Job-Killing Health

Care Law Act" (H.R.2), which, if enacted, would repeal the Patient Protection and Affordable Care Act and the health care-related text of the Health Care and Education Reconciliation Act of 2010. All Republicans and 3 Democrats voted for repeal. In the Senate, the bill was offered as an amendment to an unrelated bill, and was subsequently voted down. Before votes in both houses of the Congress took place, president Obama stated that he would veto the bill should it pass both chambers. Democrats in the House proposed that repeal not take effect until a majority of the Senators and Representatives had opted out of the Federal Employees Health Benefits Program. The Republicans voted down this measure.

Job Consequences of Repeal

A spokesman for Republican Majority Leader Eric Cantor stated, "This is a job-killing law, period. Anyone who argues otherwise is ignoring the construct of the health care law and the widely accepted facts." The House Republican leadership justified its use of the term "job killing" by contending that the PPACA would lead to a loss of 650,000 jobs, and attributing that figure to a report by the Congressional Budget Office. However, the CBO report specifically stated that the negative effect on jobs was because people would voluntarily choose to work less once they have health insurance outside of their jobs. FactCheck noted that the 650,000 figure was not in the CBO report, and said that the Republican statement "badly misrepresents what the Congressional Budget Office has said about the law. In fact, CBO is among those saying the effect 'will probably be small.'" The Republicans also cited a study by the National Federation of Independent Businesses, but PolitiFact.com said that the 2009 NFIB study had concerned an earlier version of the bill that differed significantly from what was enacted. PolitiFact rated the Republican statement as False.

Effect of Repeal Proposals on Federal Budget Projections

The CBO estimated that repealing the entire PPACA (including both its taxing and spending provisions) would increase the net 2011-2021 federal deficit projections by $210 billion. Others disagree, arguing that estimate was based on unrealistic assumptions; House Speaker John Boehner said, "I don't think anyone in this town believes that repealing Obamacare is going to increase the deficit." In May 2011, CBO analysed proposals to prevent the use of appropriated funds to implement the legislation, and wrote that "a temporary prohibition, extending through the remainder of fiscal year 2011, would reduce the budget deficit by about $1.4 billion in 2011 but would increase deficits by almost $6 billion over the 2011-2021 period... CBO cannot determine whether changes in spending under a permanent prohibition would produce net costs or net savings relative to its baseline projection, which assumes full implementation."

United Kingdom Insolvency Law

United Kingdom insolvency law deals with the insolvency of firms and individuals in the United Kingdom. The important statutes are the Insolvency Act 1986, as amended by the Enterprise Act 2002, as well as the Company Director Disqualification Act 1986 and the Companies Act 2006. Insolvency is a term which encompasses both companies and individuals, though the term bankruptcy is generally reserved for individuals in the UK. United Kingdom bankruptcy law follows a similar, but separate set of principles. This article focuses on corporate insolvency, and so is heavily connected to UK company law. Corporate insolvency is defined as either cash flow insolvency or balance sheet insolvency. The Insolvency Act 1986, s.123 gives the definition of inability to pay debts, primarily if a creditor has given three weeks to be repaid over £750, but seen nothing (s.123(1)(a)) or,

> *"(e) if it is proved to the satisfaction of the court that the company is unable to pay its debts as they fall due.*
>
> *A company is also deemed unable to pay its debts if it is proved to the satisfaction of the court that the value of the company's assets is less than the amount of its liabilities, taking into account its contingent and prospective liabilities."*

Cash flow insolvency has recently been reinterpreted in *Re Cheyne Finance plc* [2007] All ER (D) 25 (regarding a structured investment vehicle) to not only consider whether current debts are unable to be paid as they fall due, but also consider whether future debts will not be able to be paid. This makes it possible for creditors to call for insolvency earlier.

Cornhill Insurance plc v Improvement Services Ltd [1986] 1 WLR 114.

History of Bankruptcy Law

Some form of law for bankrupts can be seen tracing back to Ancient Babylon. In England, the first recognised piece of legislation was the Bankruptcy Act 1542. Bankrupts were seen as crooks, and the Act stated its aim to prevent "crafty debtors" escaping the realm. A more humane approach was developed in the Bankruptcy Act 1705.

The Lord Chancellor was given power to discharge bankrupts, once disclosure of all assets and various procedures had been fulfilled. In *Fowler v Padget* Lord Kenyon reasserted the old sentiment that,

> *"Bankruptcy is considered a crime and a bankrupt in the old laws is called an offender."*

The bankrupt was seen bonded to his creditors. Under the Insolvent Debtors Act 1813, debtors could request release after 14 days in jail by taking an oath that their assets did not exceed £20, but if any of their creditors objected, they had to stay inside.

Attitudes were changing, however, and the Bankrupts (England) Act 1825 allowed people to start proceedings for their own bankruptcy. Before only creditors could start the proceedings.

In the middle of the 19th century, attitudes towards corporations were also quickly changing. Since the South Sea Bubble disaster, companies were viewed as inefficient and dangerous. But with the industrial revolution in full swing that changed. The Joint Stock Companies Act 1844 allowed people to create companies without permission through a royal charter.

Companies had "separate legal personality", the ability to sue and be sued, and served as an easy mechanism for raising capital through the purchase of shares (an equitable title) in the company's capital. The Act's corollary, to bring the existence of these "legal persons" to an end was the Joint Stock Companies Winding-Up Act 1844. The Limited Liability Act 1855 produced a further innovation.

Before, if a corporation had gone broke, the people that lent it money (creditors) could sue all the shareholders to pay off the company's debts. But the 1855 Act said that shareholders' liability would be limited to the amount they had paid in their shares. So if you had invested £100 in a company, but now the company owed millions of pounds, the creditors could not come after you for the debts.

You would lose £100 and no more. Your liability to pay debts was limited to the value of your shares.

The Joint Stock Companies Act 1856 consolidated the companies legislation in one, and the modern law of corporate insolvency was born. In 1869, the Bankruptcy Act 1869 was passed allowing all people, rather than just traders to file for bankruptcy.

Procedures

As a company nears insolvency, UK law provides four main procedures by which the company could potentially be rescued or wound down and its assets distributed. First, a company voluntary arrangement, allows the directors of a company to reach an agreement with creditors to potentially accept less repayment in the hope of avoiding a more costly administration or liquidation procedure and less in returns overall. However, only for small private companies is a statutory moratorium on debt collection by secured creditors available. Second, and since the Enterprise Act 2002 the primary insolvency procedure, a company which is insolvent can go under administration. Here a qualified insolvency practitioner will replace the board of directors and is charged with a public duty of rescuing the company in the interests of all creditors, getting a better result for creditors, or if nothing can be done effecting an orderly winding up and distribution of assets. This was introduced following the Cork Report's recommendations that UK law should develop a rescue culture to rehabilitate companies over breaking them up.

Third, administrative receivership is a procedure available for a narrow list of companies where the insolvency practitioner is appointed by the holder of a floating charge that covers a company's whole assets. This stems from common law receivership where the practitioner's primary duty was owed to the creditor that appointed him. After the Insolvency Act 1986 it was increasingly viewed to be unacceptable that one creditor could manage a company when the interests of her creditor might conflict with those holding unsecured or other debts. Fourth, when none of these procedures is used, the business is wound up and a company's assets are to be broken up and sold off, a liquidator is appointed.

Company Voluntary Arrangement

Under the Insolvency Act 1986 sections 1 to 7, a company's directors may instigate a voluntary arrangement with creditors, that is designed to reduce the company's debt burden in the hope of restructuring the business. If already appointed, an administrator or liquidator can also propose it. The procedure takes place under the supervision of an insolvency practitioner, to whom the directors will submit a report on the company's finances and a proposal for reducing the debt. For instance, directors might propose that each creditor accepts 80 per cent of the money owed to each, and to spread repayments out over five years, in return for a commitment to restructure the business' affairs under a new marketing strategy.

The weakness of the procedure on its introduction was that the arrangement could be scuppered by a single creditor who did not agree. Since 2002 under a new section 1A, a company may apply for a moratorium on debt collection if it is smaller than two of the following criteria (1) under £6.5m in turnover (2) under £3.26m in balance sheet, or (3) fewer than 50 employees. After an arrangement is proposed creditors will have the opportunity to vote, and if 75 per cent approve the plan it will bind the whole.

Nevertheless, the introduction of the ability for administrators to be appointed out of court, and the complicated procedure for obtaining a moratorium, still only for small companies, means that the company voluntary arrangement remains considerably under-used compared to the individual voluntary arrangement available for people in bankruptcy.

10

Cash Flow Statement

In financial accounting, a cash flow statement, also known as *statement of cash flows* or *funds flow statement*, is a financial statement that shows how changes in balance sheet accounts and income affect cash and cash equivalents, and breaks the analysis down to operating, investing, and financing activities. Essentially, the cash flow statement is concerned with the flow of cash in and cash out of the business.

The statement captures both the current operating results and the accompanying changes in the balance sheet.

As an analytical tool, the statement of cash flows is useful in determining the short-term viability of a company, particularly its ability to pay bills. International Accounting Standard 7 (IAS 7), is the International Accounting Standard that deals with cash flow statements.

People and groups interested in cash flow statements include:

- Accounting personnel, who need to know whether the organisation will be able to cover payroll and other immediate expenses
- Potential lenders or creditors, who want a clear picture of a company's ability to repay
- Potential investors, who need to judge whether the company is financially sound
- Potential employees or contractors, who need to know whether the company will be able to afford compensation
- Shareholders of the business.

Purpose

***Table** : Statement of Cash Flow - Simple Example* for the period 01/01/2006 to 12/31/2006

Cash flow from operations	$4,000
Cash flow from investing	($1,000)
Cash flow from financing	($2,000)
Net cash flow	$1,000

Parentheses indicate negative values

The cash flow statement was previously known as the flow of Cash statement. The cash flow statement reflects a firm's liquidity. The balance sheet is a snapshot of a firm's financial resources and obligations at a single point in time, and the income statement summarizes a firm's financial transactions over an interval of time. These two financial statements reflect the accrual basis accounting used by firms to match revenues with the expenses associated with generating those revenues.

The cash flow statement includes only inflows and outflows of cash and cash equivalents; it excludes transactions that do not directly affect cash receipts and payments. These non-cash transactions include depreciation or write-offs on bad debts or credit losses to name a few. The cash flow statement is a cash basis report on three types of financial activities: operating activities, investing activities, and financing activities. Non-cash activities are usually reported in footnotes.

The cash flow statement is intended to

1. provide information on a firm's liquidity and solvency and its ability to change cash flows in future circumstances
2. provide additional information for evaluating changes in assets, liabilities and equity
3. improve the comparability of different firms' operating performance by eliminating the effects of different accounting methods
4. indicate the amount, timing and probability of future cash flows

The cash flow statement has been adopted as a standard financial statement because it eliminates allocations, which might be derived from different accounting methods, such as various timeframes for depreciating fixed assets.

History & Variations

Cash basis financial statements were very common before accrual basis financial statements. The "flow of funds" statements of the past were cash flow statements. In 1863, the Dowlais Iron Company had recovered from a business slump, but had no cash to invest for a new blast furnace, despite having made a profit. To explain why there were no funds to invest, the manager made a new financial statement that was called a *comparison balance sheet*, which showed that the company was holding too much inventory. This new financial statement was the genesis of Cash Flow Statement that is used today.

In the United States in 1971, the Financial Accounting Standards Board (FASB) defined rules that made it mandatory under Generally Accepted Accounting Principles (US GAAP) to report sources and uses of funds, but the definition of "funds" was not clear." Net working capital" might be cash or might be the difference between current assets and current liabilities.

From the late 1970 to the mid-1980s, the FASB discussed the usefulness of predicting future cash flows. In 1987, FASB Statement No. 95 (FAS 95) mandated that firms provide cash flow statements. In 1992, the International Accounting Standards Board issued International Accounting Standard 7 (IAS 7), *Cash Flow Statements*, which became effective in 1994, mandating that firms provide cash flow statements.

US GAAP and IAS 7 rules for cash flow statements are similar, but some of the differences are:

- IAS 7 requires that the cash flow statement include changes in both cash and cash equivalents. US GAAP permits using cash alone or cash and cash equivalents.
- IAS 7 permits bank borrowings (overdraft) in certain countries to be included in cash equivalents rather than being considered a part of financing activities.
- IAS 7 allows interest paid to be included in operating activities or financing activities. US GAAP requires that interest paid be included in operating activities.
- US GAAP (FAS 95) requires that when the direct method is used to present the operating activities of the cash flow statement, a supplemental schedule must also present a cash flow statement using the indirect method. The IASC strongly recommends the direct method but allows either method. The

IASC considers the indirect method less clear to users of financial statements. Cash flow statements are most commonly prepared using the indirect method, which is not especially useful in projecting future cash flows.

Cash Flow Activities

The cash flow statement is partitioned into three segments, namely: 1) cash flow resulting from operating activities; 2) cash flow resulting from investing activities; and 3) cash flow resulting from financing activities.

The money coming into the business is called cash inflow, and money going out from the business is called cash outflow.

Operating Activities

Operating activities include the production, sales and delivery of the company's product as well as collecting payment from its customers. This could include purchasing raw materials, building inventory, advertising, and shipping the product.

Under IAS 7, operating cash flows include:

- Receipts from the sale of goods or services
- Receipts for the sale of loans, debt or equity instruments in a trading portfolio
- Interest received on loans
- Dividends received on equity securities
- Payments to suppliers for goods and services
- Payments to employees or on behalf of employees
- Interest payments (alternatively, this can be reported under financing activities in IAS 7, and US GAAP).

Items which are added back to [or subtracted from, as appropriate] the net income figure (which is found on the Income Statement) to arrive at cash flows from operations generally include:

- Depreciation (loss of tangible asset value over time)
- Deferred tax
- Amortization (loss of intangible asset value over time)
- Any gains or losses associated with the sale of a non-current asset, because associated cash flows do not belong in the operating section. (unrealised gains/losses are also added back from the income statement).

Preparation Methods

The direct method of preparing a cash flow statement results in a more easily understood report. The indirect method is almost universally used, because FAS 95 requires a supplementary report similar to the indirect method if a company chooses to use the direct method.

Direct Method

The direct method for creating a cash flow statement reports major classes of gross cash receipts and payments. Under IAS 7, dividends received may be reported under operating activities or under investing activities.

If taxes paid are directly linked to operating activities, they are reported under operating activities; if the taxes are directly linked to investing activities or financing activities, they are reported under investing or financing activities. *Sample cash flow statement using the direct method.*

***Table** : Cash flows from (used in) operating activities*

Cash receipts from customers	9,500
Cash paid to suppliers and employees	(2,000)
Cash generated from operations (sum)	7,500
Interest paid	(2,000)
Income taxes paid	(3,000)
Net cash flows from operating activities	2,500
Cash flows from (used in) investing activities	
Proceeds from the sale of equipment	7,500
Dividends received	3,000
Net cash flows from investing activities	10,500
Cash flows from (used in) financing activities	
Dividends paid	(2,500)
Net cash flows used in financing activities	(2,500)
Net increase in cash and cash equivalents	10,500
Cash and cash equivalents, beginning of year	1,000
Cash and cash equivalents, end of year	$11,500

Indirect Method

The indirect method uses net-income as a starting point, makes adjustments for all transactions for non-cash items, then adjusts from all cash-based transactions. An increase in an asset account is subtracted from net income, and an increase in a liability account is added back to net income. This method converts accrual-basis net income (or loss) into cash flow by using a series of additions and deductions.

Rules (Operating Activities)

Table: *To Find Cash Flows* from Operating Activities *using the Balance Sheet and Net Income*

For Increases in	***Net Inc Adj***
Current Assets (Non-Cash)	Decrease
Current Liabilities	Increase
For All Non-Cash...	
**Expenses* (Decreases in Fixed Assets)	Increase

**Non-cash expenses must be added back to NI. Such expenses may be represented on the balance sheet as decreases in long term asset accounts. Thus decreases in fixed assets increase NI.*

The following rules can be followed to calculate Cash Flows from Operating Activities when given only a two year comparative balance sheet and the Net Income figure.

Cash Flows from Operating Activities can be found by adjusting Net Income relative to the change in beginning and ending balances of Current Assets, Current Liabilities, and sometimes Long Term Assets.

When comparing the change in long term assets over a year, the accountant must be certain that these changes were caused entirely by their devaluation rather than purchases or sales (i.e. they must be operating items not providing or using cash) or if they are nonoperating items.

- Decrease in non-cash current assets are added to net income
- Increase in non-cash current asset are subtracted from net income
- Increase in current liabilities are added to net income
- Decrease in current liabilities are subtracted from net income
- Expenses with no cash outflows are added back to net income (depreciation and/or amortization expense are the only operating items that have no effect on cash flows in the period)
- Revenues with no cash inflows are subtracted from net income
- Non operating losses are added back to net income
- Non operating gains are subtracted from net income

The intricacies of this procedure might be seen as,
Net Cash Flows from Operating Activities = Net Income + Rule Items

For example, consider a company that has a net income of $100 this year, and its A/R increased by $25 since the beginning of the year. If the balances of all other current assets, long term assets and current liabilities did not change over the year, the cash flows could be determined by the rules above as $100 – $25 = Cash Flows from Operating Activities = $75.

The logic is that, if the company made $100 that year (net income), and they are using the accrual accounting system (not cash based) then any income they generated that year which has not yet been paid for in cash should be subtracted from the net income figure in order to find cash flows from operating activities. And the increase in A/R meant that $25 of sales occurred on credit and have not yet been paid for in cash.

In the case of finding Cash Flows when there is a change in a fixed asset account, say the Buildings and Equipment account decreases, the change is subtracted from Net Income. The reasoning behind this is that because Net Income is calculated by, Net Income = Rev - Cogs - Depreciation Exp - Other Exp then the Net Income figure will be decreased by the building's depreciation that year. This depreciation is not associated with an exchange of cash, therefore the depreciation is added back into net income to remove the non-cash activity.

Rules (Financing Activities)

Finding the Cash Flows from Financing Activities is much more intuitive and needs little explanation. Generally, the things to account for are financing activities:

- Include as outflows, reductions of long term notes payable (as would represent the cash repayment of debt on the balance sheet)
- Or as inflows, the issuance of new notes payable
- Include as outflows, all dividends paid by the entity to outside parties
- Or as inflows, dividend payments received from outside parties
- Include as outflows, the purchase of notes stocks or bonds
- Or as inflows, the receipt of payments on such financing vehicles.

In the case of more advanced accounting situations, such as when dealing with subsidiaries, the accountant must:

- Exclude intra-company dividend payments.
- Exclude intra-company bond interest.

A traditional equation for this might look something like,

Net Cash Flows from Financing Activities =

[Divs received from 3rd parties] – [Divs paid to 3rd parties] –

{Divs paid to NCI but not intracompany div payments }

Example: cash flow of XYZ:

***Table** : XYZ co. Ltd. Cash Flow Statement(all numbers in millions of Rs.)*

Period ending	03/31/2010	03/31/2009	03/31/2008
Net income	21,538	24,589	17,046
Operating activities, cash flows provided by or used in:			
Depreciation and amortization	2,790	2,592	2,747
Adjustments to net income	4,617	621	2,910
Decrease (increase) in accounts receivable	12,503	17,236	—
Increase (decrease) in liabilities (A/P, taxes payable)	131,622	19,822	37,856
Decrease (increase) in inventories	—	—	—
Increase (decrease) in other operating activities	(173,057)	(33,061)	(62,963)
Net cash flow from operating activities	13	31,799	(2,404)
Investing activities, cash flows provided by or used in:			
Capital expenditures	(4,035)	(3,724)	(3,011)
Investments	(201,777)	(71,710)	(75,649)
Other cash flows from investing activities	1,606	17,009	(571)
Net cash flows from investing activities	(204,206)	(58,425)	(79,231)
Financing activities, cash flows provided by or used in:			
Dividends paid	(9,826)	(9,188)	(8,375)
Sale (repurchase) of stock	(5,327)	(12,090)	133
Increase (decrease) in debt	101,122	26,651	21,204

Other cash flows from financing activities	120,461	27,910	70,349
Net cash flows from financing activities	206,430	33,283	83,311
Effect of exchange rate changes	645	(1,840)	731
Net increase (decrease) in cash and cash equivalents	2,882	4,817	2,407

Statement of Retained Earnings

The Statement of Retained Earnings (and similarly the *Equity Statement*, *Statement of Owner's Equity* for a single proprietorship, *Statement of Partner's Equity* for partnership, and Statement of Retained Earnings and Stockholders' Equity for corporation) are basic financial statements.

The statements explain the changes in a company's retained earnings over the reporting period. They break down changes in the owners' interest in the organisation, and in the application of retained profit or surplus from one accounting period to the next. Line items typically include profits or losses from operations, dividends paid, issue or redemption of stock, and any other items charged or credited to retained earnings. The statements are expected by Generally Accepted Accounting Principles and explain the owners' equity and retained earnings shown on the balance sheet, where:

Owners' Equity = Assets – Liabilities.

Requirements of the U.S. GAAP

A retained earnings statement is required by the U.S. Generally Accepted Accounting Principles (U.S. GAAP) whenever comparative balance sheets and income statements are presented. It may appear in the balance sheet, in a combined income statement and changes in retained earnings statement, or as a separate schedule.

Therefore, the statement of retained earnings uses information from the income statement and provides information to the balance sheet. Retained earnings are part of the balance sheet (another basic financial statement) under "stockholders equity (shareholders' equity)" and is mostly affected by net income earned during a period of time by the company less any dividends paid to the company's owners/stockholders. The retained earnings account on the balance sheet is said to represent an "accumulation of earnings" since net profits and losses are added/subtracted from the account from period to period.

Retained Earnings are part of the Statement of Changes in Equity. The general equation can be expressed as following:

Ending Retained Earnings = *Beginning* Retained Earnings – Dividends Paid + Net Income

This equation is necessary to use to find the Profit Before Tax to use in the Cash Flow Statement under Operating Actvities when using the indirect method. This is used whenever a comprehensive income statement is not given but only the balance sheet is given.

Income Statement

Income statement (also referred to as *profit and loss statement (P&L), statement of financial performance, earnings statement, operating statement* or *statement of operations*) is a company's financial statement that indicates how the revenue (money received from the sale of products and services before expenses are taken out, also known as the "top line") is transformed into the net income (the result after all revenues and expenses have been accounted for, also known as the "bottom line").

It displays the revenues recognised for a specific period, and the cost and expenses charged against these revenues, including write-offs (e.g., depreciation and amortization of various assets) and taxes.

The purpose of the income statement is to show managers and investors whether the company made or lost money during the period being reported. The important thing to remember about an income statement is that it represents a period of time. This contrasts with the balance sheet, which represents a single moment in time.

Charitable organisations that are required to publish financial statements do not produce an income statement. Instead, they produce a similar statement that reflects funding sources compared against program expenses, administrative costs, and other operating commitments. This statement is commonly referred to as the statement of activities. Revenues and expenses are further categorised in the statement of activities by the donor restrictions on the funds received and expended.

The income statement can be prepared in one of two methods. The Single Step income statement takes a simpler approach, totalling revenues and subtracting expenses to find the bottom line. The more complex Multi-Step income statement (as the name implies) takes several steps to find the bottom line, starting with the gross profit.

It then calculates operating expenses and, when deducted from the gross profit, yields income from operations. Adding to income from operations is the difference of other revenues and other expenses. When combined with income from operations, this yields income before taxes. The final step is to deduct taxes, which finally produces the net income for the period measured.

Usefulness and Limitations of Income Statement

Income statements should help investors and creditors determine the past financial performance of the enterprise, predict future performance, and assess the capability of generating future cash flows through report of the income and expenses. However, information of an income statement has several limitations:

- Items that might be relevant but cannot be reliably measured are not reported (*e.g.* brand recognition and loyalty).
- Some numbers depend on accounting methods used (*e.g.* using FIFO or LIFO accounting to measure inventory level).
- Some numbers depend on judgments and estimates (*e.g.* depreciation expense depends on estimated useful life and salvage value).

INCOME STATEMENT GREENHARBOR LLC

For the year ended DECEMBER 31 2010

	€ Debit	€ Credit
Revenues		
GROSS REVENUES (including INTEREST income)		296,397
Expenses:		
ADVERTISING	6,300	
BANK & CREDIT CARD FEES	144	
BOOKKEEPING	2,350	
SUBCONTRACTORS	88,000	
ENTERTAINMENT	5,550	
INSURANCE	750	
LEGAL & PROFESSIONAL SERVICES	1,575	
LICENSES	632	
PRINTING, POSTAGE & STATIONERY	320	
RENT	13,000	
MATERIALS	74,400	
TELEPHONE	1,000	

UTILITIES	1,491	
TOTAL EXPENSES		(195,512)
NET INCOME		100,885

Guidelines for statements of comprehensive income and income statements of business entities are formulated by the International Accounting Standards Board and numerous country-specific organisations, for example the FASB in the U.S..

Names and usage of different accounts in the income statement depend on the type of organisation, industry practices and the requirements of different jurisdictions. If applicable to the business, summary values for the following items should be included in the income statement:

Irregular Items

They are reported separately because this way users can better predict future cash flows - irregular items most likely will not recur. These are reported *net of taxes*.

- Discontinued operations is the most common type of irregular items. Shifting business location(s), stopping production temporarily, or changes due to technological improvement do not qualify as discontinued operations. Discontinued operations *must* be shown separately.

Cumulative effect of changes in accounting policies (principles) is the difference between the book value of the affected assets (or liabilities) under the old policy (principle) and what the book value would have been if the new principle had been applied in the prior periods. For example, valuation of inventories using LIFO instead of weighted average method. The changes should be applied retrospectively and shown as adjustments to the *beginning* balance of affected components in Equity. All comparative financial statements should be restated. (IAS 8)

However, *changes in estimates* (e.g. estimated useful life of a fixed asset) only requires prospective changes. (IAS 8) No items may be presented in the income statement as extraordinary items. (IAS 1.87) *Extraordinary items* are both unusual (abnormal) and infrequent, for example, unexpected natural disaster, expropriation, prohibitions under new regulations. Additional items may be needed to fairly present the entity's results of operations. (IAS 1.85)

Disclosures

Certain items must be disclosed separately in the notes (or the statement of comprehensive income), if material, including: (IAS 1.98)

- Write-downs of inventories to net realisable value or of property, plant and equipment to recoverable amount, as well as *reversals* of such write-downs
- Restructurings of the activities of an entity and *reversals* of any provisions for the costs of restructuring
- Disposals of items of property, plant and equipment
- Disposals of investments
- Discontinued operations
- Litigation settlements
- Other reversals of provisions.

Earnings Per Share

Because of its importance, earnings per share (EPS) are required to be disclosed on the face of the income statement. A company which reports any of the irregular items must also report EPS for these items either in the statement or in the notes.

$$\text{Earnings per share} = \frac{\text{Net income} - \text{Preferred stock dividends}}{\text{Weighted average of common stock shares outstanding}}$$

There are two forms of EPS reported:

- Basic: in this case "weighted average of shares outstanding" includes only actual stocks outstanding.
- Diluted: in this case "weighted average of shares outstanding" is calculated as if all stock options, warrants, convertible bonds, and other securities that could be transformed into shares *are* transformed. This increases the number of shares and so EPS decreases. Diluted EPS is considered to be a more reliable way to measure EPS.

Sample Income Statement

The following income statement is a very brief example prepared in accordance with IFRS. It does not show all possible kinds of items appeared a firm, but it shows the most usual ones. Please note the difference between IFRS and US GAAP when interpreting the following sample income statements.

Table: *Fitness Equipment Limited*

INCOME STATEMENTS

(in millions)

Year Ended March 31	2009	2008	2007
Revenue	$ 14,580.2	$ 11,900.4	$ 8,290.3
Cost of sales	(6,740.2)	(5,650.1)	(4,524.2)
Gross profit	*7,840.0*	*6,250.3*	*3,766.1*
SGA expenses	(3,624.6)	(3,296.3)	(3,034.0)
Operating profit	*$ 4,215.4*	*$ 2,954.0*	*$ 732.1*
Gains from disposal of fixed assets	46.3	-	-
Interest expense	(119.7)	(124.1)	(142.8)
Profit *before* tax	4,142.0	2,829.9	589.3
Income tax expense	(1,656.8)	(1,132.0)	(235.7)
Profit (or loss) for the year	*$ 2,485.2*	*$ 1,697.9*	*$ 353.6*

DEXTERITY INC. AND SUBSIDIARIES

CONSOLIDATED STATEMENTS OF OPERATIONS

(In millions)

Year Ended December 31,	2009	2008	2007
Revenue	$ 36,525.9	$ 29,827.6	$ 21,186.8
Cost of sales	(18,545.8)	(15,858.8)	(11,745.5)
Gross profit	*17,980.1*	*13,968.8*	*9,441.3*
Operating expenses:			
Selling, general and administrative expenses	(4,142.1)	(3,732.3)	(3,498.6)
Depreciation	(602.4)	(584.5)	(562.3)
Amortization	(209.9)	(141.9)	(111.8)
Impairment loss	(17,997.1)	—	—
Total operating expenses	(22,951.5)	(4,458.7)	(4,172.7)
Operating profit (or loss)	*$ (4,971.4)*	*$ 9,510.1*	*$ 5,268.6*
Interest income	25.3	11.7	12.0
Interest expense	(718.9)	(742.9)	(799.1)

Profit (or loss) from continuing operations *before* tax, share of profit (or loss) from associates and non-controlling interest	$ (5,665.0)	$ 8,778.9	$ 4,481.5
Income tax expense	(1,678.6)	(3,510.5)	(1,789.9)
Profit (or loss) from associates, *net of tax*	(20.8)	0.1	(37.3)
Profit (or loss) from non-controlling interest, *net of tax*	(5.1)	(4.7)	(3.3)
Profit (or loss) from continuing operations	$ (7,348.7)	$ 5,263.8	$ 2,651.0
Profit (or loss) from discontinued operations, *net of tax*	(1,090.3)	(802.4)	164.6
Profit (or loss) for the year	*$ (8,439.0]*	*$ 4,461.4*	*$ 2,815.6*

Bottom Line

"Bottom line" is the net income that is calculated after subtracting the expenses from revenue. Since this forms the last line of the income statement, it is informally called "bottom line." It is important to investors as it represents the profit for the year attributable to the shareholders. After revision to IAS 1 in 2003, the Standard is now using profit or loss rather than *net profit or loss* or *net income* as the descriptive term for the bottom line of the income statement.

Requirements of IFRS

On 6 September 2007, the International Accounting Standards Board issued a revised *IAS 1: Presentation of Financial Statements*, which is effective for annual periods beginning on or after 1 January 2009.

A business entity adopting IFRS must include:

- a Statement of Comprehensive Income or
- *two* separate statements comprising:
  1. an *Income Statement* displaying components of profit or loss and
  2. a *Statement of Comprehensive Income* that *begins* with profit or loss (bottom line of the income statement) and displays the items of other comprehensive income for the reporting period. (IAS1.81)

All non-owner changes in equity (i.e. *comprehensive income*) shall be presented in either in the statement of comprehensive income (or in a separate income statement and a statement of comprehensive income). Components of comprehensive income may not be presented in the statement of changes in equity.

Comprehensive income for a period includes profit or loss (net income) for that period and other comprehensive income recognised in that period.

All items of income and expense recognised in a period must be included in profit or loss unless a Standard or an Interpretation requires otherwise. (IAS 1.88) Some IFRSs require or permit that some components to be excluded from profit or loss and instead to be included in other comprehensive income. (IAS 1.89)

Accumulated other Comprehensive Income

In 1997 the United States Financial Accounting Standards Board issued Statement on Financial Accounting Standards No. 130 entitled "Reporting Comprehensive Income". This statement required all income statement items to be reported either as a regular item in the income statement or a special item as other comprehensive income. It is commonly referred to as FAS130.

Comprehensive Income

Comprehensive income is the total non-owner change in equity for a reporting period. This change encompasses all changes in equity other than transactions from owners. Most of these changes appear in the income statement. A few special types of gains and losses are not shown in the income statement but as special items in shareholder equity section of the balance sheet.

Since these comprehensive income items are not closed to retained earnings each period they accumulate as shareholder equity items and thus are entitled "Accumulated Other Comprehensive Income" and is sometimes referred to as "AOCI". Accumulated other comprehensive income is a subsection in equity where "other comprehensive income" is accumulated (summed or "aggregated").

The balance of AOCI is presented in the Equity section of the Balance Sheet as is the Retained Earnings balance, which aggregates past and current Earnings, and past and current Dividends.

Other Comprehensive Income

Other comprehensive income is the difference between net income as in the Income Statement (Profit or Loss Account) and comprehensive income, and represents the certain gains and losses of the enterprise not recognised in the P&L Account. It is commonly referred to as "OCI".

In practice, it comprises the following items:

1. Unrealised gains and losses on available for sale securities [IAS 39/ *"FAS 115" - "Accounting for Certain Investments in Debt and Equity Securities"*]
2. Gains and losses on derivatives held as cash flow hedges (only for effective portions) [IAS 39/ *"FAS 133" - "Accounting for Derivative Instruments and Hedging Activities"*]
3. Gains and losses resulting from translating the financial statements of foreign subsidiaries (from foreign currency to the presentation currency) [IAS 21/ *"FAS 52" - "Foreign Currency Translation"*],
4. Actuarial gains and losses on defined benefit plans recognised (Minimum pension liability adjustments) [IAS 19/ *"FAS 158" - "Employers' Accounting For Defined Benefit Pension And Other Postretirement Plans"*]
5. Changes in the revaluation surplus [IAS 16 and IAS 38].

While the AOCI balance is presented in Equity section of the balance sheet, the annual accounting entries, as flows, are presented sometimes in a Statement of Comprehensive Income. This statement expands the traditional Income Statement beyond Earnings to include OCI in order to present Comprehensive Income.

Under the revised IAS 1, all non-owner changes in equity (comprehensive income) must be presented *either* in one Statement of comprehensive income or in two statements (a separate income statement and a statement of comprehensive income).

Reclassification to Profit or Loss (P&L)

Flows presented initially in OCI sometimes are reclassified into Earnings (Profit or Loss) when certain conditions are met. For the five types of OCI described above, the triggers for reclassification are presented in the accounting standard that gives rise to the OCI flow.

Alterations to Definition of OCI

In the United States further alterations to this OCI definition occur when a new standard (including a revision of a previously issued accounting standard) identifies an item that can be measured, should be measured in the financial statements, represents a "flow" variable rather than a stock, or snapshot, variable, and does not represent a flow variable that should be presented in the Income Statement as a component of Earnings. The flow variable that is both measurable and should be recognised is then added to the list above of items that a reporting entity would include in AOCI.

In the third quarter of 2008 the United States Securities and Exchange Commission received several proposals to allow the recognition in AOCI of certain fair value changes on financial instruments. This proposal was initially well received by representatives of the banking community who felt that Earnings recognition of these fair value changes during the concurrent "credit meltdown of 2008" would be inappropriate.

The effect of this proposal, on balance, would be to remove sizeable losses from Earnings and thus Retained Earnings of banks, and assist them in preserving their regulatory capital. The regulatory capital of banks in the US and generally worldwide includes contributed equity capital and retained earnings but excludes AOCI, even though it is reported as a component of the Equity section of the Balance Sheet.

Why is Hedge Accounting Necessary?

Many financial institutions and corporate businesses (entities) use derivative financial instruments to hedge their exposure to different risks (for example interest rate risk, foreign exchange risk, commodity risk, etc.). Accounting for derivative financial instruments under International Accounting Standards is covered by IAS39 (Financial Instrument: Recognition and Measurement).

IAS39 requires that all derivatives are marked-to-market with changes in the mark-to-market being taken to the profit and loss account. For many entities this would result in a significant amount of profit and loss volatility arising from the use of derivatives. An entity can mitigate the profit and loss effect arising from derivatives used for hedging, through an optional part of IAS39 relating to hedge accounting.

What Hedge Accounting Options are Available to an Entity?

All economic hedges aim to manage foreign currency exposure, meaning they are undertaken for the economic aim of reducing potential loss from fluctuations in foreign exchange rates. However, not all hedges are designated for special accounting treatment. Accounting standards enable hedge accounting for three different designated forex hedges:

- A cash flow hedge may be designated for a highly probable forecasted transaction, a firm commitment (not recorded on the balance sheet), foreign currency cash flows of a recognised asset or liability, or a forecasted intercompany transaction.
- A fair value hedge may be designated for a firm commitment (not recorded) or foreign currency cash flows of a recognised asset or liability.
- A net investment hedge may be designated for the net investment in a foreign operation.

The aim of hedge accounting is to provide an offset to the mark-to-market movement of the derivative in the profit and loss account. For a fair value hedge this is achieved either by marking-to-market an asset or a liability which offsets the P&L movement of the derivative. For a cashflow hedge some of the derivative volatility into a separate component of the entity's equity called the cash flow hedge reserve. Where a hedge relationship is effective (meets the 80%–125% rule), most of the mark-to-market derivative volatility will be offset in the profit and loss account. To achieve hedge accounting requires a large amount of compliance work involving documenting the hedge relationship and both prospectively and retrospectively proving that the hedge relationship is effective.

Simple Procedure of Hedge Accounting

To know simple procedure of hedge accounting, we should divide hedge into two parts. One is fair value hedge and other is cash flow hedge. When we have risk of decreasing the share prices, we take the contract of fair value hedge. We give option to other at current prices. If anybody accepts and if in future, prices of share decreases, we will get gain from option and will record like general income record.

In cash flow hedge accounting, we do hedge for reducing the risk of increasing the prices. If prices will increases, we will have to paid same but we will receive the cash profit from future contract. We also record the payment and gaining amount from such transactions.

XBRL (eXtensible Business Reporting Language)

XBRL (eXtensible Business Reporting Language) is a freely available, market-driven, open, and global standard for exchanging business information. XBRL allows information modelling and the expression of semantic meaning commonly required in business reporting. XBRL is XML-based. It uses the XML syntax and related

XML technologies such as XML Schema, XLink, XPath, and Namespaces to articulate this semantic meaning. One use of XBRL is to define and exchange financial information, such as a financial statement. The XBRL Specification is developed and published by XBRL International, Inc. (XII). XBRL is a standards-based way to communicate and exchange business information between business systems. These communications are defined by metadata set out in XBRL taxonomies, which capture the definition of individual reporting concepts as well as the relationships between concepts and other semantic meaning. Information being communicated or exchanged is provided within an XBRL instance. Early users of XBRL included regulators such as the U.S. Federal Deposit Insurance Corporation and the Committee of European Banking Supervisors (CEBS). Common functions in many countries that make use of XBRL include regulators of stock exchanges and securities, banking regulators, business registrars, revenue reporting and tax-filing agencies, and national statistical agencies. A wiki repository of XBRL projects is available to be freely explored and updated. An XBRL Adoption Survey is available as well. According to the FT "the Securities and Exchange Commission (SEC) in the US, the UK's HM Revenue & Customs (HMRC), and Companies House in Singapore have begun to require companies to use it, and other regulators are following suit."

Extensibility

Besides the creation of additional modules, XBRL International supports several methods for continuing expansion of shared XBRL functionality.

- Link Role Registry – This registry, hosted at xbrl.org, collects link roles and arc roles to promote reuse across taxonomies.
- Functions Registry – This registry collects XPath functions for reuse in formula linkbases.
- Format Registry – This registry collects common numeric formats for reuse in Inline XBRL applications.
- Best Practice RFCs – These documents will share common practices among community members to improve interoperability of design.

iXBRL

iXBRL (in-line Extensible Business Reporting Language) is a development of XBRL in which the XBRL tags are embedded in the formal document, e.g. a published report and accounts. It requires the formal document to be in XHTML format so that the XBRL tags can be invisible when the document is viewed in a web browser or printed yet be present when the electronic file is processed or viewed in an XML editor.

There are two main ways of producing iXBRL documents:

1. a program can generate the iXBRL file from source data;
2. a version of a word processing package can be used which has been enhanced to handle the XBRL tags.

However, neither of these produces a native iXBRL document which is designed as a web page and marked up with XBRL tags. A good example of this is the IASC 2007 Annual Report. In the UK, HM Revenue and Customs requires businesses to submit their report and accounts and tax computations in iXBRL format when making their Corporation Tax return. Businesses and their agents can use HMRC's Online Filing software to prepare their report and accounts and tax computations in iXBRL format or they can prepare the iXBRL files themselves and submit them to HMRC.

HMRC's Online Filing software is an example of a program which generates iXBRL from source data. This uses a series of forms in which the key data (which will appear in XBRL tags) are entered in data entry fields. Additional data (the rest of the report and accounts) are entered in text boxes. The program generates the iXBRL report and accounts in a standard sequence of sections and a standard format. All other formatting of material is lost. While the resulting report and accounts meets HMRC's requirements, it is not an attractive document to view or read.

The word processing package which has been enhanced for iXBRL most widely is Microsoft Word. This allows "round-tripping" between its own format for the precise layout of documents and HTML through the use of nonstandard extensions to HTML. The iXBRL tags are typically held as comments within the document.

One difference between XBRL and iXBRL is that in iXBRL a data item (e.g. profit) may appear repeatedly and is marked up as an XML tag each time it appears. With large and complex accounts, the resulting file may be too large for a web browser to handle. This happens more often when, as in the UK, the company report, which may contain many graphics, is combined with the accounts in a single iXBRL document. The iXBRL specification allows for a set of iXBRL documents to be treated as a single iXBRL document set ("IXDS").

Lack of Accuracy

In April 2009 a study of the North Carolina State University Department of Accounting College of Management evaluated the accuracy of XBRL filings for 22 companies participating in the SEC's voluntary filing program in 2006. Results of a comparison of XBRL filings to Forms 10-K revealed multiple errors in signage, amounts, labelling, and classification. The study considers that these errors are serious since XBRL data is computer-readable and users will not visually recognize the errors, especially when using XBRL analysis software.

Auditor's Report

The auditor's report is a formal opinion, or disclaimer thereof, issued by either an internal auditor or an independent external auditor as a result of an internal or external audit or evaluation performed on a legal entity or subdivision thereof (called an "auditee").

The report is subsequently provided to a "user" (such as an individual, a group of persons, a company, a government, or even the general public, among others) as an assurance service in order for the user to make decisions based on the results of the audit. An auditor's report is considered an essential tool when reporting financial information to users, particularly in business.

Since many third-party users prefer, or even require financial information to be certified by an independent external auditor, many auditees rely on auditor reports to certify their information in order to attract investors, obtain loans, and improve public appearance. Some have even stated that financial information without an auditor's report is "essentially worthless" for investing purposes.

Adverse Opinion Report

An Adverse Opinion is issued when the auditor determines that the financial statements of an auditee are materially misstated and, when considered as a whole, do not conform with GAAP. It is considered the opposite of an unqualified or clean opinion, essentially stating that the information contained is materially incorrect, unreliable, and inaccurate in order to assess the auditee's financial position and results of operations. Investors, lending institutions, and governments very rarely accept an auditee's financial statements if the auditor issued an adverse opinion, and usually request the auditee to correct the financial statements and obtain another audit report. Generally, an adverse opinion is only given if the financial statements pervasively differ from GAAP. An example of such a situation would be failure of a company to consolidate a material subsidiary.

The wording of the adverse report is similar to the qualified report. The scope paragraph is modified accordingly and an explanatory paragraph is added to explain the reason for the adverse opinion after the scope paragraph but before the opinion paragraph. However, the most significant change in the adverse report from the qualified report is in the opinion paragraph, where the auditor clearly states that the financial statements are not in accordance with GAAP, which means that they, as a whole, are unreliable, inaccurate, and do not present a fair view of the auditee's position and operations.

> *"In our opinion,* because of the situations mentioned above *(in the explanatory paragraph), the financial statements referred to in the first paragraph* do not *present fairly, in all material respects, the financial position of..."*

Disclaimer of Opinion Report

A Disclaimer of Opinion, commonly referred to simply as a Disclaimer, is issued when the auditor could not form, and consequently refuses to present, an opinion on the financial statements. This type of report is issued when the auditor tried to audit an entity but could not complete the work due to various reasons and does not issue an opinion.

The disclaimer of opinion report can be traced back to 1949, when the Statement on Auditing Procedure No. 23: *Recommendation Made To Clarify Accountant's Representations When Opinion Is Not Expressed* was published in order to provide guidance to auditors in presenting a disclaimer.

Statements on Auditing Standards (SAS) provide certain situations where a disclaimer of opinion may be appropriate:

- A lack of independence, or material conflict(s) of interest, exist between the auditor and the auditee (SAS No. 26)
- There are significant scope limitations, whether intentional or not, which hinder the auditor's work in obtaining evidence and performing procedures (SAS No. 58);
- There is a substantial doubt about the auditee's ability to continue as a going concern or, in other words, continue operating (SAS No. 59)

- There are significant uncertainties within the auditee (SAS No. 79).

Although this type of opinion is rarely used, the most common examples where disclaimers are issued include audits where the auditee willfully hides or refuses to provide evidence and information to the auditor in significant areas of the financial statements, where the auditee is facing significant legal and litigation issues in which the outcome is uncertain (usually government investigations), and where the auditee has going concern issues (the auditee may not continue operating in the near future). Investors, lending institutions, and governments typically reject an auditee's financial statements if the auditor disclaimed an opinion, and will request the auditee to correct the situations the auditor mentioned and obtain another audit report.

A disclaimer of opinion differs substantially from the rest of the auditor's reports because it provides very little information regarding the audit itself, and includes an explanatory paragraph stating the reasons for the disclaimer. Although the report still contains the letterhead, the auditee's name and address, the auditor's signature and address, and the report's issuance date, every other paragraph is modified extensively, and the scope paragraph is entirely omitted since the auditor is basically stating that an audit could not be realised.

In the introductory paragraph, the first phrase changes from "We have audited" to "We were engaged to audit" in order to let the user know that the auditee commissioned an audit, but does not mention that the auditor necessarily completed the audit. Additionally, since the audit was not completely and/or adequately performed, the auditor refuses to accept any responsibility by omitting the last sentence of the paragraph.

The scope paragraph is omitted in its entirety since, effectively, no audit was performed. Similar to the qualified and the adverse opinions, the auditor must briefly discuss the situations for the disclaimer in an explanatory paragraph. Finally, the opinion paragraph changes completely, stating that an opinion could not be formed and is not expressed because of the situations mentioned in the previous paragraphs. The following is a draft of the three main paragraphs of a disclaimer of opinion because of inadequate accounting records of an auditee, which is considered a significant scope of limitation: We *were engaged to audit* the accompanying balance sheet of ABC Company, Inc. (the "Company") as of December 31, 20XX and the related statements of income and cash flows for the year then ended. These financial statements are the responsibility of the Company's management. The Company does not maintain adequate accounting records to provide sufficient information for the preparation of the basic financial statements. The Company's accounting records do not constitute a double-entry system which can produce financial statements.

Because of the significance of the matters discussed in the preceding paragraphs, the scope of our work was not sufficient to enable us to express, and we do not express, an opinion of the financial statements referred to in the first paragraph.

Auditor's Report on Internal Controls of Public Companies

Following the enactment of the Sarbanes-Oxley Act of 2002, the Public Company Accounting Oversight Board (PCAOB) was established in order to monitor, regulate, inspect, and discipline audit and public accounting firms of public companies. The PCAOB Auditing Standards No. 2 now requires auditors of public companies to include an additional disclosures in the opinion report regarding the auditee's internal controls, and to opine about the company's and auditor's assessment on the company's internal controls over financial reporting. These new requirements are commonly referred to as the COSO Opinion. The auditor's report is modified to include all necessary disclosures by either presenting the report subsequent to the report on the financial statements, or combining both reports into one auditor's report. The following is an example of the former version of adding a separate report immediately after the auditor's report on financial statements.

Internal Control Over Financial Reporting

We have also audited management's assessment, included in the accompanying Management's Annual Report on Internal Control Over Financial Reporting, that the Company maintained effective internal control over financial reporting as of December 31, 20XX, based on criteria established in Internal Control—Integrated Framework issued by the Committee of Sponsoring Organisations of the Treadway Commission ("COSO"). The Company's management is responsible for maintaining effective internal control over financial reporting and for its assessment of the effectiveness of internal control over financial reporting. Our responsibility is to express an opinion on management's assessment and on the effectiveness of the Company's internal control over financial reporting based on our audit. We conducted our audits in accordance with the standards of the Public Company Accounting Oversight Board (United States). Those standards require that we plan and perform the audit to obtain reasonable assurance about whether effective internal control over financial reporting was maintained in all material respects. Our audit of internal control over financial reporting included obtaining an understanding of internal control over financial reporting, evaluating management's assessment, testing and evaluating the design and operating effectiveness of internal control, and performing such other procedures as we considered necessary in the circumstances. We believe that our audit provides a reasonable basis for our opinion.

A company's internal control over financial reporting is a process designed to provide reasonable assurance regarding the reliability of financial reporting and the preparation of financial statements for external purposes in accordance with generally accepted accounting principles.

A company's internal control over financial reporting includes those policies and procedures that (1) pertain to the maintenance of records that, in reasonable detail, accurately and fairly reflect the transactions and dispositions of the assets of the company; (2) provide reasonable assurance that transactions are recorded as necessary to permit preparation of financial statements in accordance with generally accepted accounting principles, and that receipts and expenditures of the company are being made only in accordance with authorisations of management and directors of the company; and (3) provide reasonable assurance regarding prevention or timely detection of unauthorised acquisition, use, or disposition of the company's assets that could have a material effect on the financial statements.

Because of its inherent limitations, internal control over financial reporting may not prevent or detect misstatements. Also, projections of any evaluation of effectiveness to future periods are subject to the risk that controls may become inadequate because of changes in conditions, or that the degree of compliance with the policies or procedures may deteriorate. In our opinion, management's assessment that ABC Company maintained effective internal control over financial reporting as of December 31, 20XX, is fairly stated, in all material respects, based on criteria established in Internal Control—Integrated Framework issued by COSO. Furthermore, in our opinion, ABC Company maintained, in all material respects, effective internal control over financial reporting as of December 31, 20XX, based on criteria established in Internal Control—Integrated Framework issued by COSO.

Auditor's Reports on Financial Statements in Different Countries

The auditor's report usually does not vary from country to country, although some countries do require either additional or less wording. In the United States, auditors are required to include in the scope paragraphs a phrase stating that they conducted their audit "in accordance with generally accepted auditing standards in the United States of America", and, in the opinion paragraph, state whether the financial statements are presented "in conformity with generally accepted accounting principles in the United States of America".

Some countries, such as the Philippines, use similar reports to those issued in the United States, with the exception that second paragraph would state that the audit was conducted in accordance with Philippine Standards on Auditing, and that the financial statements are in accordance with Philippine Financial Reporting Standards.

11

Accounting, Accountability and the Account

Businesses exist to provide goods or services to customers in exchange for a financial reward. Public-sector and not-for-profit organisations also provide services, although their funding comes not from customers but from government or charitable donations. While this book is primarily concerned with profit-oriented businesses, most of the principles are equally applicable to the public and not-for-profit sectors. Business is not about accounting. It is about markets, people and operations (the delivery of products or services), although accounting is implicated in all of these decisions because it is the financial representation of business activity.

The American Accounting Association defined accounting in 1966 as: The process of identifying, measuring and communicating economic information to permit informed judgements and decisions by users of the information.

This is an important definition because:

- it recognizes that accounting is a process: that process is concerned with capturing business events, recording their financial effect, summarizing and reporting the result of those effects and interpreting those results;
- it is concerned with economic information: while this is predominantly financial, it also allows for non-financial information;
- its purpose is to support 'informed judgements and decisions' by users: this emphasizes the decision usefulness of accounting

information and the broad spectrum of 'users' of that information.

The notion of accounting for a narrow (shareholders and financiers) or a broad (societal) group of users is an important philosophical debate to which we will return throughout this book. This debate derives from questions of accountability: to whom is the business accountable and for what and what is the role of accounting in that accountability?

Boland and Schultze defined accountability as: The capacity and willingness to give explanations for conduct, stating how one has discharged one's responsibilities, an explaining of conduct with a credible story of what happened and a calculation and balancing of competing obligations, including moral ones. Hoskin suggested that accountability is: more total and insistent... [it] ranges more freely over space and time, focusing as much on future potential as past accomplishment. Boland and Schultze argued that accountability entails both a narration of what transpired and a reckoning of money, both meanings deriving from the original meanings of the word account. Accounting is a collection of systems and processes used to record, report and interpret business transactions. Accounting provides an account – an explanation or report in financial terms – about the transactions of an organisation. It enables managers to satisfy the stakeholders in the organisation (owners, government, financiers, suppliers, customers, employees etc.) that they have acted in the best interests of stakeholders rather than themselves.

This is the notion of accountability to others, a result of the stewardship function of managers that takes place through the process of accounting. Stewardship is an important concept because in all but very small businesses, the owners of businesses are not the same as the managers. This separation of ownership from control makes accounting particularly influential due to the emphasis given to increasing shareholder wealth (or shareholder value). Accountability results in the production of financial statements, primarily for those interested parties who are external to the business. This function is called financial accounting.

Accounting is traditionally seen as fulfilling three functions:

- *Scorekeeping:* Capturing, recording, summarizing and reporting financial performance.
- *Attention-directing:* Drawing the attention of managers to and assisting in the interpretation of, business performance,

particularly in terms of the comparison between actual and planned performance.

- *Problem-solving:* Identifying the best choice from a range of alternative actions.

Here we acknowledge the role of the scorekeeping function while emphasizing attention-directing and problem-solving as taking place through three inter-related functions, all part of the role of functional as well as financial managers:

- *Planning:* Establishing goals and strategies to achieve those goals.
- *Decision-making:* Using financial information to make decisions consistent with those goals and strategies.
- *Control:* Using financial information to maintain performance as close as possible to plan, or using the information to modify the plan itself.

Planning, decision-making and control are particularly relevant as increasingly businesses have been decentralized into many business units, where much of the planning, decision-making and control is focused. Managers need financial and non-financial information to develop and implement strategy by planning for the future (budgeting); making decisions about products, services, prices and what costs to incur (decision-making using cost information); and ensuring that plans are put into action and are achieved (control). This function is called management accounting.

A Short History of Accounting

The history of accounting is intertwined with the development of trade between tribes and there are records of commercial transactions on stone tablets dating back to 3600 BC. The early accountants were 'scribes' who also practiced law. Stone noted: In ancient Egypt in the pharaoh's central finance department... scribes prepared records of receipts and disbursements of silver, corn and other commodities. One recorded on papyrus the amount brought to the warehouse and another checked the emptying of the containers on the roof as it was poured into the storage building. Audit was performed by a third scribe who compared these two records.

However, accounting as we know it today began in the fourteenth century in the Italian city-states of Florence, Genoa and Venice as a result of the growth of maritime trade and banking institutions. The first bank with customer facilities opened in Venice in 1149. The

Lombards were Italian merchants who were established as moneylenders in England at the end of the twelfth century. Balance sheets were evident from around 1400 and the Medici family had accounting records of 'cloth manufactured and sold'.

The first treatise on accounting was the work of a monk, Luca Pacioli, in 1494. The first professional accounting body was formed in Venice in 1581. Much of the language of accounting is derived from Latin roots. 'Debtor' comes from the Latin debitum, something that is owed; 'assets' from the Latin ad + satis, to enough, i.e. to pay obligations; 'liability' from ligare, to bind; 'capital' from caput, a head (of wealth). Even 'account' derives initially from the Latin computare, to count, while 'profit' comes from profectus, advance or progress. 'Sterling' and 'shilling' came from the Italian sterlino and scellino, while the pre-decimal currency abbreviation 'LSD' (pounds, shillings and pence) stood for lire, soldi, denarii. Chandler traced the development of the modern industrial enterprise from its agricultural and commercial roots as a result of the Industrial Revolution in the last half of the nineteenth century. By 1870, the leading industrial nations – the United States, Great Britain and Germany – accounted for two-thirds of the world's industrial output. One of the consequences of growth was the separation of ownership from management.

Although the corporation, as distinct from its owners, had been in existence in Britain since 1650, the separation of ownership and control was enabled by the first British Companies Act, which formalized the law in relation to 'joint stock companies' and introduced the limited liability of shareholders during the 1850s. The London Stock Exchange had been formed earlier in 1773 by stockbrokers, who had previously worked from coffee houses. The second consequence of growth was the creation of new organisational forms. Based on his extensive historical analysis, Chandler found that in large firms structure followed strategy and strategic growth and diversification led to the creation of decentralized, multidivisional corporations like General Motors, where remotely located managers made decisions on behalf of absent owners and central head office functions. Ansoff emphasized that success in the first 30 years of the mass-production era went to firms that had the lowest prices. However, in the 1930s General Motors 'triggered a shift from production to a market focus'.

In large firms such as General Motors, budgets were developed to co-ordinate diverse activities. In the first decades of the twentieth century, the DuPont company developed a model to measure the return on investment (ROI). ROI was used to make capital investment decisions and to evaluate the performance of business units, including the managerial responsibility to use capital efficiently.

The Role of Management Accounting

The advent of mechanized production following the Industrial Revolution increased the size and complexity of production processes, which employed more people and required larger sums of capital to finance machinery. Accounting historians suggest that the increase in the number of limited companies that led to the separation of ownership from control caused the attention of cost accounting to shift from determining cost to exercising control by absent owners over their managers.

The predecessor of management accounting, 'cost accounting', was reflected in the earlier title of management accountants as cost or works accountants. Typically situated in factories, these accountants tended to know the business and advise non-financial managers in relation to operational decisions. Cost accounting was concerned with determining the cost of an object, whether a product, an activity, a division of the organisation or market segment. The first book on cost accounting is believed to be Garcke and Fell's Factory Accounts, which was published in 1897. Historians have argued that the new corporate structures that were developed in the twentieth century – multidivisional organisations, conglomerates and multinationals – placed increased demands on accounting. These demands included divisional performance evaluation and budgeting. It has also been suggested that developments in cost accounting were driven by government demands for cost information during both World Wars. It appears that 'management accounting' is a term used only after the Second World War.

In their acclaimed book Relevance Lost, Johnson and Kaplan traced the development of management accounting from its origins in the Industrial Revolution supporting process-type industries such as textile and steel conversion, transportation and distribution. These systems were concerned with evaluating the efficiency of internal processes, rather than measuring organisational profitability. Financial reports were produced using a separate transactions-based system that reported financial performance. Johnson and Kaplan argued that by 1925 'virtually all management accounting practices used today had been developed'. They also described how the early manufacturing firms attempted to improve performance via economies of scale by reducing unit cost through increasing the volume of output. This led to a concern with measuring the efficiency of the production process. Calculating the cost of different products was unnecessary because the product range was homogeneous.

Over time, the product range expanded and businesses sought economies of scope through producing two or more products in a single facility. This led to the need for better information about how the mix of products could improve total profits. However, after 1900 the production of accounting information was largely for external reporting to shareholders and not to assist managerial decision-making. Johnson and Kaplan described how a management accounting system must provide timely and accurate information to facilitate efforts to control costs, to measure and improve productivity and to devise improved production processes. The management accounting system must also report accurate product costs so that pricing decisions, introduction of new products, abandonment of obsolete products and response to rival products can be made.

The Chartered Institute of Management Accountants' definition of the core activities of management accounting includes:

- participation in the planning process at both strategic and operational levels, involving the establishment of policies and the formulation of budgets;
- the initiation of and provision of guidance for management decisions, involving the generation, analysis, presentation and interpretation of relevant information;
- contributing to the monitoring and control of performance through the provision of reports including comparisons of actual with budgeted performance and their analysis and interpretation.

One of the earliest writers on management accounting described 'different costs for different purposes'. This theme was developed by one of the earliest texts on management accounting. Vatter distinguished the information needs of managers from those of external shareholders and emphasized that it was preferable to get less precise data to managers quickly than complete information too late to influence decision-making. Johnson and Kaplan commented that even today, organisations with access to far more computational power... rarely distinguish between information needed promptly for managerial control and information provided periodically for summary financial statements.

They argued that the developments in accounting theory in the first decades of the twentieth century came about by academics who emphasized simple decision-making models in highly simplified firms – those producing one or only a few products, usually in a onstage production process. The academics developed their ideas by logic and deductive reasoning. They did not attempt to study the problems actually faced by managers of organisations producing hundreds or thousands of products in complex production processes.

They concluded: Not surprisingly, in this situation actual management accounting systems provided few benefits to organisations. In some instances, the information reported by existing management accounting systems not only inhibited good decision-making by managers, it might actually have encouraged bad decisions.

Johnson and Kaplan described how the global competition that has taken place since the 1980s has left management accounting behind in terms of its decision usefulness. Developments such as total quality management, just-in-time inventory, computer-integrated manufacturing, shorter product life cycles and the decline of manufacturing and rise of service industries have led to the need for 'accurate knowledge of product costs, excellent cost control and coherent performance measurement'. And 'the challenge for today's competitive environment is to develop new and more flexible approaches to the design of effective cost accounting, management control and performance measurement systems'.

Recent Developments in Management Accounting

Partly as a result of the stimulus of Relevance Lost but perhaps more so as a consequence of rapidly changing business conditions, management accounting has moved beyond its traditional concern with a narrow range of numbers to incorporate wider issues of performance measurement and management. Management accounting is now implicated, to greater or lesser degrees in different organisations, with:

- value-based management;
- non-financial performance measurement systems;
- quality management approaches;
- activity-based management; and
- strategic management accounting.

Value-based management is in brief a concern with improving the value of the business to its shareholders. Management accounting is implicated in this, as a fundamental role of non-financial managers is to make decisions that contribute to increasing the value of the business. The limitations of accounting information, particularly as a lagging indicator of performance, have led to an increasing emphasis on non-financial performance measures. Non-financial measures are a major concern of both accountants and non-financial managers, as they tend to be leading indicators of the financial performance that will be reported at some future time.

Improving the quality of products and services is also a major concern, since advances in production technology and the need to improve performance by reducing waste have led to management tools such as total quality management (TQM), just-in-time (JIT), business process re-engineering (BPR) and continuous improvement processes such as Six Sigma and the Business Excellence model. Management accounting has a role to play in these techniques and non-financial managers need to understand the relationships between accounting and new management techniques. Activity-based management is an approach that emphasizes the underlying business processes that are required to produce goods and services and the need to identify the drivers or causes of those activities in order to be able to budget for and control costs more effectively.

Strategic management accounting, is an attempt to shift the perceptions of accountants and non-financial managers from an inward-looking to an outward-looking one, recognizing the need to look beyond the business along the value chain to its suppliers and customers and to seek ways of achieving and maintaining competitive advantage.

These changes to the narrow view of accountants, from 'bean-counters' to more active participants in formulating and implementing business strategy, have been accompanied by a shift in the collection, reporting and analysis of routine financial information from accountants to non-financial line managers. This decentring of accounting is evidenced by the delegation of responsibility for budgets and cost control to line managers and is the underlying reason that non-financial managers need a better understanding of accounting information and how that information can be used in decision-making.

A Critical Perspective

Although the concepts and assumptions underlying accounting are yet to be introduced, having begun this book with an introduction to accounting history it is worthwhile considering a contrasting viewpoint. While this viewpoint is one that may not be accepted by many practising managers, it is worth knowing, because it does lie at the very basis of the capitalist economic system in which we live and in which accounting plays such an important role.

The Marxist historian Hobsbawm argued that colonialism had been created by the cotton industry that dominated the UK economy and this resulted in a shift from domestic production to factory production. Sales increased but profits shrank, so labour (which was three times the cost of materials) was replaced by mechanization during the Industrial Revolution.

Entrepreneurs started with borrowings and small items of machinery and growth was largely financed by borrowings. The Industrial Revolution produced 'such vast quantities and at such rapidly diminishing cost, as to be no longer dependent on existing demand, but to create its own market'.

Advances in mass production followed the development of the assembly line, supported by railways and shipping to transport goods and communications through the electric telegraph. At the same time, agriculture diminished in importance. Due to the appetite of the railways for iron and steel, coal, heavy machinery, labour and capital investment, 'the comfortable and rich classes accumulated income so fast and in such vast quantities as to exceed all available possibilities of spending and investment'.

While the rich accumulated profits, labour was exploited with wages at subsistence levels. Labour had to learn how to work, unlike agriculture or craft industries, in a manner suited to industry and the result was a draconian master/servant relationship. In the 1840s a depression led to unemployment and high food prices and 1848 saw the rise of the labouring poor in European cities, who threatened both the weak and obsolete regimes and the rich. This resulted in a clash between the political and industrial revolutions, the 'triumph of bourgeois-liberal capitalism' and the domination of the globe by a few western regimes, especially the British in the mid-nineteenth century, which became a 'world hegemony'.

This 'global triumph' of capitalism in the 1850s was a consequence of the combination of cheap capital and rising prices. Stability and prosperity overtook political questions about the legitimacy of existing dynasties and technology cheapened manufactured products. There was high demand but the cost of living did not fall, so labour became dominated by the interests of the new owners of the means of production.

'Economic liberalism' became the recipe for economic growth as the market ruled labour and helped national economic expansion. Industrialization made wealth and industrial capacity decisive in international power, especially in the US, Japan and Germany. This 'British' capitalist system was exported throughout the world, not least with the support of a colonial expansionist Empire that lent large sums of money in return for adopting the British system. This system has since been taken over by multinational corporations, largely based in the United States. Armstrong traced the historical factors behind the comparative (in relation to other professions) pre-eminence of accountants in British management hierarchies and the emphasis on financial control. He concluded that accounting controls were installed by accountants as a result of their power base in global capital markets, which was achieved through their role in the allocation of the profit surplus to shareholders.

Armstrong argued that mergers led to control problems that were tackled by American management consultants who tended to recommend the multidivisional form of organisation... [which] entirely divorce headquarters management from operations. Functional departments and their managers are subjected to a battery of financial indicators and budgetary controls... [and] a subordination of operational to financial decision-making and a major influx of accountants into senior management positions. Roberts suggested that organisational accounting embodies the separation of instrumental and moral consequences, which is questionable. He argued:

The mystification of accounting information helps to fix, elevate and then impose upon others its own particular instrumental interests, without regard to the wider social and environmental consequences of the pursuit of such interests. Accounting thus serves as a vehicle whereby others are called to account, while the interests it embodies escape such accountability. This is a more critical perspective than that associated with the traditional notion of accounting as a report to shareholders and managers, which is a result of the historical development of capitalism in the West.

While this book is designed to help non-financial managers understand the tools and techniques of accounting, it is also intended to make readers think critically about the role of accounting and the limitations of accounting, some of which have been historically defined. One intention is to reinforce to readers that: accounting information provides a window through which the real activities of the organisation may be monitored, but it should be noted also that other windows are used that do not rely upon accounting information.

Shareholder Valu and Business Structure

Capital and Product Markets

Since the seventeenth century, companies have been formed by shareholders in order to consolidate resources and invest in opportunities. Shareholders had limited liability through which their personal liability in the event of business failure was limited to their investment in shares.

Shareholders appointed directors to manage the business, who in turn employed managers. Shareholders have few direct rights in relation to the conduct of the business. Their main powers are to elect the directors and appoint the auditors in an annual general meeting of shareholders. They are also entitled to an annual report containing details of the company's financial performance.

The market in which investors buy and sell the shares of companies is called the capital market, which is normally associated with the Stock Exchange. Companies obtain funds raised from shareholders (equity) and borrowings from financiers (debt). Both of these constitute the capital employed in the business. The cost of capital represents the cost incurred by the organisation to fund all its investments, comprising the cost of equity and the cost of debt weighted by the mix of debt and equity. The cost of debt is interest, which is the price charged by the lender.

The cost of equity is partly dividend and partly capital growth, because most shareholders expect both regular income from profits (the dividend) and an increase in the value of their shares over time in the capital market. Thus the different costs of each form of capital, weighted by the proportions of different forms of debt and equity, constitute the weighted average cost of capital. The management of the business relationship with capital markets is called financial management or corporate finance.

Companies use their capital to invest in technologies, people and materials in order to make, buy and sell products or services to customers. This is called the product market. The focus of shareholder wealth, according to Rappaport, is to obtain funds at competitive rates from capital markets and invest those funds to exploit imperfections in product markets. Where this takes place, shareholder wealth is increased through dividends and increases in the share price. The

1990s saw a growing concern with the role of accounting in improving shareholder wealth.

Value-based Management

Since the mid-1980s, there has been more and more emphasis on increasing the value of the business to its shareholders. Traditionally, business performance has been measured through accounting ratios such as return on capital employed (ROCE), return on investment (ROI), earnings per share and so on. However, it has been argued that these are historical rather than current measures and they vary between companies as a result of different accounting treatments.

Rappaport described how companies with strong cash flows diversified in the mid-twentieth century, often into uneconomic businesses, which led to the 'value gap' – the difference between the market value of the shares and the value of the business if it had been managed to maximize shareholder value. The consequence was the takeover movement and subsequent asset stripping of the 1980s, which provided a powerful incentive for managers to focus on creating value for shareholders. The takeover movement itself led to problems as high acquisition premiums (the excess paid over and above the calculated value of the business, i.e. the goodwill) were paid to the owners and financed by high levels of debt. During the 1990s institutional investors (pension funds, insurance companies, investment trusts etc.), through their dominance of share ownership, increased their pressure on management to improve the financial performance of companies.

Value-based management (VBM) emphasizes shareholder value, on the assumption that this is the primary goal of every business. VBM approaches include total shareholder return, market value added, shareholder value added and economic value added. Recent research into the use of value-based management approaches by UK companies is covered by Cooper et al..

Total shareholder return (TSR) compares the dividends received by shareholders and the increase in the share price with the original shareholder investment, expressing the TSR as a percentage of the initial investment. Market value added (MVA) is the difference between total market capitalization (number of shares issued times share price plus the market value of debt) and the total capital invested in the business by debt and equity providers. This is a measure of the value generated by managers for shareholders.

Rappaport coined shareholder value added (SVA) to refer to the increase in shareholder value over time. He defines shareholder value as the economic value of an investment, which can be calculated by using the cost of capital to discount forecast future cash flows (which he called free cash flows) into present values.

The business must generate profits in product markets that exceed the cost of capital in the capital market for value to be created (if not, shareholder value is eroded). Rappaport developed a shareholder value network. Through this diagram, he identified seven drivers of shareholder value: sales growth rate, operating profit margin, income tax rate, working capital investment, fixed capital investment, cost of capital and forecast duration. Managers make three types of decisions that influence these value drivers and lead to shareholder value:

- Operating decisions – product mix, pricing, promotion, customer service etc., which are then reflected in the sales growth rate, operating profit margin and income tax rate.
- Investment decisions – in both inventory and capacity, which are then reflected in both working capital and fixed capital investment.
- Financing decisions – the mix of debt and equity and the choice of financial instrument determine the cost of capital, which is assessed by capital markets in terms of business risk.

The value growth duration is the estimated number of years over which the return from investments is expected to exceed the cost of capital. The seven value drivers determine the cash flow from operations, the level of debt and the cost of capital, all of which determine shareholder value. A detrimental consequence of the emphasis on shareholder value is that it has led to a continued focus on short-term financial performance at the expense of longer-term strategy.

Economic Value Added (EVA) is a financial performance measure developed by consultants Stern Stewart & Co. It claims to capture the economic profit of a business that leads to shareholder value creation. In simple terms, EVA is net operating profit after deducting a charge to cover the opportunity cost of the capital invested in the business. EVA's 'economic profit' is the amount by which earnings exceed (or fall short of) the minimum rate of return that shareholders and financiers could get by investing in other securities with a comparable risk.

EVA accepts the assumption that the primary financial objective of any business is to maximize the wealth of its shareholders. The value of the business depends on the extent to which investors expect future profits to be greater or less than the cost of capital. Returns over and above the cost of capital increase shareholder wealth, while returns below the cost of capital erode shareholder wealth. Stern Stewart argues that managers understand this measure because it is based on operating profits. By introducing a notional charge based on assets held by the business, managers (whether at a corporate or divisional level) manage those assets as well as the profit generated.

EVA also has its critics. For example, the calculation of EVA allows up to 164 adjustments to reported accounting profits in order to remove distortions caused by arbitrary accounting rules and estimates the risk-adjusted cost of capital, both of which can be argued as subjective, although Stern Stewart argues that most organisations need only about a dozen of these. The increase in shareholder value is reflected in compensation strategies for managers whose goals, argues Stern Stewart, are aligned to increasing shareholder wealth through bonus and share option schemes that are paid over a period of time to ensure consistent future performance.

Accounting and Strategy

This book treats accounting as part of the broader business context of strategy, marketing, operations and human resources. The focus of accounting in business organisations is shareholder value – increasing the value of the business to its shareholders – through dividends from profits and/or through capital growth. Strategy both influences and is influenced by shareholder value. Strategy is reflected in the functional business areas of marketing, operations and human resources, through the actions the business wants to take to achieve, maintain and improve competitive advantage. Financial management is concerned with raising funds from shareholders or financiers to provide the capital the business needs to sell and produce goods and services. Financial accounting represents the stewardship function, that managers are accountable to those with a financial interest in the business and produce financial reports to satisfy that accountability.

Management accounting provides the information for planning, decision-making and control. Therefore, the main content of this book is the interaction between the functional areas of marketing, operations and human resources – driven by strategy – and how accounting provides a set of tools and techniques to assist functional managers.

Management accounting both influences and is influenced by the functional areas and by business strategy.

The importance of strategy for management accounting and the information it provides is that a strategic perspective involves taking a longer-term view about the business than is usually provided by traditional accounting reports. Management accounting comprises a set of tools and techniques to support planning, decisionmaking and control in business organisations.

Accounting is – or at least should be – integrated with business strategy. However, these same accounting tools and techniques can be used to help evaluate the performance of customers, suppliers and competitors in order to improve competitive advantage. Accounting should also extend beyond a narrow concern with financial measurement and encompass non-financial performance measurement, a subject of steadily increasing importance for those managers who are responsible for achieving performance targets, as well as for accountants.

Strategy is concerned with long-term direction, achieving and maintaining competitive advantage, identifying the scope and boundaries of the organisation and matching the activities of the organisation to its environment. Strategy is also about building on resources and competences to create new opportunities and take advantage of those opportunities and manage change within the organisation.

There is also a link between strategy and operational decisions in order to turn strategy formulation into strategy implementation. An economic perspective is added by Grant, who saw the value created by firms distributed among customers, suppliers and equity risk-takers. In order to provide this value, business firms establish profit as the single dominant objective. The purpose of strategy 'is to pursue profit over the long term'. Strategy is thus linked to performance by setting performance targets for the business as a whole and for individual business units and then measuring performance against those targets. It is to the divisionalized organisational form that we now turn.

12

Competition Defined

The word competition is frequently heard and with various implications. Literally it means "seeking-together," with the suggestion of rivalry, of mutual exclusion of the seekers. As applied to trade, competition means the attempt of two or more persons to get the same thing, each being guided by his own valuation and not restrained by any outside force. Thus there is an element of competition in the simplest case of barter, for whatever ratio is more favourable to one is less favourable to the other party and gives to one what the other fails to get.

But the idea of competition more frequently is applied to a group of traders buying or selling the same class of goods. All the members of the group are thought of as being on one side of the trade, either the buyer's or the seller's side. If in such case there is on the other side but one trader (or some agreement or limitation of competition) there is one-sided competition. When there are two groups of competitive traders, one of buyers and one of sellers, there is two-sided competition.

Naturalness of Competition

Competition has been implied in previous chapters in such words as rivalry, emulation, bidding, least eager buyer, or seller, price-adjustment, etc. Competition is spoken of as a force raising or lowering prices, as a motive acting upon the traders, etc., but competition is not a different force, or a separate motive, apart from the desires of the traders. (Some minor exceptions occur where the motive is the mere wish to outdo for the fun of the game.) Rather competition ordinarily is but an expression for the situation where each trader is exercising his choice in a market without restraint from others of the same group. For unless there is introduced a new personal factor of collusion, conspiracy, agreement not to bid against each other, the market price will be competitive, and a condition of competition exist. Such agreements, being dependent always on the good faith of the parties, often also on secrecy, and being provocative of jealousies in the division of the gains, are dependent on personal factors, and create a more artificial state of price than is found in competitive price, which has a more impersonal character. Hence competitive prices have, since the days of Adam Smith, commonly been spoken of as "natural" prices.

The word natural must, however, be used with caution. It can not be said that the choice any trader makes in entering into an agreement not to compete, when he sees that he can gain by so doing is, in one sense, any less "natural" than his choice of the thing when he competes. The choice might be called natural but the situation and the price resulting are not so, viewed from our present standpoint; they are artificial in the sense that they result from an agreement to abstain from the competition which otherwise would take place.

Conflicting Interests of Competition

The buyers have the common interest of low prices; the sellers, the common interest of high prices; and buyers' interest as a group is opposed to sellers' interest as a group. The competition of interests is thus in two dimensions, but competition is applied particularly to the rivalry within the group on either side. If there are more would-be buyers than sellers (or vice versa), some on the buyers' side will be forced out by the competition of the others; and even if the numbers are equal in each group, and all succeed in trading, it will probably be at a ratio altered by the competition. The presence of competing buyers, having different valuations, raises the price at which some sellers will be able to sell and, vice versa, the presence of competing sellers lowers the price which some buyers must pay.

It would always be to the advantage of the traders on one side (say the sellers) if some of their number would cease to produce, or would produce less, as this would raise the price that those remaining could get. Sometimes the rise of price through decreased production is so great that the total price of the whole supply is greater than the total price of the larger supply (and vice versa, in case of increased production).

This is the paradox of value applying to a whole market and to the buyers' curve of composite demand, rather than to the individual and to his valuation curve. For example, the total amount of money received by all the farmers of a country for a large crop of corn, wheat, tobacco, cotton, may be less than what would be received for a smaller crop. Abundance is good for the purchasers of farm products, but not always advantageous to the farmers as a class. This appears in the comparison of amount produced, price per unit, and value of the total crop, in successive years; for example, of cotton in the United States. This phenomenon appears frequently in the case of many kinds of products. To the sellers it is very disagreeable to get less for a large crop than for a smaller one, and it constitutes a motive for attempting to control the prices to their own advantage whenever they can.

Nature of monopoly. Monopoly is derived from the Greek roots, monos (sole, only) and polein (to sell), whence the abstract noun monopolia (exclusive power, or condition of sale). It originally meant the exclusive legal right of selling some article in some market. The typical monopoly of later medieval and early modern times was the power (or person or company granting it) granted in a patent by the sovereign. The name patent survives as the special name for the monopoly granted by law to an inventor. Patents and franchises of public corporations, such as street railways, etc., are the main modern forms of legal monopoly. The idea was extended in one direction to include the right to deal in some article, and has been extended in modern usage in another direction to mean economic power to become (within limits) the sole seller (or buyer) of an article, whether this power is derived from law or springs from the economic conditions. It is applied also to the group of persons, or to the business company or corporation, which has this power.

Monopoly, therefore, is essentially opposed to competition, but only within a group on one side of the market, not in the market as a whole. It suggests always the limitation or absence of that rivalry within the group of buyers or of sellers, respectively, which constitutes competition. In nine changes that occurred (as compared with the preceding year) production and prices moved in opposite directions eight times, and in the other case (in 1910) price rose but little the same year that production increased a little. No doubt cotton prices would have been on a lower level the last few years (1909-1912) but for two factors: (1) The increasing scale of general prices due to gold production, and (2) the increasing population and the corresponding need for more cotton.

Competition and Monopoly

In five of the nine changes the paradox of value appeared; three times (1904, 1908, and 1911) when production increased, and two times (1909 and 1911) when production declined; and in still another year (1905), this nearly occurred, for a crop smaller by 20 percent had a total value only two-thirds of a percent less than the year before.

Competition and Monopoly

Types of monopoly-price: receipts vs. profits. These petty devices develop, in the case of larger markets and of many important articles of sale, into the systematic practice of manipulating prices artificially. The explanation of the motives and of the limits of monopolistic price-fixing would best be reserved in large part until a later stage of our study, where it can be considered in connection with enterprise. It is in the sale of the products of a business that the most important problems of monopoly are found. There the monopolist Is seeking the highest net gain over a considerable period in the sale of a continuous output of goods.

The cost per unit is the minimum seller's valuation and the monopoly-price sought is that which in the long run yields the largest gain (the product of units of sales times margin of gain per unit). Let us here consider merely the case where the monopoly (seller or group of sellers) is seeking the maximum total price (not net gain) for a stock of goods which have no minimum seller's valuation. Such is the classic example of monopoly in colonial trade related by Adam Smith: "In the spice islands the Dutch are said to burn all the spiceries which a fertile season produces beyond what they expect to dispose of in Europe with such a profit as they think sufficient." "We may call this price which concerns the gross receipts from sales, crude monopoly-price. It is that which yields the monopolist (with complete control of supply) the maximum gross receipts.

This type of cases is of not infrequent occurrence. Such a case is presented whenever the unsold portion of a supply would go to waste, such as perishable goods after they have come to market (fruits, vegetables, etc.), such as vacant seats in an opera house, at athletic games, etc., where the expense of the whole performance has been incurred and will not be increased by more spectators. This control of all the seats at a single entertainment is a very restricted kind of monopoly, and does not present a social problem. There is still intense competition among artists of all kinds to provide entertainments having the merits to attract spectators.

Uniform Monopoly-price

In all such cases the competitive price would be fixed solely by the buyers' scale of valuation, as in an auction without reserve. If the supply of goods be large, approaching the saturation point of desires, whether there be one seller (without reserve valuation) or competing sellers, the price will tend toward the valuation of the marginal buyer, and in the extreme case may sink to zero. The only way sellers can prevent this is to reserve a part of the supply, even if it has to be burned up or thrown away (fish, fruit, etc.), or remains unused (as the empty seats in a theater).

In the case shown if there were 7 units for sale, the unit price would be 1, the total price 7, and each of the 7 sellers would get 1. But if the owners of these 7 units unite and withhold 3 units, the total receipts are 16, which divided equally, gives 22/7 units of price to each seller. It is a general truth, that monopoly power can be made effective to raise a uniform market-price above what it would be if the monopolistic competed, only by artificially increasing scarcity, by limiting supply. Shown graphically, the maximum crude monopoly-price obtainable is always the largest rectangle that can be inscribed within the coordinate axes and the hypothetical demand-curve.

Uniform Monopoly-price, Inelastic Demand

With a more inelastic demand, where buyers' demand increases very little with a rapid fall in price, the monopolist must restrict his offers more narrowly to attain a total price above the competitive. The offer of 3 units would at the price 6 yield the maximum proceeds (18), and any supply below that would be tapping only the lower levels of valuation. If a few valuations are high, and the others fall very rapidly, the price can be raised very much more, if the demand curve were AEFG the monopoly-price would be 9. This is the type of demand for articles of great luxury, limited to the very rich. Note that as demand means number of units demanded, at a price, an elastic demand means a large change of demand with a small change in price. With given scales of price and of quantities of goods, the more elastic the demand, the flatter the demand-curve.

Uniform monopoly-price: elastic demand. The more elastic the demand the more nearly a monopolistic price approaches a competitive price with a given number of units of supply. It appears that with any number of units up to 4, the monopolistic and the competitive market-prices would be the same, and any restriction would involve a loss to the monopolist. The motive for monopoly lies in the range of supply of 5 units and beyond. With a more elastic type of demand as in scale A-B where there is less difference in the valuations of the most urgent (or capable) and of the less urgent buyer, competitive and monopolistic market-prices are the same up to 7 units (7 X 41/3 = 301/3 total). With a still more elastic demand represented by a more flattened curve, as in C-D, the competitive and monopolistic price are the same up to 11 units (11 X 31/3 = 36% total) and either 10 or 11 units will yield the same total. Beyond that is the region of possible monopolistic price.

Compound types of demand scales, made up of different levels of demand, would further strengthen or weaken the motive to limit supply. If the demand curve, after rapidly falling, flattens to a new broad field of demand, a lower price will yield a larger total than the previous monopoly-price. This is the type of non-essential goods which remain luxuries when price is high, but rapidly become looked upon as comforts and necessities when price falls.

Perfect Competition

In economics, perfect competition occurs in markets in which no participant has market power. Because the conditions for perfect competition are strict, there are few if any perfectly competitive markets. Nonetheless, the concept of perfect competition can serve as a useful benchmark against which to measure real life, imperfectly competitive markets.

Approaches and Conditions

Historically, in neoclassical economics there have been two strands of looking at what perfect competition is. The first emphasis is on the inability of any one agent to affect prices. This is usually justified by the fact that any one firm or consumer is so small relative to the whole market that their presence or absence leaves the equilibrium price very nearly unaffected. This assumption of negligible impact of each agent on the equilibrium price has been formalized by Aumann (1964) by postulating a continuum of infinitesimal agents.

The difference between Aumann's approach and that found in undergraduate textbooks is that in the first, agents have the power to choose their own prices but do not individually affect the market price, while in the second it is simply assumed that agents treat prices as parameters. Both approaches lead to the same result. The second view of perfect competition conceives of it in terms of agents taking advantage of-and hence, eliminating-profitable exchange opportunities. The faster this arbitrage takes place, the more competitive a market.

The implication is that the more competitive a market is under this definition, the faster the average market price will adjust so as to equate supply and demand (and also equate price to marginal costs). In this view "perfect" competition means that this adjustment takes place instantaneously. This is usually modelled via the use of the Walrasian auctioneer. The widespread recourse to the auctioneer tale appears to have favoured an interpretation of perfect competition as meaning price taking *always*, i.e. also at non-equilibrium prices; but this is rejected e.g. by Arrow (1959) or Mas-Colell et al.

Steve Keen notes, following George Stigler, that if firms do not react strategically to one another, the slope of the demand curve that a firm faces is the same as the slope of the market demand curve. Hence, if firms are to produce at a level that equates marginal cost and marginal revenue, the model of perfect competition must include at least an infinite number of firms, each producing an output quantity of zero. As noted above, an influential model of perfect competition in neoclassical economics assumes that the number of buyers and sellers are both of the power of the continuum, that is, an infinity even larger than the number of natural numbers. K. Vela Velupillai quotes Maury Osborne as noting the inapplicability of such models to actual economies since money and the commodities sold each have a smallest positive unit.

Thus nowadays the dominant intuitive idea of the conditions justifying price taking and thus rendering a market perfectly competitive is an amalgam of several different notions, not all present, nor given equal weight, in all treatments. Besides product homogeneity and absence of collusion, the notion more generally associated with perfect competition is the negligibility of the size of agents, which makes them believe that they can sell as much of the good as they wish at the equilibrium price but nothing at a higher price (in particular, firms are described as each one of them facing a horizontal demand curve).

However, also widely accepted as part of the notion of perfectly competitive market are perfect information about price distribution and very quick adjustments (whose joint operation establish the law of one price), to the point sometimes of identifying perfect competition with an essentially instantaneous reaching of equilibrium between supply and demand.

Finally, the idea of free entry with free access to technology is also often listed as a characteristic of perfectly competitive markets, probably owing to a difficulty with abandoning completely the older conception of free competition. In recent decades it has been rediscovered that free entry can be a foundation of absence of market power, alternative to negligibility of agents (Novshek and Sonnenschein 1987.)

Free entry also makes it easier to justify the absence of collusion: any collusion by existing firms can be undermined by entry of new firms. The necessarily long-period nature of the analysis (entry requires time!) also allows a reconciliation of the horizontal demand curve facing each firm according to the theory, with the feeling of businessmen that "contrary to economic theory, sales are by no means unlimited at the current market price" (Arrow 1959 p. 49). Sraffian economists see the assumption of free entry and exit as characteristic of the theory of free competition in Classical economics, an approach that is not expressed in terms of schedules of supply and demand.

The Principle of Proportionality; Its General Nature

In what has been said in regard to scarcity as an element in value it was implied that value involves, in the simplest case of direct or immediately enjoyable goods, a certain proportionality between goods and the desires of men. The more abundant are goods, relative to the desire for them, the less is their value. Similarly, in connection with the principle of evaluation, we encountered, in the relations between the stimuli and the reactions of the nervous system, a certain quantitative relation, or principle of proportionality.

In the whole process of trade, also, which is the adjusting of a ratio between two or more goods in a group of traders seeking to buy and sell, an element of proportionality is plainly involved. And still later in discussing the improvement of productive processes we have touched upon the important problem of proportionality in the use and development of indirect agents. We saw that the development of new inventions, new processes, etc., was largely a matter of bringing things together in the most effective way-that is, in the best proportions for the accomplishment of certain physical, mechanical, chemical, or other desired technical results.

Cost and Sacrifice Defined

In our evaluations there are usually certain negative items variously referred to as cost or as sacrifice. In its broadest sense cost may be defined as that which must be given up to get another thing. This is its original, and still general, meaning. This would include, on the one hand, sacrifices of a purely psychic nature-disappointments, regrets, etc., caused by doing or by giving up a thing; and, on the other hand, the prices of things-whether expressed in money or in other goods. Usually, however, in business the word cost is given a more specialized meaning, and we shall take this in order to distinguish it from price in general on the one hand, and from sacrifice on the other.

In this narrower connotation cost means the outlay (considered as a business expense and expressed in money terms) which a person must make in order to obtain a certain product from goods. Sacrifice may be defined as that less definitely measured, psychic, alternative good (whether of enjoyment or of freedom from effort) which must be given up to get another good. Finally, price is the good surrendered in a trade with another person.

Sacrifice is involved in every choice and in every price in barter or sale; but cost, in this business man's sense, only when the outlay for a good up to date is compared with its value or with its selling price.

The Principle of Proportionality

The doctrine of separable uses: "We may think of the use of an object not as one undivided whole, but as a group of uses, separable each from the other. Likewise anyone of these uses is separable from the use-bearer considered as a concrete object. Every economic good, the use of which can be spread throughout a period of time, may be looked upon as consisting of groups of uses. The simplest case of this results from mere physical divisibility. A basketful of peaches is eaten piece by piece; each peach may be counted as one use. In this case the use is consumptive: it is not separable from the using up of the use-bearer itself.

The truly separable use, however, is found in the case of a durable agent which continues through a period of time to render a series of durative uses. A very perfect example is a diamond necklace, the sparkle and charm of which is a use which is absolutely without detriment to the use-bearer (i.e., the necklace, who perhaps not to the wearer). Many agents have this enduring quality more or less fully, and in all such cases the durative use may be treated practically and theoretically in economics as something separable from the use-bearer, in matters of valuation, of trade, and of price. The peaches may be gathered without harming the fitness of the trees to produce another crop. Shelter is furnished, once the house is built, without destroying the house more than disuse would, if it stood tenantless. The horse is the better if driven moderately each day, and the carriage lasts for years. In every such case, the use is something different from the "using up" of a limited number of goods, for there is left in the use-bearer the power to go on yielding indefinitely some more of the same product or use if it is kept in repair.

Some of the uses contained in a use-bearer may be actual or realized; others may be and may remain merely potential. Or they may all be realized in the course of a period of time, at the end of which the good is entirely consumed or worn out. The uses of a suit of clothes, for example, may be realized only day by day for a considerable period. Some men go on wearing a suit until it is almost completely worn out before discarding it; others discard clothing while there are still many possibilities of use in it. It may perhaps be safely asserted that the great majority of things have potentialities of which the owner for one reason or another does not avail himself. As already indicated, it does not pay to squeeze all possible uses out of a good. Uses 8, 9, etc., are quite possible of realization, but the attendant inconvenience or sacrifice is so great that they are valueless, and they will be ignored. The owner will not forego his sleep because he dislikes to have the piano go unused through the hours of the night. In the case of a durable good circumstances may warrant a very slight utilization at one time and a very much more complete utilization at another. The factory which has been running on half-time may later be operated day and night to meet a great increase in demand.

More intensive utilization: The uses of a good at a given time are actual or realized up to a point, limit, or margin beyond which further uses would not be worth the outlay of effort or of other goods. This point in the utilization is called the intensive margin. Using the thing more and more, while uniting other things with it, is using it more intensively. Getting more use out of the book by effort, out of the farm by applying more fertilizer, out of the factory by employing two or three shifts and working longer hours, out of the house by putting more people in it, is intensive utilization. The superior uses come easily, naturally; the inferior ones are to be secured only with increasing difficulty. When some change comes-such as an increase in demand for the product of an agent-which causes that agent to be more intensively utilized, this change is said to have lowered the (intensive) margin of utilization. The inferior grades of uses are being resorted to. The use a is the highest in the sense that it is the most easily obtained. Like results are to be had by the use of b to g successively only at greater costs; or less valuable results at the same costs.

More extensive utilization: This same change of demand may, however, bring about a simultaneous change of a different sort. If there are various agents of different degrees of excellence, and only the better grades are being used to meet this particular demand, then an increase in the demand is likly to result not only in a more intensive utilization of the superior agents, but also in the calling of some of the inferior agents into use. The best agents that are available at the time are used first, but as they are more intensively used, there is increasing inconvenience. This may be relieved by using either physical duplicates of the better agents or by using inferior agents. If there is more than one of a certain kind of agents, the duplicates are distributed so as to be where most valued by the owner. A man having two umbrellas keeps one at his office and the other at home; a student having two books of the same kind keeps one at his room and the other at the university; a farmer having two hoes keeps one at the barn and the other in a distant field, and by this method the additional units have higher uses than if they were used in the same way or at the same place as the earlier units.

It may finally be necessary to have recourse to agents which as a whole are inferior to the other agents, but whose first uses are better than the remaining intensive uses of the better grades of agents. This employment of inferior agents is also called lowering the margin of utilization. But it is a different margin with which we have to do-the margin between superior and inferior agents. It is the extensive margin. At the same time that an increase in demand causes the use of double shifts in the efficient factory, another factory, of inferior efficiency, which has been completely idle, may be brought into use, who possibly not to its full capacity. There has then occurred a change or lowering of both margins. At the same time that the cultivation becomes more intensive on the better fields, it becomes more extensive if there are other areas which have just come to have valuable uses. The intensive margin of use is in the particular thing; the extensive margin is the line between the superior and the inferior good. The inferior agent which is not utilized is spoken of as "below" or "beyond" or "outside of" the (extensive) margin of utilization. The interrelations between the two margins are shown in the diagram.

Intensiveness and exten-siveness of utilization are relative terms. The utilization of one machine or of one piece of land is more or less intensive as compared with another when more of other agents (e.g., labour) is used with or upon it; or the utilization of an agent becomes more or less intensive than it was before if more or less complementary agents are used than before. One might say that the use of an agent is intensive in one place as compared with another (e.g., land in New Jersey compared with that in Kansas), yet extensive as compared with still another place (with that in western Europe). In the same way extensive utilization is relative.

The rectangles, M, N, O, P, Q, represent agents of various grades, each consisting of strata of uses. The best uses are a, b, and c, in M; but after M has been utilized intensively down to d, N will begin to be utilized at its highest point. When utilization goes down to f, O comes into use, and so on. Therefore it will be seen that until the intensive margin takes in d, M is on the extreme margin of utilization, and N is just outside it; when the intensive margin falls to g and h, P is inside the extensive margin, and Q is just outside.

Application of complementary agents at the two margins: It is not our purpose at this point to emphasize the fact (important as it is) that changes of demand occur, and that these changes cause the best economic proportion to change. Rather we use illustrations of change to make clear that in any given set of conditions there is a best proportion in which to combine agents.

There is a right degree of economic utilization in that particular situation. Where this best proportion is attained, is a point of economic equilibrium, in the sense that there is in the situation itself (and until some other conditions change, as invention, increased demand, etc.) no motive to change the proportion. In such a case the effort is made to repeat the process, to maintain just that proportion which has been found to be on the whole best. If either of two complementary agents is used in greater or less amount than this best proportion, a loss results, something less than the possible maximum of value is obtained. Now the case of the two margins always occurs when one of the complementary agents is present in more than one quality or grade, as respects stuff, form, or place.

Then the supply of the complementary agent is distributed over the different grades of uses, now to the lower uses in the better agent, now to the upper uses of the poorer grades. In this way the effectiveness of each unit of the complementary agent is kept equal on the intensive and on the extensive margins of utilization of goods. As the value of the added product in the more intensive use of a particular agent decreases, a point finally is reached where it is better to transfer the outlay to another agent, to shift from the intensive to the extensive margin, by going over to the use of another field or of another machine not so good.

As the effectiveness of the labour, of the machinery, of the lands, of complementary agents of every kind, that men have to apply to two grades of another agent is being compared constantly, the uses of the complementary agents are distributed along the two margins. The margin of utilization is marked by a line of uses valued at zero. When used to that point the total value obtainable from the agent is at its maximum. If utilization is less intensive the value of the last possible use is lost, and if it is more intensive there is a net loss on the outlay.

Intensive use of Ground Space

The principle of proportionality applies to ground-space in all industries. Some space is needed for any activity, even for mere existence, and a limited area cannot afford an unlimited number of uses. If a large library is accumulated in one small room, a point is reached where there is scarcely room to stand, and much energy is wasted in trying to find the books.

In a university the psychical product, education, may be limited by the need of space. School-rooms, laboratories, and college class-rooms, if used all day and all night, would accommodate several times as many students as they do; but the "wee sma' hours" would not be popular; and, therefore, as students increase, buildings must be added. One cannot conveniently increase the business of a lumber-yard without a larger yard-space, or of a factory without a larger floor-space.

But the added space may be gotten by spreading horizontally or piling up vertically. Even in agriculture vertical addition is possible by the use of greenhouses in which mushrooms are grown below the tables and tomatoes above, and where artificial heat gives a more intensive utilization throughout the winter. Therefore, with more space and also more time a single foot of ground can be made to yield half a dozen crops in the year.

In the production of food, however, on account of the need of sun, light, and air, the limits of space are more quickly felt, and are less elastic than in most other industries; the difference, however, is one of degree, and not of kind. In mercantile, commercial, and manufacturing businesses 10 acres or 60 acres of usable floor-space may be had by putting a building of that number of stories upon an acre of land, and installing elevators and moving stairways, parcel carriers, and telephones.

Not only is the initial cost high, but the cost of maintenance likewise, and it is economically warranted only when land-space is very high priced. Business adapts itself to this law, but does not escape its operation. Neither the law of gravitation nor the principle (or law) of proportionality is violated or broken when materials are lifted to build the upper stories. Both "laws" are at work, even when the building is rising from the ground.

Intensive use of tools and implements

All the implements used in agriculture are subject to the limitation of the principle of proportionality. Why will not one hoe, one rake, one plow, one scythe, one horse, one wagon, do for all the farmers of a neighbourhood?

It might, in many cases, but it would be with much labour and time in carrying the things back and forth and in waiting for others to get through using them; it would require work to be continued all night, on Sundays and on holidays, and even then the plowing, hoeing, harvesting, and other farm operations could not be performed when most needed.

Even now there is much loss in just these ways because, the every farmer has at least one, and some have many, of these tools, there are brief periods when there are not tools enough. "Why, then, not have more tools? Because they cost. Between the extremes of no tools and a multitude a balance is struck at a point where the last additional tool adds to the price of the crop at least as much as the tool costs. The mode of estimating these costs we have later to study more closely.

In manufacture, whether by hand tools in small shops or by machinery, in transportation, whether by boat or railroad, there is, in the mind of the manager, the same ideal point of equilibrium between the price of the uses to be added and the price of the other agents (labour, tools, materials) that must be expended to secure the additional product. To do nothing with a tool, implement, machine, for the purpose of saving the things that would have to be used with it, is to lose the use of it.

Bearings of the principle

It is plain that this principle of proportionality must be taken account of in all practical affairs by those who are directing the processes of productive industry, whether on a large or on a small scale. Their problem is both technical and economic. They must make effective technical use of goods, and they must combine things in ways that will pay.

To the student of economics a clear understanding of this most fundamental principle of proportionality is essential to the solution of the complex problems of valuation. Things are not valued in isolation from each other. The great mass of complementary agents act and react upon each other. The valuation put upon one agent is due in part to the presence in certain proportions of other agents. Many evidences of this truth will appear to us as our study proceeds.

Bibliography

Arora, Shyam Lal : *A Textbook of Hotel Accounting*, Cyber Tech, Delhi, 2011.

Bazilevskii, Y. Y.: *The Theory of Mathematical Machines*, Pergamon Press, Macmillan Co., New York, 1963.

Bernstein, Peter L.: *Against The Gods – The Remarkable Story of Risk*. John Wiley and Sons. New York, NY, 1996.

Burke, Frank M., *Valuation and Valuation Planning for Closely Held Businesses*, Englewood Cliffs, NJ, Prentice Hall, 1981.

Chandra, Krishna : *Accounting for Managerial Control*, Sarup, Delhi, 2002.

Cootner, Paul : *The Random Character of Stock Market Prices*, MIT Press, 1964.

Dimson, Elroy: *Stock Market Anomalies*, Cambridge University Press, 1988.

Farmer, Mayuri J. : *An Accounting Evaluation of Performance of Indian Public Sector Banks*, Shanti Prakashan, Delhi, 2003.

Goodman, Rae Jean B., *An Assessment of Recent Changes and Proposals in S&L Taxation*, Invited Research Working Paper No. 43, Washington, DC: Federal Home Loan Bank Board, 1983.

Gupta, Nirmal and Chhavi Sharma: *Cost Accounting : Theory and Practice*, Ane Books, Delhi, 2009.

Harrigan, K. R.: *Strategies for Declining Businesses*. Lexington, MA: Heath, 1980

Hayek, F. A. *Individualism and Economic Order*, The University of Chicago Press, Chicago, 1948.

John M.: *How The Stock Market Works,* Prentice Hall Press. New York Institute of Finance, 1988.

Kar, Subrata : *Corporate Depreciation Accounting : A Critical Study*, SBS Pub, Delhi, 2008.

Lehman, C.R.: *Accounting's Changing Roles in Social Conflict*, New York, Markus Weiner Publishing, 1992.

Mayer, Thomas : *The Political Economy of American Monetary Policy*. Cambridge University Press. Cambridge, 1990.

Mishkin, Frederic S. and Stanley G. Eakins: *Financial Markets and Institutions,* Addison-Wesley, 2000.

Patrick G.: *Master Financial Statements: Who Murdered Savings and Loans,* Washington, DC: Palindrome Press, 1991.

Pramanik, Alok Kumar : *Accounting Standards and Convergence Scenario,* Deep and Deep Publications, Delhi, 2011.

Rana, Girish : *Practical Cost Accounting : Modern Methods and Techniques,* ABD, Delhi, 2006.

Ritchken, Peter: *Derivative Markets: Theory, Strategy, and Applications.* HarperCollins. New York, 1996.

Sarker, J.B. : *Accounting and Finance : Contemporary Issues,* Deep and Deep, Delhi, 2001.

Schumpeter, J. A., *The Theory of Economic Development,* Harvard University Press,Cambridge, Massachusetts, 1934.

Selznick, P.: *Leadership in Administration, A Sociological Interpretation,* New York, Harper & Row, 1957.

Sharma, B.S. : *Accounting Management : Information for Decisions,* Global India, Delhi, 2009.

Singh, Kavaljit: *Taming Global Financial Flows: A Citizen's Guide.* New York: St Martin's Press, 2000.

Stewart C. Meyers: *Principles of Corporate Finance,* Irwin, McGraw-Hill, 2000.

Tietenberg, Tom, *Environmental Economics and Policy,* New York, HarperCollins, 1994

Vataliya, K S : *Accounting Information Systems : Theory and Applications,* Paradise Pub, Delhi, 2007.

Veale, Stuart R.: *Stocks, Bonds, Options and Futures.* Prentice Hall Press – New York Institute of Finance, 2000.

West, Thomas L.: and Jeffrey D. Jones: *Handbook of Business Valuation,* New York: Wiley, 1992.

Index

❑❑❑